CONSUMER SHiFT

MEET THE AUTHOR

http://bit.ly/mQc60U

CONSUMER SHIFT

How Changing Values Are Reshaping The Consumer Landscape

Andy Hines

PUBLISHING

No Limit Publishing Group
60 East Rio Salado Parkway, Suite 900
Tempe AZ 85281
info@nolimitpublishinggroup.com

This book was printed in the United States of America

CONTENTS

ACKNOWLEDGEMENT TO SPONSORS

Much of the research and analysis for this work was done in support of a "New Dimensions of Consumer Life" Futures Consortium meeting held on 10 November 2009 at the Willard Hotel in Washington DC. These meetings are held twice annually for the sponsors of one or both of Innovaro's Futures Consortium's two research streams, Global Lifestyles and Technology Foresight. I would like to recognize the sponsoring organizations as their support is what made this work possible.

Alticor	Hasbro	Research in Motion
Boeing	IHG	State Farm Insurance
Brown and Forman	Kellogg	Tekes
Centra	Kohler	UPS
Ford	Kraft	Wyeth
GM	Nissan	
Gensler	Reed Elsevier	

The following individuals participated in the meeting:

Bob Arko, *Coalesse*

Christine Barber, *Gensler*

Nona Beining, *Kohler Company*

Matthew Benson, *Faurecia*

Lance Boge, *Gensler*

John Bricker, *Gensler*

Leigh Anne Capello, *Hasbro*

Bill Cawley, *UTEK Corporation*

Henrik Christensen, *Miller Coors*

Carol Csanda, *State Farm Insurance*

Linda DeBerardinis, *Western Union*

Bea De Paz, *Gensler*

Howard Katz, *Kohler Company*

Kate Kirkpatrick, *Gensler*

Anne Marie Kroisi, *Hasbro*

Regina Lewis, *InterContinental Hotels*

Kimberly Maxwell, *Spike TV*

Sammy McCubbins, *State Farm Insurance*

Gina Melona, *Hasbro*

Seth Minsk, *Pfizer Consumer Healthcare/Wyeth*

Patricia Morrissey

Angela Ojeda, *Nissan North America*

Gina Pais, *Kohler Company*

Marilyn Parrett, *Brown-Forman*

Joseph Dvorak, *Research in Motion*

Julie Eller, *Lowe's*

Elena Falcone, *Consumers Union*

Nancy Fitzgerald, *Kraft Foods*

Jackie Fradin, *Hasbro*

Joetta Gobell, *Nissan North America*

Donald Goh, *InterContinental Hotels*

Soili Helminen, *Tekes*

Mary Henkener, *Procter & Gamble*

Jennifer Hsieh, *Marriott*

Andres Jordan, *Deutsche Telekom NA, Inc.*

Magnus Karlsson, *Telefonaktiebolaget LM Ericsson*

Virginia Pettit, *Gensler*

Betsy Quint-Moran

Ed Rogers, *UPS Corporate Strategy*

Peter Skazynski, *Strategos*

Ilene Strongin-Garry, *InterContinental Hotels*

Mike Suman, *Research in Motion*

Robin Uler, *Marriott*

Emily Ulrich, *Steelcase*

Paul Vassallo, *UPS Corporate Marketing*

Katie Waterson, *Peer Insight*

Peter Westerstrahle, *Tekes*

Terresa Zimmerman, *UTEK Corporation*

Thanks to Lisa Robinson of Nissan for pointing the author toward the excellent work of Manfred Max-Neef on universal human needs. Thanks also to Pero Micic of Future Management Group for pointing the author toward the equally outstanding work of Steven Reiss in the area of human needs and motivation. A huge thanks to Chris Carbone of Innovaro for contributing a significant piece of the work on catalysts in Chapter 5.

And, of course, a huge thank you to my former colleagues at Social Technologies (now Innovaro), who provided the research and inspiration for so much of this work: Don Abraham, Malissa Bennett, Josh Calder, Chris Carbone, John Cashman, Denise Chiavetta, Sara Chilcote, Tom Conger, Bill Croasmun, Jason Forrest, Roumiana Gotseva-Yordanova, Terry Grim, Christina Hawkins, Sam Jones, Mark Justman, Christopher Kent, Daniel Klein, Laura Leenhouts, Kristin Nauth, Mark Niles, Kevin Osborn, Scott Reif, Gail Siegel, Matt Sollenberger, Kyle Spector, Simeon Spearman, Gio Van Remortel and Peter Von Stackelberg.

Finally, thanks to my most important mentors, Joe Coates and Peter Bishop.

PREFACE

Over a dozen years ago, I was tasked with looking at how values changes might provide opportunities for the North American cereal market. My first reaction to the task was "uh-oh," as the world of values, at the time, was something of a wasteland in terms of foresight. Nonetheless, I explored the question and found a few promising leads. Jay Ogilvy of the Global Business Network directed me to the VALS (Values and Lifestyles) program at SRI (Stanford Research Institute), but noted that its psychographic approach (psychographics refers to attributes relating to personality, values, attitudes, interests, or lifestyles) in defining eight segments was struggling to keep up with rapid changes in consumer behavior.[1] That is, consumers were not behaving according to type! He also mentioned that Professor Ronald Inglehart at the University of Michigan had been doing some interesting survey work in values, but that it was rather academic. The Inglehart work, called the World Values Survey,[i] was indeed academic, i.e., not exactly user-friendly, but it showed promise for providing data support that would back up the idea of discernible patterns in shifts of global values. My subsequent mining of that data has proved incredibly rewarding. One early connection was my finding that this data overlapped with Maslow's Hierarchy of Human Needs. That initial investigation launched the journey culminating in the research for this book. The next key advance in the story was my introduction to the outstanding work of Don Beck and his colleague Christopher Cowan, inspired by their mentor Clare Graves, called Spiral Dynamics. The fact that their different approach to explaining human development led to similar findings launched yet another phase of the journey—looking across human development systems to see if the explanations found common themes. Happily they do. This research formed the conceptual basis for the book, which is greatly enhanced by the research and analysis of my colleagues at Social Technologies (now Innovaro). It enabled me to build on the research and expand its scope and apply it to the issue at hand of describing the ConsumerShift.

---

i   See http://www.worldvaluessurvey.org/

A NOTE ON THE GREAT RECESSION

At the time of publication, thinking about the consumer landscape is dominated by the impact of the Great Recession. Any work describing the consumer landscape would be incomplete without attention to the question of the impact of the Great Recession. The obvious question is whether consumer behavior will return to normal once the recession is over.

As will be shown, the shifts are driven in part from improving economic prospects and a feeling of economic security. The arrival of the Great Recession would at first glance seem to threaten that. The values changes driving the reshaping of the consumer landscape described here have been gaining strength over the course of a generation (roughly the last 30 years). The long-term pattern has been a long, gradual movement from "older" to "newer" values (i.e., from traditional to modern to postmodern to integral, as will be explained).

Recessions, depending on their severity, may slow or even temporarily reverse the values changes. In times of economic stress, people are less inclined to adopt new values or may even "fall back" to previous values. In general, the values changes comprising the consumer shift are stronger than a typical recession; that is, there is little if any long-term impact on the values shift from a business cycle recession. Even a more severe recession, such as the dot.com bust over a decade ago, had little impact or long-term influence on the values shift.

There have been significant impacts from major politico-economic disruptions. For instance, there were clear reversals in the values changes after the collapse of the former Soviet Union and after the end of apartheid South Africa. But even here, as those situations stabilized several years later, the values changes resumed. Put simply, in times of stress, people tend to avoid change and revert to what's comfortable. Thus, one would expect that consumers who have been newly embracing postmodern values, for example, would be reverting back to modern values given the Great Recession. Alas, here is where things get interesting.

The arrival of "new values"—described here as postmodern and integral—appears to be bucking the pattern; that is, the Great Recession may be reinforcing the emergence of the new. In a nutshell, these new values suggest a consumer lifestyle that puts less emphasis on economic success and material goods achievement, and more emphasis on quality-of-life concerns. The constraints imposed by the Great Recession actually make it "easier" to put less emphasis on economic matters. For example, let's say one is forced to take a pay cut. One response might be to take a second job to make up the lost income. A postmodern values family, however, may make that pay cut an opportunity to "downsize" their lifestyle and prepare them for a parent to take another job more in sync with their values—since they can now live at a lower income level. To be clear, this is one example and not meant to suggest that all postmodern values holders will embrace less money. They are looking for ways to sync up their values and lifestyles. Ironically, the Great Recession is more likely to enable rather than inhibit change.

1

INTRODUCTION

THE CASE FOR "THE RETHINK"

"**W**e just don't understand our consumers anymore." "We need to do a better job of anticipating where our consumers are heading." "Our old approaches to consumer understanding just aren't working anymore." These and similar statements have become increasingly common over recent years among my clients—ranging from multinational corporations, government agencies, nonprofits, and associations, and including analysts, managers, directors, and senior leaders. The old confidence is gone. Something is clearly happening in consumer life that suggests that the landscape of the next decade is likely to be quite different from the previous one. What's worked before, or may still be working now, will not work with consumers at the leading edge of the changes described in this study. Not only will they not work, but they will antagonize these consumers and have them working against these organizations stuck in the past. The changes are characterized as "the rethink."

GATEWAY

ENTER

ONE

http://bit.ly/q85s7y

The seeds of the rethink were planted in the social fringes of the late 1960s and 1970s and are finally bearing fruit with the mainstream today. Many visionaries at the time suggested a coming transformation.[ii] It simply took much longer than they hoped and expected. Nonetheless, forces are lining up to suggest that

Values defined

An individual view about what is most important in life that in turn guides decision-making and behavior. Values are the ultimate decision-making criteria—what an individual falls back upon when making important life decisions.

It is worth noting that many definitions also include an individual's sense of "what is right and wrong." My approach assigns this aspect to virtues.

Further, core personal values, borrowing from Simon, are those: one thinks one has, one feels at a deep level, and one has acted on, borrowing Simon's concept that a value becomes a value when it is *felt, analyzed,* and *expressed* in terms of behavior.

Source: Simon, S., Howe, L., & Kirschenbaum, H. (1972). Values Clarification: A Practical, Action-Directed Workbook.

the next decade will see these changes expressed in the consumer landscape. The visionaries were not wrong; it's just that the changes turned out to be more evolutionary than revolutionary. By 2020, the changes should be in full force.

An interesting paradox is taking place. The values changes and the external factors reinforcing them have been growing but have not yet reached critical mass.

ii   For example: Mead, M. (1974, June). Ways to Deal with the Current Social Transformation. *The Futurist*, 122; Platt, J. (1974, June). Transformation: Changes in Belief Systems. *The Futurist*, 124; Harman, W. (1977, February). The Coming Transformation: Part One. *The Futurist*, 105; (1977, April). The Coming Transformation: Part Two. *The Futurist*, 106.

Along comes the Great Recession, and normally difficult times slow down the adoption of new values; thus one would expect consumers to fall back on older and more comfortable values. The paradox is that the Great Recession may have the opposite effect and actually provide a boost to the adoption of new values among those consumers predisposed to be at the leading edge of change. In this particular case, the crisis, rather than triggering people to fall back on comfortable values, is enabling the "rethink" that nets out in a way that reinforces the changes taking place. In simple terms, and as will be demonstrated, the values changes have an aspect of anti-consumerism brewing underneath them, and the Great Recession will help to solidify and strengthen it.

At the core of the rethink are shifts toward postmodern values, and behind these are integral values reinforced by the Great Recession. In this work, these changes in values are combined with related external trends in the form of emerging need states and future personas. Five key themes form the core of these changes, making a case for the consumer shift (note the acronym "A CASE"):

- *Authenticity.* One of the costs of modern life, with its focus on economic growth and consumerism, is that everything and anything can be seen as a marketing opportunity; thus messaging and spin are ubiquitous. It has become more and more difficult to have an experience that isn't manufactured, managed, or otherwise staged to some degree. The truly authentic experience has become a rare commodity, and thus, an object of desire. People are tired of being managed and manipulated and hunger for the straight story, warts and all.

- *Connection.* Related to the feeling of life being out of control is the desire to get reconnected with what is really important in life. In its extreme form, this could manifest as a sense of angst. The busyness of daily life and the need to "keep up with the Joneses" has reached a point where people feel they've lost touch with their priorities. Thus they are seeking to scale back and get more involved in the activities that remain. They want to spend more time with family and friends, get more involved in their community, know who their neighbors are and who they do business with—in general they want to become more reengaged with their daily lives.

- *Anti-consumerism.* A disenchantment with consumerism has been gaining momentum. The rapid pace of modern life has taken its toll on lifestyles and relationships. People are recognizing those costs and, given their relative affluence, are increasingly willing to trade off money and material goods for time to enjoy experiences and invest in relationships. This is not necessarily extreme, e.g., recycling underwear—they appreciate the need for goods and services—but rather a sense that the consumption relationship needs to be reoriented such that consumption is not the end goal but a means to various ends.

- *Self-expression.* Disillusionment with modern life and consumerism has led individuals to turn inward and reassess the meaning of their lives. There is a sense of emptiness with adding yet another material possession—and the data shows that having more money and goods, beyond poverty level, adds nothing to one's happiness. Thus, there is a search for deeper meaning and purpose in one's life. This pursuit is seen as a worthy one that has intrinsic value, and people want to tell the world about it. They shift from a passive to an active orientation; they want to express their views, their values, their purpose, and their creativity.

- *Enoughness.* Think of this as voluntary simplicity with a bit of an edge to it. Whereas voluntary simplicity suggested a benevolent, altruistic adoption of a simpler lifestyle, enoughness gets to a similar end point, but only partly from choice, as necessity in the form of the Great Recession is mixed into the equation. There is a sense of one "having enough" or being fed up with the status quo. There is an acceptance and embrace of the need for limits. People feel their lives are getting out of control, and they want to take back that control and set limits.

Thus a key challenge is emerging in that these "consumers" don't want to be thought of primarily as consumers. It's not that they no longer want to buy goods and services, but they want to reconfigure or rebalance the relationship between buyer and seller. They don't want things they don't need and are scrutinizing just what they do need. They don't want buyers pushing, marketing, spinning, and hard selling. They see a difference between transactions and relationships. They want an authentic connection, and they want their viewpoint to be acknowledged.

Think this is a bunch of touchy-feely gobbledygook? Read on. Your future may literally depend on it. Organizations that fail to grasp these changes will miss connecting to the leading edge of change set by these consumers, for they will set the tone for the mainstream eventually to follow. As Clay Christenson suggested in his work on the *Innovator's Dilemma*,[iii] being overly focused on today's customers, even one's best customers, can lead organizations to miss the market shifts and innovations of the future.

While the focus is on consumers, the findings here are applicable to "citizens" in general. In other words, while the consumer aspect is emphasized, the analysis

---

iii   Clay Christenson, *The Innovator's Dilemma: The Revolutionary Book that Will Change the Way You Do Business,* Harper, 2003.

can be interpreted for other aspects of life, such as social or political life. Self-expression in consumer life may mean buying fair trade coffee. In social life it may mean patrolling with the neighborhood watch team. In political life, it may be joining a citizen's group to work against a proposed new interstate highway that crosses a wetland. In fact, these aspects are interrelated.

To help place these ideas in context, consider the "Diffusion of Innovation" model of Everett Rogers that suggests how, why, and at what rate new ideas and technology spread through cultures. For the percentage of people in each of the five "adopter" categories, see Figure 1.

The leading postmodern nations have about 25% of their population with a postmodern orientation, suggesting that postmodern values have gone beyond the early adopters and reached the early majority. At the same time, integral values are estimated at less than 2% of these populations, suggesting they are still primarily in the camp of the Innovators.[2]

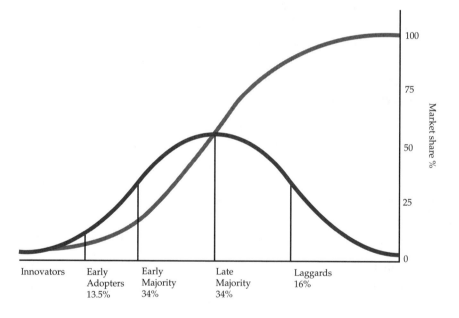

Innovators: first to adopt

Early Adopters: 2nd fastest to adopt; have highest degree of opinion leadership.

Early Majority: time of adoption is significantly longer than the innovators and early adopters

Late Majority: adopt only after the average member of the society

Laggards: last to adopt

Figure 1. Rogers' "Diffusion of Innovation"

THE FOCUS

Why values

An important assumption of this work is that values come together in relatively coherent patterns. This does not mean all consumers hold these patterns consistently but that there is enough consistency across populations to suggest that these patterns exist. Moreover, the presence of these patterns enables some useful generalizations in the study of values that would not otherwise be possible at the micro level, in the spirit of every consumer holding a unique set of values.

Emphasis on the future and the new

A human development approach is taken. It assumes directionality in values changes; that is, it assumes that values are changing in a consistent direction over time. Understanding these changes provides critical insight into changes in the future consumer landscape. As Hall suggests, "the critical factor in the transformation of people and organizations is their values."[3]

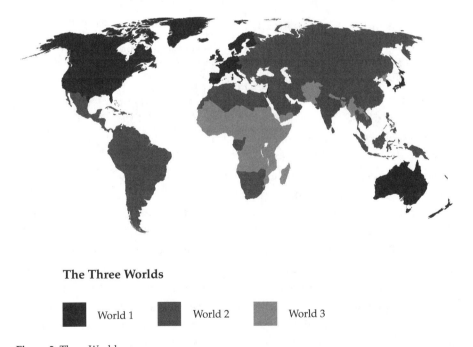

The Three Worlds

World 1   World 2   World 3

Figure 2. Three Worlds

These changes are most evident in the affluent nations such as the United States, most of Europe (especially Northern Europe), Japan, Korea, Australia, and others [see Figure 2 and Appendix 1 for details on the sorting of nations into categories: World 1 (W1) Affluent, World 2 (W2) Emerging Market, and World 3 (W3) Poor].[iv] This does not mean that the changes are exclusively happening in the affluent W1 nations; they are, however, in greater evidence there or in greater percentages of the populations than in the rest of the world. Indeed, there are significant values changes going on in the emerging markets, but they are following a similar trajectory as the affluent nations have already passed through. They will express these values changes differently; but structurally, the changes are similar to what has gone before. The focus on new values patterns means that the primary focus is on changes in the affluent W1 nations most prominently associated with the leading edge of change. In the United States, for instance, the postmodern values are more prominent on the coast than in the heartland. In Europe, they are more prominent in Scandinavia and Northern Europe.

THE APPROACH

The bulk of the research sources are in Chapters 2 through 5. Chapters 2, 3, and 4 lay the conceptual groundwork, which informs the rest of the analysis. Chapter 5, "How Catalysts of Change Are Shaping and Being Shaped by Consumers," provides data support in the form of the individual trends and values

> **The value of secondary research**
>
> Interestingly, it may be that secondary research is more helpful than primary in the case of understanding future consumer life. For instance, consumers seem to be pretty poor at forecasting their own futures. Dan Gilbert's *Stumbling on Happiness* lampooned consumer follies in this regard: "Our ability to imagine our personal future happiness is flawed, drawing upon psychology, cognitive neuroscience, philosophy, and behavioral economics." Asking people about how they might behave differently is a risky endeavor.

that were subsequently synthesized into larger forces of change called catalysts. Many of the trends are qualitative in nature, and the evidence is in the form of observations or examples of the trend appearing in "real life." Quantitative data is used where it exists, but it should be noted that numbers are subject to interpretation, as is qualitative data. Economic statistics, for instance, are often used to support a certain case, perhaps to mask negative developments that support a political case, e.g., understating unemployment or overstating economic growth. Chapters 6 and 7 rely on analysis based on the conceptual ideas referenced in Chapters 2, 3, and 4, as well as the trends and values informing the catalysts in Chapter 5.

---

iv   The Three Worlds concept was originally developed by Coates & Jarratt in the mid 1990s as part of our *2025* book (co-authors Joseph Coates and John Mahaffie) and project and was further refined by colleagues at Social Technologies in the 2000s. Josh Calder was instrumental in developing and maintaining the instrument in both firms.

Visual guide to the approach

Figure 3 summarizes the process used to generate the personas that are the culmination of the work. The New Dimensions of Consumer Life conceptual model (Chapters 2 and 3) provides the basis for the inner dimension changes (Chapter 4). The inner dimension changes are combined with the outer dimension changes (Chapter 5) to form the basis of the emerging need states (Chapter 6), which in turn provide the basis for the personas (Chapter 7). Thus, there is a dual tone to this work. Part One, "Why the Consumer Landscape Is Changing," includes Chapters 2 through 5, which take a more scholarly approach and lay the conceptual groundwork. Part Two, "What the Changing Consumer Landscape Will Look Like," includes Chapters 6 through 8 that aim to illustrate how the theory will manifest in daily life. Thus the tone of these chapters is lighter, more informal, and story-like. Chapter 8, "Customizing the Personas: A Persona Construction Kit," is a reference guide or how-to manual that guides readers to apply the insights from this work to their particular context or situation.

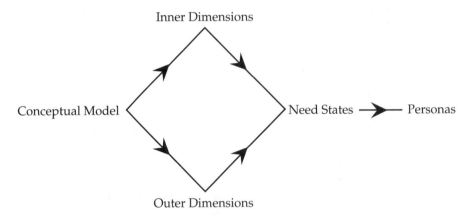

Figure 3. Visual guide to the approach

The nine chapters in two parts are briefly characterized below:

Part One, "Why the Consumer Landscape Is Changing," presents the case for change. It develops the *New Dimensions of Consumer Life Model*, which is a framework for understanding why the consumers are changing. The most theoretical part of the book, it makes the case for the emphasis on values and provides the foundation for mapping out the consumer landscape in Part Two.

- Chapter 1, "Introduction," introduces the work and provides an overview of what the work intends to accomplish.

- Chapter 2, "What's Going on [Deep] Inside Consumers," introduces the *New Dimensions of Consumer Life Model* and focuses on the inner dimension's interior aspect, including identity, mind, and body. It makes the case for the emphasis on values, along with needs and worldviews, as key to understanding future consumer changes. Readers might choose to accept this argument and simply skip or skim this chapter and move right into the description of the values changes in Chapter 4. Those seeking a more in-depth and richer understanding of the various influences on the inner life of consumers will likely find this chapter of greater interest.

- Chapter 3, "What's Being Said to Consumers," explores the various ways that society or culture tries to influence the values of individual consumers.

- Chapter 4, "How Changing Values Are the Single Biggest Influence on Consumers," explains the changes in the inner dimensions of consumer life, emphasizing the role of values, and how values changes are likely to transform consumer life in the future. These inner-dimension changes will be combined with changes in the outer dimensions in Chapter 5 to produce the emerging need states identified and described in Chapter 6.

- Chapter 5, "How Catalysts of Change Are Shaping and Being Shaped by Consumers," explains the changes in the outer dimensions of consumer life captured as catalysts of change. Thirteen catalysts are identified and described. These outer-dimension changes are combined with changes in the inner dimensions to produce the emerging need states identified and described in Chapter 6.

Part Two: "What the Changing Consumer Landscape Will Look Like" builds upon the conceptual foundation described in Part One to paint a picture of how the future consumer landscape will be different. It maps the future in two different ways, identifying emerging consumer need states, and developing representative personas to help bring those need states to life. Finally, it provides a mechanism for individuals and organizations to customize the personas for their specific purposes.

- Chapter 6, "Consumer Sweet Spots: Identifying Emerging Need states," identifies and describes emerging consumer need states based on changes in the inner and outer dimensions of consumer life. These emerging need states are presented as inviting targets for market researchers, new product developers, and new business development. It assumes that insight into emerging consumer needs provides clues to the types of products, services, and experiences that consumers will desire in the future.

- Chapter 7, "Future Personas: Bringing the Future to Life," brings the emerging need states to life in seven future consumer personas. The personas represent likely combinations of the need states. They describe the characteristics of consumers who embody the particular combination of need states. The intent of creating a single representation is to provide a more concrete target against which to aim product, service, and experience development than a more abstract treatment is capable of, recognizing that there will be variations around this projected "average" representation.

- Chapter 8, "Customizing the Personas: A Persona Construction Kit," is intended to help translate the generic personas in Chapter 7 to the more specific needs of individual organizations. It provides a step-by-step approach to fine-tuning the personas to particular organizations, markets, customers, products, etc.

- Chapter 9, "Conclusion," concludes the work with a call-to-action on how to apply the insights and recaps the key points. The work seeks to fill a void in consumer understanding by providing a model, a theory, and data on how consumers are changing. It then paints a picture of what that change looks like with emerging need states and future personas. It seeks to inspire action. Put simply, organizations that fail to understand and act on these changes will be left behind.

An appendix, glossary, annotated bibliography, references and index conclude the work.

PART ONE

WHY THE CONSUMER LANDSCAPE IS CHANGING

Part One explains why the consumer landscape is changing. It may be tempting to skip directly to Part Two: "What the Changing Consumer Landscape Will Look Like." While readers could take the Part One case on faith, understanding the "why" is critical to successfully preparing and responding to the proposed changes. Intent matters. This is a big shift from an emphasis on the bottom-line outcome. These consumers want to partner with organizations they believe in, so the intent of the organization is important to them. Is this an organization that is "doing the right things" or "one that I believe in"? Simply trying to adjust behavior without understanding the "why" will come through as phony and insincere. "This company tries but they just don't get it."

The growing sophistication of consumers at the leading edge of these proposed changes means that they will expect to be dealt with by those who understand where they are coming from and what they need. **While it may indeed be possible to design products or services to address an emerging need state, as proposed in Part Two, a lack of understanding of why that need state is important to consumers may lead to slight missteps or miscalculations that could undermine an otherwise well developed campaign.** For instance, a branding approach that relies heavily on authenticity must understand why that authenticity is important. Simply paying lip service to authenticity will likely be detected by consumers and will undermine the campaign. Part One provides the conceptual understanding that will lead to informed strategic responses. The "why" is indeed important.

The explanation in the next two chapters on the inner dimension serves a two-fold purpose. First, it establishes a consistent framework and terminology for talking about and understanding consumer life. Some organizations may find this the most valuable chapter in the book. They may be stuck in the morass of widely varying assumptions and perspectives and be unable to find common ground. There may be value in simply agreeing on the model as a basis for discussion, even if there is disagreement on some of the particulars.

Second, it establishes the complexity involved in understanding consumer life. It shows how the various coordinates and their associated units each make a contribution to consumer life. The focus on how consumer life is changing led to the focus on values with related needs and worldviews. Simply jumping right in to a values-based explanation would lead readers to rightly criticize the neglect of many other important factors. Therefore an attempt was made to provide enough of an explanation of these factors to give readers a sense of their contribution, while obviously not doing justice to their full richness, which would merit a separate book for each factor. Their links to values was emphasized as appropriate, to keep the work focused and not drown the reader in too much complexity.

2

WHAT'S GOING ON
[DEEP] INSIDE CONSUMERS

The first step in understanding any complex phenomenon is to map the system.[4] This involves setting the boundaries of the topic to be explored—deciding what's in and what's out of scope. There are different ways to represent systems, and in this case there are lots of interpretations of how consumers operate. Consumer life is mapped here by the *New Dimensions of Consumer Life Model*.

Consumer life is a complex phenomenon. Understanding it is further complicated by the fact that one person's values are another's virtues. For some, attitudes are the key, for others it's personality, or identity. Ten people in a room would probably all describe identity differently, so even a simplified model can be confusing. The approach here is to choose a model that is consistent in sorting out the different components of consumer life. It is not suggested that this model is *the* "correct" one—there are different ways to slice the pie—but there is value in being up front and consistent in how the components are defined and related. This will cut down on confusion. For some organizations that have long labored with different groups having different interpretations, simply agreeing on this model may have tremendous value by enabling conversations to take place based on a common understanding.

Values are the focal point of the model, reflecting the view that this component best helps one understand future changes in consumer life. This is not saying that values are more important than other components, but that they are most useful for understanding long-term changes in consumer life. As will be described later, data from the World Values Survey tracks long-term changes in values, which will be shown to be instrumental in reshaping the consumer landscape. Nonetheless, a different focus might emphasize a different component. For example, a market research effort to understand what motivates consumer decision making at the point of purchase might emphasize emotional states instead of values. Our emphasis on the future suggests a focus on values.

Values provide background context in a consumer's decision-making process. Consumers do not consciously call upon their values in daily life before they go shopping. But those values influence whether to consume or not; the "enoughness" trend above suggests that more consumers are consciously choosing to do with less. When they decide to consume, values influence selection as well. For instance, consumption has long been seen as a means of expressing one's identity. When consumers self-express by buying a hybrid vehicle or organic coffee, they tell others what they stand for, and often become advocates for the products, services, and organizations they really believe in. Values will play a lesser role in influencing decisions about products consumers don't really care about. In those instances, price is the deciding factor. And values also play less of a role in impulsive decisions that are attitudinal or situational; these are more reflective of transient mood than enduring values.

Each component is described briefly below and specifically defined in the glossary. Terminology for the model can be troublesome—even agreeing on what to call the categories, components, elements, etc., requires thought to ensure consistency. The concepts of inner and outer dimensions frame the model. The dictionary says that the dimension of a space or an object is the minimum number of coordinates needed to specify each point within it. In this case then, a minimum number of four "coordinates" comprises the inner dimension: identity, mind-body, external influences, and behavior. The outer dimension comprises three coordinates: engaged consumers, blurring boundaries, and bounded consumption.

GATEWAY
ENTER
TWO
http://bit.ly/oAalUw

The parts of the model are referred to as follows:

- Consumer life is the *phenomenon* being studied.

- It is simplified to two *dimensions*: inner and outer.

- The inner dimension has two aspects (interior and exterior) and four *coordinates*: identity, mind-body, external influences, and behavior.

- Each of the coordinates has one to several *units*:

    o Identity has five units: purposes, needs, beliefs, values, and worldviews. Mind-body has six mind-based units—mental model, feelings, memory, imprints, thinking style and intuition—and three body-based units: genetic predisposition, moods, and emotions.

    o External influences has three interior units—morals, norms and ethics—and five exterior units—culture, paradigm, ideology, generations, and archetypes.

    o Behavior has six units: personality, attitudes, character, traits, and virtues, and lifestyles.

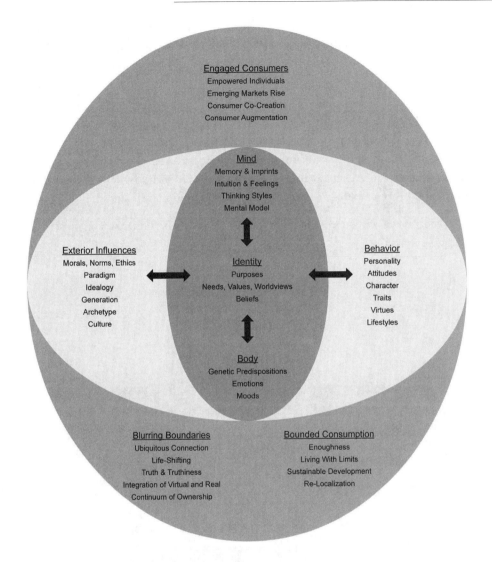

Figure 4. *New Dimensions of Consumer Life Model*

To repeat, the goal is not to claim absolute correctness, but consistency. There are many places where the lines get very blurry. For instance, the behavior units—personality, attitudes, character, traits, and virtues—could also have been categorized as exterior aspects of identity.

Values, the focal point of the model, are located under identity. Identity is how consumers define, think about, and describe themselves. It is often not explicit but implicit—a point that recurs frequently in this work and hints at why it is so difficult to understand these phenomena. A consumer's concept of identity is influenced by the three other major coordinates of the model: mind-body, external influences, and behavior. The way the model is laid out suggests a flow where one starts at the left with external influences, moves right to mind-body and then identity, and then turns down to behavior. While there is some truth in that in terms of an information flow, in reality the process is highly iterative and the coordinates repeat and feed back on one another. The intent is not to assert logical, linear, deterministic progress through each of the coordinates, but it might be easier to think of this linear flow, while keeping the iterative nature in mind. A quick summary reveals that **values are at the core of identity, which emerges from mind and body, as influenced by external forces, and manifested in behavior.**

The role of the coordinates and units of the inner dimension is described below.

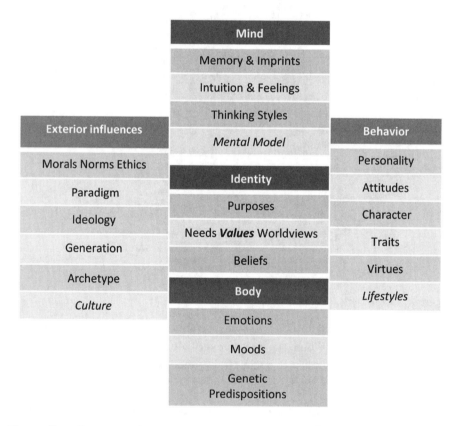

Figure 5. Inner Dimension of the *New Dimensions of Consumer Life Model*

IDENTITY

Values are an integral part of identity. Maslow asserts that "ultimately the search for identity is in essence the search for one's own intrinsic authentic values."[5] Values also serve as guides to meeting consumer needs and influencing consumer decisions and behavior. As Rokeach notes, "The functions served by a person's values are to provide him with a comprehensive set of standards to guide actions, justifications, judgments, and comparisons of self and others and to serve needs for adjustment, ego defense, and self-actualization. All these diverse functions converge into a single overriding, master function, namely, to help maintain and enhance one's total conception of oneself."[6]

Values can be thought of as a translator mechanism for identity (along with beliefs) into behavior and expressed in lifestyles. As one has multiple values, it can be said that one has multiple identities. William James writes of a material self, a social self, and a spiritual self, depending on the situation.[7] Values are the building blocks of identity. Berger observes that "while it is possible to say that man has a nature, it is more significant to say that man constructs his own nature, or more simply, that man produces himself."[8]

What all these experts are saying is that identity is who we think we are, and our values are key building blocks of our identity. When most people describe who they are, they start with their occupation and their roles, e.g., I'm a parent. It usually takes time to get people to reveal their values, as this is viewed as personal and is not easily shared with people we don't know well. For organizations trying to understand their consumers, gaining insight into identity is critical as the shift in values suggests that consumers are more aware of their identity and express it in the products and services they buy and in the organizations they choose to associate with. It takes some work to gain this understanding. This work attempts to provide a solid starting point.

Purpose

Values may implicitly or explicitly serve a higher purpose. Some people have a clear sense of purpose while others do not. It can be said that purpose unconsciously guides one's life. It is not suggested that consumers live their lives in strict adherence to purpose but that it can provide a guide or direction along with values. Three examples of common purposes are described below.

Happiness (a.k.a. well-being). The pursuit of happiness is perhaps the most common purpose in the United States. The U.S. Declaration of Independence cites the pursuit of happiness as an "unalienable right." The pursuit of happiness is a natural phenomena. As Layard suggests, "The function of happiness... is our overall motivational device... We are programmed to seek happiness."[9]

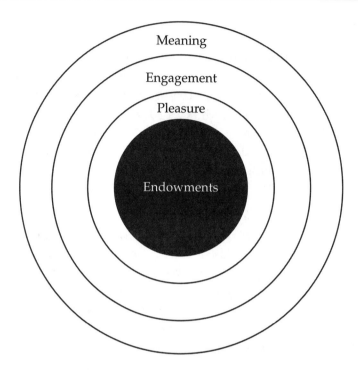

Figure 6. A model of happiness

This happiness model was adapted and slightly modified from Martin Seligman, the Positive Psychology guru, as part of the research for the MTV *Future of Youth Happiness* project. Four components of happiness are present in individuals to varying degrees.

- Endowments (In The Genes), which relate to one's physical status, e.g., health, genetics, age.

- Pleasure (Feels Good), which is purely about pleasure in the moment.

- Engagement (Connections), which relates to family, work, romance, and hobbies.

- Meaning (Bigger Picture), which relates to applying oneself to serve a larger purpose.

Source: Willis, C. (2005, January). *The New Science of Happiness*, Time.

GATEWAY

ENTER

THREE

http://bit.ly/o6lrOF

A challenge is that happiness is vaguely defined and means different things in different contexts. It can be characterized as an emotion; that is, it is situational and relatively short-lived, or as a purpose in terms of long-term well-being. For instance, Stefan Klein asserts in *The Science of Happiness*, "Happiness is what we feel at the same moment in which we have an experience. It exists only in the present. Satisfaction [a.k.a. well-being] is that which remains in the mind."[10] So when someone talks about happiness, it is useful to distinguish between the short-term emotion and the longer-term sense of well-being.

This suggests that understanding what makes people happy over the long term provides insight into how to relate to them in the present.

Service to God or others. Many cite service to God or a higher power as a purpose. Religions have long advocated this as the proper purpose. Several popular books have recently been published on this topic, such as *The Purpose Driven Life*,[v] *The Power of Intention*,[vi] and *The Highest Goal*.[vii] The emergence of 12-step programs in the 20th century suggest that staying free from addiction and helping other addicts to recover are the primary purposes of a recovering addict. These consumers may apply a criterion of alignment with their purpose to organizations they choose to patronize. At a minimum, they may avoid organizations they see as hostile to their purpose.

Creative expression. An emerging purpose accompanying the rise of post-modern values is an individual's creative expression. People with this purpose feel that they have a reason for being on this earth, a special talent or contribution to make, and their mission is to find that purpose and pursue it. Richard Florida, in his popular book *The Creative Class*, cites, "The rise of human creativity as the key factor in our economy and society."[11] Similarly, Julia Cameron suggests creative expression as a purpose in her popular book *The Artist's Way*: "Creativity is the natural order of life."[12] It's not just the pursuit of creativity but the expression of it to others that in part explains the boom in social media. People want to share their creative purpose with others.

v   Warren, R. (2007). *The Purpose Driven Life: What on Earth Am I Here For?* Zondervan.
vi   Dyer, W. (2005). *The Power of Intention. Hay House.*
vii Ray, M. (2004). *The Highest Goal: The Secret That Sustains You in Every Moment.* San Francisco, CA.

Beliefs

Beliefs are what one holds to be true about the world. They are in effect one's personal knowledge base. Berger notes, "As long as my knowledge works satisfactorily, I am generally ready to suspend doubts about it."[13] Beliefs are typically consistent with needs-values-worldviews[viii] and purpose. Changes in beliefs will in turn influence these units. If one changes a belief about the proper role of an individual within a society, this will influence one's needs-values-worldviews and larger purpose where one is present. For example, people with traditional values may change their belief that their proper role is to follow the rules of their established social class and move to a belief that they ought to be able to change their roles or status through hard work. In fact, this is a key change that takes place in the evolution from traditional to modern values. This change in values doesn't happen without an accompanying change in beliefs, suggesting that changes in our identity are a package deal—not just one thing changes, but changes have ripple effects. Or as systems theorist Draper Kaufman puts it, "You can never do just one thing… Everything is connected to everything else."[14]

Needs

Needs are the motivators for action that values often address. The four categories used here are drawn primarily from Maslow's Hierarchy of Human Needs, which has been the most widely accepted system for categorizing needs. While it may have flaws and has been criticized by many, this is common for any conceptual scheme that achieves a leading status. For the purpose of this work, the overall scheme hangs together well and merits its position as a starting point in exploring needs. It fits with other approaches to categorizing needs, such as those of Max-Neef and Reiss, which will be described in more detail in Chapter 6, "Consumer Sweet Spots: Identifying Emerging Need States." In addition, Maslow's hierarchy relates well with the data from the World Values Survey and the Spiral Dynamics Worldviews, the other primary inputs into the inner dimensions models.

Values

The *New Dimensions Values Inventory* presented in Chapter 4 has been constructed over the last several years based on input from eight formal values systems and several other informal ones—more than 20 systems in total. While the overlap between the various systems is not 100%, it is very close. Many researchers coming at the question of values from different perspectives have come to similar conclusions. This is certainly not proof of being correct, but it is

---

viii   Needs, values, and worldviews are suggested as fitting together into a coherent pattern. This relationship is described in more detail in Chapter 4, How Changing Values Are the Single Biggest Influence on Consumers.

more comforting than if they were coming to completely different conclusions. The *New Dimensions Values Inventory* uses the traditional, modern, and postmodern values from Inglehart's World Values Survey as its base. The World Values Survey has been consistently tracking changes in values via surveys about every five years since the 1970s in over 100 countries. Even though the choice of values may be fairly limited, it is expanded here by adding values to the three types based on the other systems and on subsequent research. Another enhancement to this foundational work is the addition of a fourth type of emerging values called Integral, suggested by Beck in his Spiral Dynamics system, and reinforced by additional research. These Integral values have not yet been validated in the field and thus are more conjectural than the traditional, modern, and postmodern values.

These values will be covered in depth in Chapter 4, "How Changing Values Are the Single Biggest Influence on Consumers."

Worldviews

Spiral Dynamics offers an excellent approach and system for understanding worldviews. The system has nine categories of vMemes (value memes), which are defined as a worldview, a valuing system, a level of psychological existence, a belief structure, an organizing principle, a way of thinking, or a mode of adjustment.[15] "Worldview" is used as shorthand here, serving as an umbrella concept to synthesize the essence of the underlying related values and to capture the central theme of one's values. For example, a Green Communitarian worldview will include values such as sustainability, community, and authenticity.

Table 1. Spiral Dynamics Worldviews		
Color	What they seek	Percent
Beige (survival)	Biogenic needs satisfaction; reproduction	0.1%
Purple (safety)	Protection from harm; tribal/family bonds	10%
Red (power)	Asserting self to dominate others; control	20%
Blue (Order)	Obedience to earn later reward; meaning	40%
Orange (competitve)	Competing to achieve results; influence	30%
Green (communitarian)	Joining together for mutual growth; awareness	10%
Yellow (integrative)	Fitting a living system; knowing	1%
Turquoise (holistic)	Survival of the Earth; consciousness	0.1%
Coral	Not clearly emerged yet	

Source: A. Hines, based on Beck & Cowan, *Spiral Dynamics*

The Spiral Dynamics system does not focus much on individual values per se, but there is strong overlap in the worldview concept and the four types of values identified in this work. These values are in turn based on similarly related groups of needs, with Maslow's hierachy as the core organizing system. In a nutshell, Maslow's needs overlap Inglehart's values, which in turn overlap Beck's Worldviews. Different researchers and research approaches have focused on different apects of a phenomenon, with one of this work's core insights being to look across these multiple interpretations and see common patterns.

The Spiral Dynamics team has developed an assessment instrument for identifying one's worldview. They claim to have administered around 50,000 of them over the years in a wide range of cultures and thus believe they have a representative picture of their representation among the global population.

Other researchers use the worldview concept as well. Hall, for instance, says, "The phrase world view is another way of saying 'the way we see the world through our values. Each person's world view is associated with a specific set of values.'"[16]

MIND-BODY

In the model, identity emerges from mind and body, is influenced by external forces, and is expressed in behavior. Mind-body is considered as a single coordinate. While one could argue that mind and body have always been strongly linked in some cultures, in the West they have been separated, at least conceptually, by reductionist thinking. The model puts them back together, recognizing that the mind-body connection is strong. As Houston notes, "We can no longer escape the understanding that psyche and soma are inextricably woven together."[17] She goes on to acknowledge, however, that the body has been alienated by Western culture as a result of our increasing reliance on the word, the concept, the abstraction.[18] In fact, a central assertion of the model is that all the coordinates and units are interconnected. One cannot separate cognition from the body or from the external environment, as they each influence one another and in turn influence identity and thus values.

MIND-BASED UNITS

More is being learned about how the mind works in terms of hardware (neuroscience) and software (psychology, consciousness studies, etc.). Popular books by Klein[19] and Lehrer[20] provide highly readable accounts of how neuroscience is aiding understanding in happiness and decision making, respectively. Following on that knowledge, more is being learned on how to influence the mind, again from both perspectives. From the hardware side, more and more therapeutics are available to influence the mind—as well as the body. Prozac® is revolutionary in the sheer numbers of people who have used it and made it "okay" to admit to depression. On the software side, research is revealing that meditation influences the brain's performance. An enhanced understanding of the mind components is useful in understanding how values emerge and play a role in decision making. The model focuses on five units of analysis within the mind.

Memory

Memory, the ability to store, retain, and recall information, is shaped by context. An individual's sense of identity and current moods influence what memories are called forth. For example, people who are feeling a strong sense of self and are in a good mood are more likely to call up a positive memory of a situation than when the reverse is true. Zaltman notes that not only do people recall an experience differently depending on the triggering cue but that they are unaware of any difference.[21]

Memory is also incomplete. One does not typically fully recall a memory, and thus has to fill in some of the blanks. Zaltman talks a great deal about how our memories are imperfect in the sense of not necessarily reflecting back a 100% accurate storage of what we remember. The memory fills in gaps, and that "filling-in" process is influenced by the individual's context and current emotional state—and, in many cases, values: if our memory isn't sure about an interpretation, the interpretation will tend to be in line with that our current state and sense of identity and values. Friends with common memories often joke about "selective recall," which is the tendency to fill in the blanks with (usually) favorable information. Many times we remember an experience as being much more fun or happier than it really was. We remember the wonderful baseball game that went into extra innings but forget that at the time we were freezing cold, hungry, and actually glad when the game was over! Organizations may deliver a message one way, but consumers may later recall that message differently as it is shaped by other factors. What comes out from memory may not be the same as what went in, since even what goes in is shaped by values, emotions, and context.

Advances in neuroscience are also revealing more about how the brain and the memory work. It is gradually moving beyond simply understanding that this part of the brain lights up when someone thinks or does "x," to a more sophisticated understanding of how and why the circuitry works, which will assist neuroscientists. This type of information is likely to appeal to postmodern and integral values holders who tend to be interested in this level of self-analysis and self-improvement. Being more aware of their values, they are thus more likely to take advantage of insights from this research.

Imprints

Imprints are a type of memory storage. The experiences that create imprints are those with a strong emotional component that is deep and meaningful; such memories are stored deep in the subconscious. Rapaille has done pioneering work in how to identify and uncover these imprints. He believes that they are associated with "cultural codes" or points of view regarding particular entities: "The culture code is the unconscious meaning we apply to any given thing—a car, a type of food, a relationship, even a country—via the culture in which we are raised… It all comes down to the worlds in which we grew up."[22] He has developed a methodology that employs a three-hour workshop in which participants engage in three different activities to probe for and uncover imprints.[23] He suggests that memories can be influenced by cultural conditioning. For instance, the cultural code for cars in America is "identity," while in Germany it is "engineering." What he's saying is that Americans tend to choose vehicles that represent who they are—perhaps a sports car to signify youth—while Germans tend to be more focused on the engineering. Taking it a step further, he suggests that organizations can learn these codes and target their messaging accordingly. This imprinting process may also be associated with how one learns about or is conditioned to think about values.

Intuition

Intuition is about surfacing knowledge held in the subconscious. Zaltman suggests that 95% of thinking is unconscious. He goes so far as to suggest that "rather than actually guiding or controlling behavior, consciousness seems mainly to make sense of behavior after it is executed."[24] Similarly, Capra refers to Lakoff and Johnson's *Philosophy in the Flesh*, which says most of our thought is unconscious, operating at a level that is inaccessible to ordinary conscious awareness. This cognitive unconscious includes not only all our automatic cognitive operations but also our tacit knowledge and beliefs. Without awareness, the cognitive unconscious shapes and structures all conscious thought.[25]

Consumers do not typically consciously call on their values when making decisions—most are not even conscious of their values. When people are asked why they made a particular decision, it may take a few seconds for them to revisit the process, and even then they may not be sure. The influence of values operates largely at the subconscious level most of the time, although for important or major decisions—part of Zaltman's 5%—consumers may consciously invoke values to help them make a decision.

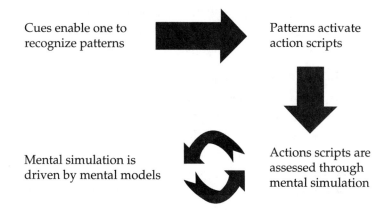

Cues enable one to
recognize patterns

Patterns activate
action scripts

Mental simulation is
driven by mental models

Actions scripts are
assessed through
mental simulation

Figure 7. Intuitive decision making
Klein's process of intuitive decision making. Klein, G. (2003). *The Power of Intuition: How to Use Your Gut Feelings to Make Better Decisions at Work*. NY: Currency Doubleday, . 28.

Klein observes that, "Because pattern matching can take place in an instant, and without conscious thought, we're not aware of how we arrived at an intuitive judgment."[26] Intuition tends work better in situations where one has experience. In effect, aspects of the experience are stored in memory, and they get triggered when a similar situation arises, and come to the aid of the decision—all this operating largely unconsciously. One may wonder "where did that come from?" Similarly, Lehrer advises using one's conscious mind to acquire all the information related to a decision and to then let the unconscious mind digest it, as he believes that whatever intuition emerges is almost certainly going to be the best choice.[27] This is not to suggest that intuition is infallible; it's not. It does demonstrate that the influence of deeply held memories, experiences, beliefs, and values is alive and well at the subconscious level. It influences consumer life from there as well as more explicitly at the conscious level. Values also operate at an unconscious and intuitive level.

Thinking style

People have different styles of thinking, which can also influence how values are expressed. Styles tend to follow certain patterns, and many different schemes for explaining these patterns have emerged. Consumers with different styles will interpret and process the same information in a different way. My interest in these instruments arose from my observation in leading training workshops that participants with similar backgrounds, education, and a seemingly large collection of things in common approached problem solving in completely different ways. The popular Meyers-Briggs personality instrument explained a certain amount of the difference, but not enough. People with the same Meyers-Briggs personality type still seemed to be coming from completely different places. Further investigation revealed the genre of thinking style differences, which helped fill in the blanks.

There are many different instruments for assessing thinking styles, including the Kirton Adaptation-Innovation instrument (KAI) and the Herman Brain Dominance Instrument (HBDI). I generally use the simple but elegant four-style system developed by Gerald "Solutionman" Haman[ix] and others. Their instrument, adapted from the more complex HBDI,[x] assesses thinking style in terms of an individual's preferred approach to innovation. Haman pioneered a 30-minute "Know Your Brain" exercise that is a quick and effective way to identify an individual's preferred thinking style. The four styles are characterized in Chapter 8, "Customizing the Personas."

Feelings

Feelings are considered to be at the intersection of mind and body. They are in effect the mind's recognition of the body's emotional response to a situation. Emotions precede feelings. Whereas an emotion is the body's automatic response to a specific stimulus, the feeling is how one interprets that emotion. People tend to mix the two together, but distinguishing them is helpful: emotions operate subconsciously while feelings are conscious. The relationship between the two shows how we bridge the conscious-unconscious divide. People routinely access the unconscious to aid the conscious. This bridge is not always a perfect crossing. As noted with intuition, there are often errors in the intuitive decision-making process.

Similarly, people are often not sure what emotion they felt or are feeling. And as Klein notes, "Emotions can remain hidden from us, for example, when we blush[an indicator of embarrassment] and no one brings it to our attention."[28] Gilbert adds, "Research shows that physiological arousal can be interpreted in a variety of ways, and our interpretation of our arousal depends on what we believe caused it. It is possible to mistake fear for lust, apprehension for guilt, shame for anxiety."[29] Feelings are powerful in the moment and can be an important factor in influencing whether we express our true values or go counter to them. For example, people who are feeling depressed may act in opposition to their values and buy a cheaper product that is bad for the environment when they are depressed, feeling at the particular moment that their support for environmentalism is a lost cause.

---

ix   See www.solutionpeople.com
x   See www.hbdi.com

Mental model

The mental model is how one believes and represents the way things work. People cannot represent every aspect of a situation they are trying to understand, so they rely on informal models that capture the key aspects of the situation and run simulations of how they might interact. At the highest level, mental models represent one's view of how things work. Klein observes that "mental models are our beliefs about how various processes work. They direct our explanations and expectations."[30]

Mental models are powerful in that they shape what one sees and what one doesn't see. People will tend to seek out information that confirms their mental model and tend to overlook contradictory information. It takes a concerted effort to challenge one's own mental model. Scharmer notes that "we see problems, then 'download' our established mental models to both define the problem and come up with solutions. For example, when we listen, we usually hear very little other than what we have heard before. 'There she goes again,' calls out the voice in our heads. From that point forward, we selectively hear only what we recognize, interpret what we hear based on our past views and feelings, and draw conclusions much like those we have drawn before."[31]

Hofstede uses the concept of "software of the mind" synonymously with our mental models. He notes that "as soon as certain patterns of thinking, feeling, and acting have established themselves within a person's mind, he or she must unlearn these before being able to learn something different, and unlearning is more difficult than learning for the first time."[32]

We typically have to train ourselves to see contradictory information. This is the essence of creative thinking. At the heart of creativity tools are different mechanisms to "trick" the brain out of its default pattern. This was a key insight of creativity guru Edward de Bono with his lateral thinking concept.[xi] The modeling process operates largely unconsciously; thus, one may be unaware of this filtering process.

The reliance on mental models and the difficulty in changing them is part of the reason that values are difficult to change as well. For most people, it is more common and comfortable to rely on established routines. At the same time, since it plays such a vital role in decision making and behavior, influencing the mental model is a high leverage point. In terms of role of the mind in thinking about the future, Pierre Wack, the Shell pioneer in scenario planning, popularized the

---

xi   De Bono says he invented the term in 1967 and it first appears in *The Use of Lateral Thinking*. London: Jonathan Cape, 1967. My personal favorite of his many books is *Serious Creativity: Using the Power of Lateral Thinking to Create New Ideas*. HarperBusiness, 1993.

importance of understanding mental models,[xii] suggesting that the goal of scenario planning was ultimately to influence the mental model of decision makers.

BODY-BASED UNITS

The body, of course, is the hardware for the inner dimension. It can be separated into three units, with emotions and moods grouped together, and genetic predispositions. In terms of relating to values, emotions and moods have their origins in the body and influence consumer decision making, but their influence is short-term and situational. Genetic endowments and predispositions are a big influence on how consumers behave over the long term. More is being learned about their influence, although the learning seems to reveal ever greater complexity and the need to learn more.

Emotions and moods

Emotions are placed in the body in the model as they can be physically felt, e.g., the heart rate speeds up. Emotions are strong motivators, and many have been identified as universals (see text box "A Note on Universals"). They are the body's automatic, typically unconscious response to stimuli that one often describes as feelings, and when these emotions last a long time, at a lower level of intensity, they can be described as moods. Ekman notes the difference between emotions and moods:[33]

A note on "universals"

Needs, values, and worldviews are universal in the sense that they apply across geographies and cultures. The seminal work in universals was done by Brown. He suggests that because universals are universal, they aren't noticed and are taken for granted. Although the long list he identifies doesn't explicitly include values, they are suggested by the inclusion of several other components of the *New Dimensions of Consumer Life Model*, e.g., worldviews, cultures, and emotions.
Source: Brown, D. (1991). *Human Universals*. McGraw-Hill, vii, 139.

Berlin, however, does include values: "Universal values... are values that a great many human beings in the vast majority of places and situations, at almost all times, do in fact hold in common, whether consciously and explicitly or as expressed in their behavior." Source: Jahanbegloo, R. (1991). *Conversations With Isaiah Berlin*. McArthur & Co. Reprinted 2007. Halban Publishers.

Ekman found that seven emotions share universal facial expressions: anger, disgust, fear, happiness, sadness, surprise, and contempt. Four others—embarrassment, guilt, shame, envy—appear universal, but do not share a common facial expression.
Source: Ekman, P. (2003). *Emotions Revealed: Recognizing Faces and Feelings to Improve Communication and Emotional Life*. Times Books, 58.

Finally, Wilber: "Evolutionary psychology gives much more interesting and compelling explanations of human behavior than the standard postmodern claim that all behavior is culturally relative and socially constructed. Evolutionary psychology made it clear that there are indeed universals in the human condition.
Source: Wilber, K. (2000). *A Theory of Everything*. Boston: Shambhala, ix.

---

xii   Wack, P. (1985, September–October). Scenarios: Uncharted Waters Ahead. *Harvard Business Review*.

- Emotions are much shorter; moods can last a long time.

- Moods resemble a slight but continuous emotional state.

- A mood activates specific emotions—the world is interpreted via one's moods.

- Moods don't have their own signal in either the face or the voice.

- Whereas we can usually identify the trigger for emotions, the "why" is often elusive in moods—they just happen.

Emotions and their counterpart feelings are powerful in the sense that they can override the "logic" of the mind. While they are important, their influence is primarily at a particular point in time. Thus, they don't provide a very robust source of clues to long-term change in consumer life. That is not to say emotions and values are not related. Research has suggested links between values and emotions.[xiii] Our emotional state is highly influential and can "override" values or other components in the heat of the moment. In other words, emotions have the ability to influence us toward decisions or behaviors that are contrary to our values. For example, they might lead us to shut a colleague out of a decision process when we're angry, going against our value of collaboration. In particular, emotions tend to favor short-term gains at the expense of a longer-term, more rational decision.[34]

Typically, product developers assume a rational, or at least a nonemotional, consumer. But what is the typical state of an individual making choices relevant to an organization? It may be that certain products or services are highly emotional choices (e.g., chocolates) about which consumers will make impulsive or perhaps even destructive choices to indulge because of an existing emotional state.

Genetic predispositions

New research and tools are improving the understanding of inner life. Genetic research is undermining the notion that people are born as a blank slate. Personal genetic screening, gene surveys, and identification of links between genes and behaviors are revealing new insights into the nature-versus-nurture debate. The last decade brought steady progress in understanding the role of genes in disease. More recent advances have made it easier for geneticists to find links between an individual's genes and their complete phenotype—the total package of physical and behavioral characteristics that have historically been attributed to chance, free will, and environment. Researchers are increasingly finding genetic markers not only for disease but also for behavioral traits. This raises questions about how much control we as individuals have over our

xiii   See Laverie, D., Kleine, R., & Schultz Kleine, S. (1993). Linking Emotions and Values in Consumption Experiences: An Exploratory Study." *Advances in Consumer Research*, 20, 70–75.

personalities. For instance, researchers have identified the specific location of genes related to alcohol, nicotine, and heroin addictions. What does this say about our degree of control over addictive substances? If we are programmed genetically for addiction, would the development of genetic therapies "fix" the bad genes be a cure, or would there still be a significant role for environmental influences? Instead of going to the typical 28-day rehab, would addicts go for gene therapy?

The debate will continue over the role of free will and the extent to which "human nature" can be changed by environmental interventions. Klein observes that "the effect of a specific gene on the organism depends to a large extent on its interactions with the external world."[35] He goes on to observe that Lykken's studies of more than 4,000 identical twins concluded that happiness was "at least 50% inherited."[36] Finally, Layard suggests that "all that our genes do is provide or not provide some predisposition. Most of our traits come from a mixture of genes and experience; the genes affect how we respond to our experience."[37] If so much of our happiness is derived from our genes, this suggests that the development of relevant genetic tests could provide useful insight into meeting people's needs—assuming consumers would be willing to share such information. Interesting questions arise: would most people want to know if they were genetically predisposed to be unhappy?

Key points

- The *New Dimensions of Consumer Life Model* is introduced to provide a comprehensive framework to understand consumer life and how it is changing. Its intent is to provide a common understanding to help align organizational understanding of consumer life. This alignment is critically important. So many times organizational conversations about consumers circle endlessly because different participants are using different definitions or different models. This model provides a starting point to gain the agreement that can enable more productive conversations, planning, and action.

- Consumer life is divided into an inner and an outer dimension. This chapter focuses on the inner dimension, putting identity at the center, and suggesting that the values at the core of identity constitute the key element to study in order to understand how consumers change. Values are fundamental influences on people's decision and behavior. They are particularly valuable here because research has revealed that they change in predictable patterns over time, thus providing valuable assistance in anticipating how consumer life will change into the future.

- The units of consumer life are identified and described, in particular, noting their relationship to values. These details are important for avoiding the confusion that comes from overlapping definitions, interchangeable use of terms, and the differences that people from different backgrounds and training bring to the table. They also help tie the concepts together in a systematic manner, both in how they relate to one another and to the focal point of values.

- This chapter focuses on the interior aspect of the inner dimension. Identity is at the core, as influenced by the mind and body. Each of these units is unique to the individual. On the one hand, external influences described in Chapter 3 are trying to influence the interior, such as what values one should hold. On the other hand, this interior—again, values in particular—influence the behavior that the world sees.

3

WHAT'S BEING SAID TO CONSUMERS

The previous chapter described the interior aspect of individuals—minds, bodies, and identities—which is uniquely theirs. Only they can reveal it should they choose to. Students of consumer life must rely on interpretation for understanding it—there is no instrument available to attach and provide a subjective measurement. There is a second aspect of the inner dimension that is more or less an intersection or boundary between the inner and outer dimensions. It is positioned here on the inner-dimension side of the fence, but could just as easily be placed on the other side, or it could be described as the fence itself.

A key distinction between the exterior and the interior is that one can "see" these units to a much greater extent. Not completely, as one can with the outer dimensions, but they are not as invisible as the inner-interior dimensions. It's possible to see, for instance, a community's morals, ethics, or norms in the textbooks approved for teaching its children or in the laws it passes. That is not the whole story, of course, as there is an informal transmission of these units as well. But it is not completely interpretive; there is something measurable that can be seen, thus a distinction worth making.

The exterior aspect is sorted into two coordinates: the external influences, with six primary units, and behavior, also with six primary units.

External influences

The external influences on the inner dimension are on the boundary with the outer dimensions. They are included on the inner side because they directly influence values. Culture, for instance, takes aim at people's values, attempting to provide them with guidance on the values they ought to adopt. It passes on the "right" values from one generation to the next. Culture does adapt to changes in circumstances or life conditions (described below) to provide its members with the tools to navigate the world successfully. Cultures that fail to adapt to change often fade away or die out.

A key distinction here is that values are what the individual ultimately chooses to live by, and norms/morals/ethics are attempts by outside groups within the culture to dictate or influence what those values choices should be. Culture is in turn influenced by new or potential paradigms and ideologies. And there are fundamental stories that explain how the culture makes sense of the world in the form of archetypes, "The American Dream" being an example.

Life conditions

The concept of life conditions is borrowed from Beck's *Spiral Dynamics*. Beck observes that "life conditions awaken value memes [a.k.a. worldviews]."[38] In other words, people's needs-values-worldviews are influenced by the conditions in which they live. The "best" values are those most appropriate to the life conditions in which they find themselves. For example, for someone living in a part of Afghanistan characterized by conflict, it may be that the Spiral Red (Power) worldview and related values are the most appropriate to the situation, and that a Spiral Green (Communitarian) worldview could be dangerous. This approach of needs-values-worldviews fitting the life conditions provides a response to those who object to the hierarchical models of development that imply that the top of the hierarchy is the "best." The top is indeed the most complex, and people have access to a wider range of thinking and options at that level, but it will not be the most appropriate approach for every set of life conditions.

Table 2. Spiral Dynamics Worldviews		
Color	What they seek	Percent
Beige (survival)	Biogenic needs satisfaction; reproduction	0.1%
Purple (safety)	Protection from harm; tribal/family bonds	10%
Red (power)	Asserting self to dominate others; control	20%
Blue (Order)	Obedience to earn later reward; meaning	40%
Orange (competitve)	Competing to achieve results; influence	30%
Green(communitarian)	Joining together for mutual growth; awareness	10%
Yellow (integrative)	Fitting a living system; knowing	1%
Turquoise (holistic)	Survival of the Earth; consciousness	0.1%
Coral	Not clearly emerged yet	

Source: A. Hines, based on Beck & Cowan, *Spiral Dynamics*

This suggested match between values and life conditions is borne out in the world at large as well. Inglehart observes, "We find remarkably strong linkages between macro-level characteristics such as stable democracy, and micro-level characteristics, such as trust, tolerance, post-materialist values, and subjective well-being."[39] The influence of life conditions on values is strong. Berger notes that "Identity [and thus values] is formed by social processes. Once crystallized, it is maintained, modified, or even reshaped by social relations. The social processes involved in both the formation and the maintenance of identity are determined by the social structure. Identity is a phenomenon that emerges from the dialectic between individual and society."[40] In other words, values are influenced by culture as well as living conditions. One may choose to have values that are at odds with both, but that is the exception, not the rule. One may choose frugality in a culture that emphasizes material goods acquisition but is likely to face social pressure to conform: "Why don't you ever come to dinner with us [at the expensive five-star restaurant]?"

Morals, norms, and ethics

Morals, norms, ethics, and values are often treated as synonymous. While this could be attributed to mere sloppiness, it may be fairer to observe that different researchers coming from different perspectives bring different interpretations. Universal definitions and distinctions have not clearly emerged. The distinctions are fine, as these units are typically synchronized. For example, an individual may adopt a value of family-orientation in response to a cultural norm around family-orientation that favors this.

The stake in the ground here is first between morals-norms-ethics and values; that is, the former are external forces attempting to influence the latter. Morals, norms, and ethics have their roots in the prevailing culture and groups within the culture while values are distinguished as individual choices. There is little practical distinction between morals and norms—they are essentially cultural views on right and wrong. They are directly related to virtues and have an indirect role in providing guidance on values as well. Ethics are a subset of morals and norms: they refer to rules or standards of conduct for specific groups, such as professional codes of ethics. Lawyers, doctor, architects, and most professions establish these codes to guide their members on the proper conduct as it relates to their profession. Professional codes are set up as standards for the individual to observe, but it is still up to individuals whether to observe them or not; that is, individuals still make the choice of which related values they will observe.

Ideology and paradigm

This brief plunge into the dangerous territory of ideologies and paradigms is deemed useful as they can influence people's values. The danger lies in the many conflicting views of what they are; thus a brief synthesis may be viewed as an oversimplification. As the term suggests, an ideology is a collection or system of ideas. It often prescribes the appropriate ideas—including values—that adherents ought to maintain. As Williams notes, "When we can identify interconnected sets of values and beliefs which describe a preferred or obligatory state of a social system, we speak of an ideology."[41]

The most common forms of ideologies are political, although it can be said that religions are a type of ideology as well. Marxism in the former USSR is a classic example of a dominant political ideology holding sway over a large group of people. Its control over the nation was comprehensive to the point that it was very difficult for its citizens to even be exposed to or aware of other ideas or values. The control of information was perhaps unprecedented. Many experts feel that the USSR's ultimate collapse was in large part due to advanced communications technologies having made it possible for new ideas to more easily infiltrate, which in turn led the citizenry to rebel. One could argue over the extent to which every citizen actually adhered to the officially prescribed values versus paying lip service to them to survive. Inglehart's World Values Survey data suggests Marxism indeed had a strong influence on the people's values.

The classic notion of the paradigm comes from Kuhn's *The Structure of Scientific Revolutions* in which he described it as a set of practices that define a scientific discipline at a particular time. The paradigm includes a set of beliefs or orthodoxies in which contrary views will tend to be filtered out. He suggests that the only way a paradigm can be overcome in science is when the existing group of adherents is replaced with new ones with the passage of time.

Futurist Joel Barker gained notoriety for applying the concept of paradigms to business. He suggests that a paradigm is a problem-solving system: "A paradigm is a system of rules and regulations (written or unwritten) that does two things: (1) it establishes or defines boundaries; and (2) it tells you how to behave inside the boundaries in order to be successful."[42] He notes the importance of paradigms in telling the story of the decline of the Swiss watch-making industry with the advent of digital watches, which led to their market share declining from 65% to less than 10% because they had missed a paradigm shift in the fundamental rules of watch-making.[43]

Values-related paradigm

Paradigms, too, are defined and applied in different ways. Futurist Willis Harman identified three types of paradigms, based on metaphysical perspectives:

- m-1 Materialistic monism (matter giving rise to mind)

- m-2 Dualism (matter plus mind)

- m-3 Transcendental Monism (mind giving rise to matter)

He suggests that five values emphases are implied in the emerging switch to the m-3 paradigm:

- humans in harmony with nature

- humans in harmony with one another

- individual self-realization

- decentralization and an ecology of cultures

- globalization of global issues

Source: Harman, W. (1998). *Global Mind Change: The Promise of the 21st Century*. San Francisco: Berrett-Koehler, 30.

These descriptions of ideologies and paradigms suggest that they are powerful forces to be reckoned with in terms of influencing values, albeit their influence may be a bit tangential or indirect in terms of the focus on consumer values.

Archetypes, myths, and metaphors

Archetypes, myths, and metaphors exist at the deepest levels of the unconscious. They are deep stories that provide explanations of various phenomena—they help one to make sense of the world. They are held so deeply that one is not consciously aware of them. Jung suggests that archetypes are the components of a collective unconscious: "In addition to our immediate consciousness, which is of a thoroughly personal nature... there exists a second psychic system of a collective, universal, and impersonal nature which is identical in all people. This collective unconscious does not develop individually, but is inherited. It consists of pre-existent forms, the archetypes, which can only become conscious secondarily and which give definite form to certain psychic contents."[44]

While the idea that archetypes are inherited has been largely discredited, his work popularized the notion of universal archetypes available to individuals. Jung saw myths as a projection of this collective unconscious.

Campbell's work on myths suggests their importance as a way of making sense of the world and communicating wisdom via stories and metaphors. His *The Hero with a Thousand Faces* explored the role of myths in providing a guide to spiritual transformation. Vogler's *The Writer's Journey* extended Campbell's work to screenwriting and noted the pervasiveness of traditional myths in contemporary Hollywood cinema, citing *Star Wars* as a famous movie closely adhering to this script.

Futurist Sohail Inayatullah developed a methodology called Causal Layered Analysis that puts myths and metaphors at the foundation of understanding the unconscious and often emotive dimensions of a problem or issue. He notes that they bring a gut-emotional level perspective, and observes that "believing that the future is like a roll of dice is quite different from the Arab saying of the future, 'Trust in Allah but tie your camel,' which differs again from the American vision of the future as unbounded, full of choice and opportunity. For the Confucian, choice and opportunity exist in the context of family and ancestors and not merely as individual decisions."[45] The key point is that these myths or stories have a strong influence on one's identity and values.

These archetypes/myths/metaphors can both influence as well as reflect values. For example, when looking at the issues of environmentalism, fundamental archetypes/myths/metaphors are at play. Lovelock's *Gaia*[xiv] notion suggests that the Earth is a fragile, living organism that requires a stewardship approach, whereas the more common notion is that "Earth is made for man."[xv] People with strong environmental values are likely to be influenced by or supportive of the Gaia notion. Thus, understanding the prevailing archetypes/myths/metaphors can provide insight into cultural influences on one's values, or changing values may challenge prevailing archetypes.

Generation-based approaches

Generations are cohorts of individuals born in the same date range and sharing a similar cultural experience. Strauss and Howe popularized the notion that there was cyclicality in generational archetypes and outlined their theory of generational cycles in their 1991 book *Generations*.[46] They claim that the patterns go back some 500 years. These archetypes are briefly characterized in Chapter 8: "Customizing the Personas: A Persona Construction Kit," where they are suggested as potential ingredients in crafting personas.

Strauss and Howe's work is limited to the United States. There does not appear to be an explanation that transcends cultures—it is not clear if this is because one doesn't exist or simply that one has not yet been uncovered by research. The relevant point for this work is that one's generation is yet another potential influence on one's values.

The table on the right captures some of the key differences among the three American generations where values change is most likely to take place (the Mature generation is less likely to be at the vanguard of values change and thus are not included).

---

xiv   See http://www.ecolo.org/lovelock/
xv   For an excellent critique of "the Earth is made for man," see Quinn, D. (1992). *Ishmael* Bantam.

Table 3. Comparing the generations			
	Boomers (1946–1964)	**Gen X** (1965–1976)	**Gen Y** (1977–1994)
Childhood	Treated as special	Neglected, criticized	Admire parents
Young adults	Rebellious then narcissistic	Risk takers, alienated	Heroic achievers
Mature adults	Moralistic, detached	Pragmatic, exhausted	Powerful, arrogant
Elderly adults	Visionary, civilization focus	Reclusive, caustic	Busy, community focus
Family life	Nuclear family	Single-parent family	Single-parent family
Defining value	Youth	Diversity	Duty
Goals sought	Self-fulfillment	Self-sufficiency	World improvement
Leading style	Righteous	Pragmatic	Expansive
Spending	Spenders, principled, and creative	Hedgers, savvy, and practical	Savers, rational, and competent
Personal traits	Resolute, perceptive, selfless	Ruthless, amoral, overbold	Arrogant, pecuniary, and insensitive

Source: Strauss and Howe

Culture

The topic of culture is the subject of many books, and it is somewhat presumptuous to synthesize its role in influencing values in just a few paragraphs. The focus of this work, however, necessitates these choices. Several excellent characterizations of culture include these:

- "Culture is mental software... culture is a catchword for all those patterns of thinking, feeling, and acting... It is the collective programming of the mind that distinguishes the members of one group or category of people from others."[47]

- "Culture consists of the conventional patterns of thought, activity, and artifact that are passed on from generation to generation in a manner that is generally assumed to involve learning rather than specific genetic programming."[48]

- "Culture is the way in which a group of people solve problems."[49]

The important point is that culture decides what morals/norms/ethics are to be socialized and thus influences what the available values choices are. This influence is both explicit and implicit. As Hofstede observes, "The sources of one's mental programs lie within the social environment... The programming starts within the family; it continues within the neighborhood, at school, in youth groups, at the workplace, and in the living community."[50] Williams adds,

"Values always have a cultural content, represent a psychological investment, and are shaped by the constraints and opportunities of a social system and of a biophysical environment."[51]

The influence of culture is strong, particularly if the society tends to be more closed. There may be few other options for individuals in terms of access to values outside the culture or society. This is why cults, for example, typically keep members from being exposed to outsiders. New ideas are "dangerous" to those who want to maintain thought control. Thus, one of the big impacts of globalization and the communication revolution is that it provides access to a greater pool of ideas and values. The recent revolutions in the Arab world are an example of how the spread of new ideas and the communication of their impact can spread in viral fashion.

Even in the face of widely available ideas, the influence of culture remains strong. Inglehart notes that "although the value systems of different countries are moving in the same direction under the impact of powerful modernizing forces, their value systems have not been converging... Cultural change is path dependent."[52] This suggests that the world is not in any imminent danger of homogenization. Values changes can be thought of as structurally similar, with different cultural interpretations. The value of self-expression, for example, is increasingly prevalent in many different cultures, but self-expression in the Unites States is quite different than self-expression in Japan, owing to the differences in cultural heritages. In short, self-expression in the United States tends to be much louder and flashier than in Japan, where the cultural heritage favors individual restraint. Put simply, the same value can be expressed differently in different cultures.

BEHAVIOR

Whereas values are what one aspires to, behavior is what one does. "Behavior may be viewed as the manifestation of attitudes and values."[53] They are not, of course, always in sync. As Loehr and Schwartz observe, "Too often our motivation for a behavior is expedient rather than value-driven."[54] One might have a value of wellness, for example, but then dine out with friends and choose a cheeseburger rather than ask for a special-order vegan burger.

Behavior is easier to study than interior units, as it can be observed and measured while interior units, such as values, rely on interpretation. The argument here is that to understand long-term change, one must understand what is driving behavior—thus the focus on values.

The operational definition of core values here is that one has to have acted on it—it has to manifest in behavior—in order to be considered a core value. Values influence behavior in combination with other components of the model, such as one's attitude, which is a context-specific orientation. As Williams notes, "Values influence but do not determine behavior.[55]

Traits

Traits are habitual patterns of behavior. They are the way a person typically responds to a particular situation. They are a mix of hardware and software. Layard suggests, "Most of our traits come from a mixture of genes and experience; the genes affect how we respond to our experience."[56] Traits will thus influence how values are expressed. Examples of traits are shyness or a sense of humor—or lack thereof. For example, a person with the trait of shyness and the value of self-expression would likely exhibit self-expression in a more restrained fashion than would someone with the trait of extroversion. While we can self-report our traits, they can also be directly observed and identified by others; values, in contrast, must be inferred from our behaviors. Our collection of traits comes together to form our personality.

Virtues

Virtues are placed in the realm of right and wrong. Our collection of virtues comprises our character. Virtues are the positive traits in relation to what is considered good or proper within a cultural context and are manifested as character. Individuals can rely on different authorities or arbiters in terms of virtues. Sometimes it is the culture at large, or it can be more focused, such as an ideology or a religion. In most cases it is a mix. One can, of course, choose whom to listen to, though there may be indirect influences that one may not be aware of. People immersed in a particular culture during childhood are likely to be influenced by that culture's sense of virtues, even if they eventually decide on a different set. They may move far away from their hometown, but they are likely to remain influenced by that childhood culture indirectly. As the Confucian line from *The Adventures of Buckaroo Banzai Across the Eighth Dimension* reminds us, "No matter where you go, there you are."

Virtues are influenced by values—and vice versa. There is a fine line between values and virtues. In fact, Loehr and Schwartz suggest that "a value in action is a virtue."[57] As defined here, values and virtues are separate, with virtues focused on the aspect of distinguishing between right and wrong. Values are often defined as including the aspect of "right" and "wrong," but here they relate to "what is important in life," and virtues to "right and wrong." This brings conceptual clarity that will aid the discussion of values in the next chapter and beyond. This distinction also helps keep the size of the values inventory more manageable.

There is also a sense of "timelessness" to virtues, which is less compatible with the human development approach to understanding values changes pursued here. For example, it is argued that love, justice, and honesty are timeless and unchanging "goods" and thus they are classified as virtues. Virtues as defined here are less likely to change over time than values, and the interest in this work is in exploring change as it relates to values and consumer life.

Character

Character is one's collection of virtues. Cultures or ideologies suggest the appropriate collection of virtues or character to which we "ought" to aspire. The culture or ideology will often measure the strength of a person's character by comparing how that behavior measures up to the standard. Personal character then is the collection of virtues or the degree to which one possesses the proper virtues. Of course, individuals may have their own personal definitions of character. There is an aspirational aspect to character, and thus it is at the boundary of values and behavior.

The "splitting" of values and virtues creates something of an artificial distinction in regard to character, as most people would include some of their prominent values when asked to describe their character, or when describing the character of others. One might say, for example, that "justice" is one of their key values. It would be silly for any researcher to claim that justice cannot be a value. Individuals can define their terms however they see fit. The position here is that the *New Dimensions Values Inventory* makes a distinction between values and virtues that labels justice a virtue. The reason is that justice and other virtues, such as cleanliness or love, have a timeless quality to them that does not provide insight into how consumers are changing over time, which is the goal of this work.

Attitudes

Values are distinguished from attitudes in terms of values being general guiding principles and attitudes focusing on specific objects and situations. The two are often lumped together, but they are separated here to specify a focus on values as more useful in understanding long-term change—and thus receiving greater emphasis in this work than attitudes. The two influence one another, but the view here is that values are more influential in the long term.

Attitudes can be seen as a bridge between values and behavior. They are specific orientations to a particular situation and thus closely linked to behavior. Attitudes sometimes express and are least likely to reflect and be consistent with values, but not in all cases. For example, one may hold the value of sustainability and in most cases have favorable attitudes to situations such as conservation, the use of alternative energy, etc. But the same person might also have an attitude against recycling, perhaps seeing that approach as encouraging more waste rather than limiting it in the first place. It would be unusual for someone to have many attitudes at odds with their values.

Personality

Personality is one's collection of characteristic traits, including behavioral, emotional, temperamental, and mental/psychological. Personality is what the outside world can see. It encompasses one's typical patterns of behavior or tendencies. In terms of values, personality is an indirect reflection of people's values and may not always provide insight into them. Knowing whether someone is shy or has a great sense of humor, for example, doesn't tell you much about someone's values. Shy people may appear passive on the surface but hold a value of being fiercely competitive. There is debate about the extent to which personality is "fixed." That is, if one is born with, say, a high degree of intuition, there are arguments over the extent to which that can be changed. It is safer to say that one's personality has a greater influence on how one expresses their values rather than on the formation of one's values.

There are common patterns in personality. The Meyers-Briggs typology is a popular tool for identifying these patterns. It categorizes personality types using different combinations of four traits that represent the poles of a continuum, with most people falling somewhere in between; that is, one typically has varying degrees of the trait, with a tendency toward one pole of the continuum or the other. The Meyers-Briggs assessment tool uses these descriptive poles:[xvi]

- *Extraversion or introversion.* Do you prefer to focus on the outer world or on your own inner world?

- *Sensing or intuition.* Do you prefer to focus on the basic information you take in or do you prefer to interpret and add meaning?

- *Thinking vs. feeling.* When making decisions, do you prefer to first look at logic and consistency or first look at the people and special circumstances?

- *Judging or perceiving.* In dealing with the outside world, do you prefer to get things decided or do you prefer to stay open to new information and options?

---

xvi   See http://www.myersbriggs.org/my-mbti-personality-type/mbti-basics/

Because the Meyers-Briggs type indicator is commonly used and highly useful, many people know their four-letter types. Each type has an identifying letter (most are the first letter of the word). For example, an INTP is introverted, intuitive, thinking, and perceiving. These people tend to be analytical and thoughtful and often appear aloof (because they are deep in thought). This tool provides insight into personality of a person, but it does not provide insight into their values. For this reason, it acts more as a snapshot—types can shift over time—than as a predictive tool of how individuals may change over time.

Lifestyles

Lifestyles are aggregates of individual behavior, personality, and character influenced by values and attitudes. Researchers have identified common patterns in lifestyle patterns. Arnold Mitchell and colleagues at the Stanford Research Institute created a popular system for categorizing lifestyles with their VALS (Values and Lifestyles) system. They segmented the U.S. population into eight distinct lifestyle patterns, backing up their system with survey analysis. Mitchell suggested the relationship between values and attitudes: "One's interior set of values—numerous, complex, overlapping, and contradictory though they are—find holistic expression in a lifestyle."[58] SRI later developed versions for the United Kingdom and Japan.[xvii] The personas that will be described in Chapter 7 are in some ways similar to the eight lifestyle profiles in the old VALS system.

Key points:

- The exterior aspects of the inner dimension are at the boundary between the individual and the outside world. Their influence is partly measured and partly subject to interpretation. An important consideration here is that most people, even professional market researchers, tend to be much more comfortable with the "measurability" of exterior aspects. It produces empirical data that fits with traditional tools. It fits with the "if you can't measure it, it doesn't exist" ethos that pervades many organizations today. The interior aspect, by comparison, is inherently subjective and more difficult to measure. One of the goals of this work is to raise the profile of the interior aspect.

- Individuals are under almost continual pressure to conform to social views of the "right" values and behavior. While these influences are indeed powerful, it is still ultimately the individual who chooses which values to hold and how to behave. That said, while individuals have the ability

---

xvii   See http://www.strategicbusinessinsights.com/vals/international.shtml

to choose, some have been so inundated by these influences, they may not be conscious of them. Similarly, individuals may behave without any conscious recognition or incorporation of their values, though they may have an unconscious influence.

- The link between values and behavior is tightest with so-called "core values." These are the values that, in addition to being identified as values, have actually been acted upon and the individual has actually behaved in accordance with the value.

4

HOW CHANGING VALUES ARE THE SINGLE BIGGEST INFLUENCE ON CONSUMERS

A definitional challenge becomes clear early in doing values research. There is a wide range of definitions in the literature, and they often cross-reference each other. Values are morals and ethics, ethics are moral values, etc. Sometimes nouns become adjectives, e.g., morals and moral values. One of the goals of this work is to provide a consistent framework, as well as to avoid sending readers on frequent trips to the dictionary.

Beyond definitions, there are also several interpretations, frameworks, and models. Some works acknowledge and build upon others, but a great proportion pay surprisingly little homage to predecessors or complementary works. The problem is not new. Milton Rokeach, a pioneer in the study of values, wrote in 1973 that "the increased currency of explicit value concepts among psychologists and social scientists has unfortunately not been accompanied by corresponding gains in conceptual clarity or consensus. We talk about altogether too many probably different things under one rubric."[59] The topic of values has not generated enough critical mass for researchers to put in the time and effort required to sort through the differences and come to at least some degree of agreement or standardization. Rather, the topic has generated sporadic interest over the last few decades, with significant works largely derived independently of one another.

There is, however, agreement on the central importance of values. Simon notes that, "Everything we do, every decision we make and course of action we take, is based on our consciously or unconsciously held beliefs, attitudes, and values."[60] As Lewis says, "Without values human behavior would be directionless, chaotic, and ultimately self-destructive."[61]

SYSTEMS FOR EXPLORING VALUES

Compounding the definitional challenge is that the many closely related concepts give rise to "separate" systems that are conceptually very close to one another. The initial assessment in exploring the various values-related systems was that they were often sloppy in classifying the different concepts, but sloppiness is a good reflection of what's going on. It is difficult, perhaps impossible, or at least highly subjective to separate

> **Values polarities**
>
> Values are often considered as pairs in opposition. For the value "change," the opposite would be permanence or stability. For simplicity, this work assumes there is an implicit opposite. Most of the pairs suggest a positive-negative pairing. In those cases, the item of the pair chosen is the "positive" one, based on the assumption that people choose to aspire to the positive—for instance, convenience over inconvenience. This rule does not comply 100%; for instance, both conformity and nonconformity could be conceived of as values, and thus they would each be listed separately.

out needs, values, worldviews, norms, virtues, etc. It is not a matter of simply finding the right answer. Consensus does not exist, and various systems and researchers are taking their best shot at it, as does this work.

There is value in presenting a consistent system despite the many hours of going back and forth over whether something is a need or a value or a fill-in-the blank. That said, some distinctions are more useful than others, and the consistency in framework and terminology will aid understanding.

Existing systems

In recognition of this overlap and interconnectedness, some of the systems included here do not directly touch on values. The research attempted to identify systems relevant to the inner dimension of consumer life. Those included here were judged to provide a useful contribution to the values discussion. There is also a bias toward the developmental schemes, as the ultimate purpose driving this work is to gain insight into change and the future. "Static" systems that do not address changes over time are still useful in aiding understanding, but for this work, they are complementary and considered primarily in terms of how they fit with developmental approaches.

Table 4. Systems for exploring values

Name of system	Principal author	What it covers	Year (est.) developed
Hierarchy of Human Needs	Abraham Maslow	Needs	1943
Spiral Dynamics	Don Beck/Clare Graves	Value memes/ worldviews	1950s
Values Inventory	Robin Williams	Values	1950s
World Values Survey	Ronald Inglehart	Values	1970s
Cultural Dimensions	Geert Hofstede	Cultural differences	1970s
Rokeach Value Survey	Milton Rokeach	Instrumental and terminal values	1973
Hall-Tonna Inventory	Brian Hall and Benjamin Tonna	Values	1979
LOV (List of Values)	Lynn Kahle	Instrumental values	1983
Human Scale Development Needs	Manfred Max-Neef	Needs and "satisfiers"	1986
VALS	Arnold Mitchell	Psychographics	1987
Mental Modes	Hunter Lewis	Mental modes	1990
Human Values Project	Encyclopedia of World Problems and Human Potential	Values	1991

Name of system	Principal author	What it covers	Year (est.) developed
SVI (Schwartz Value Inventory)	Shalom Schwartz	Individual and cultural values	1992
Cultural Value Dimensions	Fons Trompenaars	Cultural differences	1994
Transnational Consumer Cultures/ Social Milieus	Jorg Uelltzhoffer	Segmentation around values/attitudes/ behaviors	1998
Theory of 16 Basic Human Desires	Steve Reiss	Motives/Desires (needs, purposes)	1998
Cultural Creatives	Paul Ray	Creatives, Moderns, and Traditionals	2000
Deepest Values	Jim Loehr and Tony Schwartz	Deepest values	2003
Value Populations	Ken Beller, Louis Patler and Steve Weiss	Values sorted into five generational segments	2005

For this project, eight of the systems had an explicit focus on values. The rest either included values as one of several foci, or values could be inferred from them. For instance, integral values were inferred from the Yellow-Integrative Worldview of Spiral Dynamics Worldview system.

Several of the sources above were used for a first iteration that enabled the creation of an initial inventory of 132 values, which was streamlined over time to 113. The next significant evolution was to sort the values into Inglehart's World Values Survey segments of traditional, modern, and postmodern values. This was accompanied by further pruning and reduced the inventory to 93 values. The most recent revision took place as part of

Pool of values considered	
Original New Dimensions values	132
Inglehart	32
Williams	20
Rokeach	36
Hall-Tonna	125
Kahle	9
Human Values Project	230
Schwartz Values Inventory	56
Loehr/Schwartz	32
Beller/Weiss	44

the specific research for this book. The initial list of 93—along with the 39 that were culled—contained the starting points against which additional systems uncovered by research were considered. The key upgrades in the latest revision (the revision process will continue into the future) included these:

- The addition of the inner dimension model that included other components associated with values, in effect putting values in their appropriate context; this context enabled consideration of a wider range of values.

- Sharpening the focus on what a value is by distinguishing them from needs, norms, traits, virtues, etc.

- Associating values with related needs and worldviews.

- The addition of a fourth major type, integral values, to match with the Spiral Dynamics "Integral/systemic" worldview, which in turn was mapped against Maslow's proposed needs segment of self-transcendence. The integral values are not "vetted" to the degree of the three established types owing to their newness but seem to fit the same pattern and thus a leap is made to move forward with incomplete data in the interest of understanding the future.

The total number of values in the revised New Dimensions Inventory is 110, broken down into the four types of traditional, modern, postmodern, and integral, with the total number of values in parentheses and the names of the individual values in each segment in the column at the far right.

Table 5. New Dimensions Values Inventory		
Type	**Description**	**Values**
Traditional (19)	Focused on following the rules and fulfilling one's predetermined role, with priorities such as respect for authority, religious faith, national pride, obedience, work ethic, large families with strong family ties, and strict definition of good and evil.	acceptance, authority, balance, class, comfort, conformity, down-to-earth, duty, family orientation, heroism, home orientation, ordinariness, patriotism, propriety, protection, religion, security, thrift, tradition
Modern (41)	Focused on achievement, growth, and progress, with priorities such as high trust in science and technology (as the engines of progress), faith in the state (bureaucratization), rejection of out-groups, an appreciation of hard work and money, and determination to improve one's social and economic status.	achievement, action, adventure, affordability, ambition, attractiveness, belonging, challenge, change, choice, competition, confidence, control, convenience, curiosity, determination, do-it-yourself, efficiency, energy, equality, flexibility, growth, health, independence, luxury, materialism, performance, practicality, prestige, pride, quality, realism, recognition, resourcefulness, secularism, speed, style, subversion, technology orientation, time

Type	Description	Values
Postmodern (34)	Focused on the search for meaning in one's life, with priorities such as self-expression, including an emphasis on individual responsibility as well as choice, imagination, tolerance, life balance and satisfaction, environmentalism, wellness, and leisure.	access, appropriateness, authenticity, collaboration, community, cool, creativity, customization, design, discovery, diversity, empowerment, enjoyment, experience, experimentation, fitness, freedom, individuality, nonconformity, novelty, open-mindedness, passion, self-expression, simplicity, skepticism, smartness, sophistication, spirituality, spontaneity, sustainability, thrill seeking, unconventionality, understanding, uniqueness, wellness
Integral (16)	Emerging as the leading edge of values change, with a more practical and functional approach to employing values that best fit the particular situation, enabling one to pursue personal growth with an understanding and sensitivity to larger systemic considerations.	assistance, co-creation, commitment, connectivity, contentment, functional, influential, integration, interdependence, personalization, questioning, systematic, thoughtfulness, tolerance, transcendence, vision

The developmental approach suggests these values change over time in predictable patterns, as has been convincingly shown by Inglehart's World Values Survey. It is reasonably clear that macro level values change has taken and is taking place, from traditional to modern to postmodern to integral. But what about at the micro level of individual values themselves? A nuance to this broad generalization is to suggest how individual values themselves may morph over time. To be clear, there is no empirical data to back this up. The first insight came in sorting the "mass" inventory into the three, and eventually four types. Some values looked so similar to one another that it was difficult to separate them. In some case, redundancies were eliminated. In others, distinctions were made and similarities noted.

On further iterations of the inventory, with the values sorted into the types, trends or patterns across the types and values were identified. Again, this is highly subjective and reflects an interpretation. The viewpoint is that it is useful to consider this micro-level concept to bring a more nuanced understanding to changes in consumer life in the absence of empirical data (perhaps this can be done at a later time). Research has consistently suggested that old values do not simply disappear, but are sorted into new priorities. Beyond just being reprioritized, it is likely that values are reimagined and emerge in new forms, in effect being reinterpreted in a new way to fit the new circumstances of one's life.

For example, in the second row of Table 4, comfort is a core traditional value. This does not suggest that someone with modern or postmodern values no longer seeks comfort. Rather, it suggests new priorities will take precedence. Modern values will come to value change over comfort. Change is positive and often changes for the sake of change is valued. Thus, postmodern consumers value "appropriateness," where change is seen as useful in suitable circumstances. To a degree, each of the four types is akin to course-correction of the previous system. Modern values correct the perceived excesses of tradition, postmodern corrects the perceived excesses of modern, and integral corrects postmodern.

Table 6. Example of values preferences evolving over time			
Traditional	**Modern**	**Postmodern**	**Integral**
Balance →	Growth →	Sustainability	
Comfort →	Change →	Appropriateness	
Propriety →	Confidence →	Authenticity	
Protection →	Health →	Wellness	
Religion →	Secularism →	Spirituality	
Security →	Belonging →	Self-expression	
Thrift →	Luxury →	Simplicity	
Tradition →	Materialism →	Experiences →	Transcendence
Down-to-earth →	Practicality →	Creativity →	Integration
Duty →	Achievement →	Enjoyment →	Contentment
	Do-it-yourself →	Smartness →	Assistance
	Convenience →	Customization →	Personalization

Let's look at an example within the integral realm, integration. Its modern incarnation is practicality—it's all about results and the bottom line. Postmodern consumers put more emphasis on the means and value the creative process. Integral is a blend of practical and creativity—creativity as a good thing when it can be harnessed for practical purposes.

What Table 4 suggests is that there is a sense of continuity over time in how values priorities shift at the macro and micro levels. The values shifts are accompanied by underlying shifts in needs and changes in the overall umbrella of the worldviews. The emerging need states were crafted from postmodern and integral values since they are the newer approaches. The need states emerged from various combinations of how these values might come together in concert with other changes in the inner and outer dimensions, although they are clearly the important driving factor.

NEEDS-VALUES-WORLDVIEWS

Values are closely linked to needs and worldviews. Needs are the motivators for action that values often address, and values cluster together into fairly coherent patterns or worldviews. Table 5 shows these linkages via four segments that our firm uses. The four segments of needs are drawn primarily from Maslow's Hierarchy of Human Needs, the values from Inglehart's World Values Survey (with the addition of the fourth segment of Integral), and the Worldviews from Beck's Spiral Dynamics (which actually has nine categories). A consumer focused on belonging needs is likely to hold modern values organized into a "competitive" or "orange" worldview.

Table 7. How needs-values-worldviews fit together		
Needs	**Values**	**Worldviews**
Survival	Traditional	Order (Spiral Blue)
Belonging	Modern	Competitive (Spiral Orange)
Self-Actualization	Postmodern	Communitarian (Spiral Green)
Self-Transcendence	Integral	Integrative (Spiral Yellow)

The prevalence of each needs-value-worldviews types is estimated below. The first percentage is the estimate of their prevalence in the W1 affluent nations. The percentages in parentheses are across all nations. The estimates for the first three segments reflect an interpretation drawn from Inglehart's World Values Survey; the fourth Integral category comes from Beck's Spiral Dynamics.

- Traditional 33% (40%)

- Modern 40% (30%)

- Postmodern 25% (10%)

- Integral 2% (0.1%)

CHARACTERISTICS OF VALUES

This section describes several characteristics of values for those who want to deepen their understanding of why the changes in the consumer landscape are occurring.

How values emerge

Children are at the mercy of their parents, peers, and the cultural context when it comes to the origins of values. Inglehart observes, "Parents' education level has a greater influence on values than the individual's own education level."[62] The values we begin with come from others, and it's not until we develop the appropriate cognitive abilities and maturity that we can begin to question these received values and make choices of our own. Inglehart's Theory of Intergenerational Value Change asserts that a key determinant of structural changes of an individual's values over time relates to the conditions of their upbringing: "One's basic values reflect the conditions that prevailed during one's pre-adult years."[63] His data supports this hypothesis. Generations researchers such as Strauss and Howe[xviii] identify this pattern as well, albeit from their vantage point of generations.

As nations develop economically, the conditions under which children are raised will tend to improve. These children generally grow up with a greater sense of security than did previous generations. This feeling of greater security enables them to explore a wider range of values. Inglehart observes that the shift from modern to postmodern values "springs from the fact that there is a fundamental difference between growing up with an awareness that survival is precarious, and growing up with a feeling that one's survival can be taken for granted."[64] Many children are regaled with tales of how difficult their parents' upbringing was. These tales often fall on deaf ears because the children have grown up in much different circumstances and cannot relate. They believe their eyes over their ears.

Childhood experiences have a strong and lasting influence, but they do not determine the values that people will hold for the rest of their lives. People can change their values as they mature and become capable of making their own decisions.

As described in the previous chapter, values are a key part of our identity. Joas observes that values "arise in experiences of self-formation and self-transcendence."[65] Simon suggests people come to their values in three ways:[66]

---

xviii   Strauss, W. and Howe, N. (1991). *Generations: The History of America's Future*, 1584 to 2069. NY: HarperCollins.

  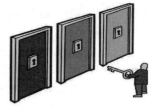

- *Teaching*: the culture tries to instill and perpetuate its values to individuals by explanation, moralizing, rules, rewards, punishments, and other methods.

- *Modeling*: individuals see demonstrations of values in action by others, often by role models.

- *Deciding*: individuals can make their own conscious choices about the values they want.

The cultural demands about the "correct" values are strong. Rokeach observes that "persons raised within the context of society are caught from the moment of birth between their own individual needs somehow cognitively represented as values, and so also to societal goals and demands. Thus, we may come to view the value system that each person internalizes to be just as much a reflection of individual needs as of societal goals and demands."[67]

In sum, people's initial values emerge from their immediate and larger social, economic, and cultural contexts in the process of identity formation.

Value priorities

People may be able to cite a long list of values, but there is a much shorter one that provides the important guide to decision making and behavior. The right question is not necessarily "What are your values?" but "What are your value priorities?" Rokeach observes, "After a value is learned it becomes integrated somehow into an organized system of values wherein each value is ordered in priority with respect to other values."[68]

The nature of changes in values is reprioritizing rather than replacing. Old values do not necessarily disappear but simply become seen as less important. Williams suggests that "differences among individuals may not be so much in the presence or absence of particular values as in the arrangement of values, their hierarchies or priorities."[69] Similarly, Inglehart suggests that the changes that take place are in terms of priorities. Just because well-being becomes a higher priority does not mean that individuals no longer value economic security.[70]

Our focus is on consumers, and there is a discernible difference between so-called consumer values and values in a more generic sense. There are distinctions that can be made about specific types of values within more narrow categories, e.g., beyond political, religious, technological, etc. The goal is to find those values that transcend particular categories. For example, self-expression is a value that will show up in and influence the political, religious, and technological realms. Thus, the New Dimensions values are important to one's conception of identity and provide insight into the decisions and behaviors that a consumer is likely to exhibit in the present and over the long term.

Number of values

As suggested above, some values are more important than others. People may hold dozens of values, but the number of core values is likely much smaller. Research suggests the number of core values is not much beyond a dozen. Rokeach sorts values into two types: terminal and instrumental. Instrumental values are equivalent to means, and terminal values to ends. The instrumental values suggest how we go about the process of achieving terminal values. He observes that "on various grounds—intuitive, theoretical and empirical—we estimate that the total number of terminal values that a grown person possesses is about a dozen-and-a-half, and that the total number of instrumental is several times that, perhaps five or six dozen."[71]

Brian Hall's Hall-Tonna Inventory comes to a similar conclusion in focusing his inventory instrument at getting individuals to identify 12 to 15 core values that are most important in their lives.[72] While their inventory has 125 values, he asserts that at any given time, individuals probably do not have room for more than about 10 priorities.[73] An additional data point comes from Inglehart's World Values survey in which the materialist/post-materialist values battery has just twelve items, which he believes is sufficient to gain insight into overall values preferences.[74]

Values have a center of gravity

Real life is messy, and people typically do not fit into neat little boxes with values any more than they do in other dimensions. For instance, using the New Dimensions four-type framework, people may have some core values in more than one segment. An individual said to have postmodern values, for example, may still identify some modern values as priorities and possibly may have incorporated some integral values as well. It is more accurate to suggest that if someone has postmodern values, those represent the individual's center of gravity.

The developmental approach suggests that some values get left behind over time—as noted, one doesn't lose them but rather shifts them down in the list of priorities. Similarly, some values are future-oriented or aspirational; in that case, an individual is moving toward them but hasn't quite incorporated them yet. Wilber observes that when a person (or society) is on the ladder of development, "it is an average, acting as an upward pull on those below, and a downward pull on those above."[75] Hall reinforces this notion with his experience in administering his Hall-Tonna Values Inventory: "Everyone tested had values in all four stages (each with two sub-stages) of development, but two stages on which each person was currently focused, called the focus area. The values in the stages preceding the focus values are called foundational values, and the values that fall beyond the focus values we call future values."[76] This concept is further validated by Beck's Spiral Dynamics approach, which talks about worldviews emerging in phases—entering, peak, and exiting.[77] It is helpful to think of the set of values on a continuum with loosely defined boundaries but an identifiable center of gravity.

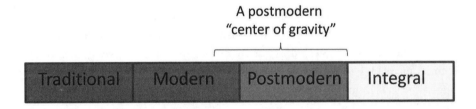

Values are not always conscious

It could be argued that values are mostly held unconsciously. If most people are asked to name their values without prompting, they would likely find it difficult (try it!). Even once they generated an initial list, it would still take some time to sort them out, and they would likely require some help. Thus, most approaches to identifying values have some sort of battery or list to choose from.

And even with that help, it is still difficult to precisely identify priorities. When people make decisions, it is not as if they jot down a list of values, compare, and then decide. Some might do something along these lines for really big and important decisions, but for most daily decisions, values act at the unconscious level. Hofstede suggests, for example, that "many values remain unconscious to those who hold them… They can only be inferred from the way people act under various circumstances."[78] And he goes on to lament that "inferring people's values from people's actions only is cumbersome and ambiguous."[79]

Thus the recommended approach to identifying core values, borrowed from Simon, includes three "tests:"

- Do they say they have it?

- Do they feel strongly about it?

- Have they acted on it?[80]

Values are not always expressed consistently

Because values are largely unconscious, people may not always act in accordance with them. And sometimes they consciously decide to act at odds with their values. Other factors suggested by the Inner Dimensions model may be more influential regarding a decision or behavior. It may be that people are emotionally triggered in a certain situation and the emotion dictates the decision or behavior, and it may lead people to act counter to their values. For example, take someone who has a value of sustainability and community and needs to dispose of an apple. The person may be in a bad mood and unable to find a trash bin, and in that case may rationalize that "it's biodegradable" and toss it on the ground.

The New Dimensions approach to values agrees with those who suggest that values must be acted on if they really are to be considered core values. That is, if they are held in the abstract and not acted on, they may be closer to ideals rather than values. The approach here holds that if people say it's their value, it "counts" as one. From there, it is admittedly a fine line regarding the extent to which a value must be expressed to be considered a core value. For instance, it can be argued that many held environmental values over the last few decades, but there were relatively few outlets on a major scale for expressing them, whereas today, one has many options for acting on their environmental values and thus they are now core values for a significant number of people.

Another factor contributing to inconsistent expression of values is the desire to project a certain image in particular circumstances. Goffman's classic work, *The*

Presentation of Self in Everyday Life, suggests that people present alter the way in which they present themselves given their assessment of particular situations. Thus, one may appear eager or enthusiastic about a particular issue in front of a potential boss even though they privately hold the opposite view, hoping to make a good impression. He observes that there can be many different motives for trying to control the impression others receive of the situation. The front can be intentional or unwitting.[81]

As Schwartz and Loehr observe, "Too often our motivation for a behavior is expedient rather than value driven."[82] When confronted with behavior that is inconsistent with their values, either by others or in their own reflections, people will often attempt to rationalize the behavior. Rapaille observes that "alibis give rational reasons for doing the things we do."[83] It may be tempting to toss the baby out with the bathwater and conclude that consumers live hopelessly contradictory lives, but the research for this work suggests that consumers are largely, but not exclusively, consistent in their values and behavior.

PATTERNS IN CHANGING VALUES

Values are influenced by changes in life conditions. These changes in context lead people to question their values. They set off an interplay between the internal and external dimensions that gets resolved when they adopt a set of values more appropriate to their new life conditions.

What causes the individual to change values

The primary impetus to values change comes from a change in what Beck calls "life conditions," or more generally changes in life situations or environment. While the change itself manifests internally, it is triggered externally. If individuals are moving about their life successfully and happily, they have little or no incentive to change, unless something comes along that leads to a reevaluation process. For instance, people might see a television ad depicting starving children abroad, which touches or jars their complacency and leads them to examine their lives and value priorities. These kinds of trigger events do not have to be negative. They could be positive or neutral, such as an opportunity to work in a new job or career or accept a transfer to a new location.

These changes in life conditions confront people in several ways. Rokeach suggests three principal ways people may be influenced to change:[84]

- Persons are induced to behave in a manner incompatible with their values.

- Persons are exposed to new information, including evaluations from significant people in their lives, that is inconsistent with one or more of their central values.

- Persons are exposed to information about inconsistencies already present among their values.

These changes spur a reexamination of priorities. Rokeach notes that values change is "assumed to be initiated as a result of some felt experience of self-dissatisfaction.[85] Maslow calls it a "felt dissatisfaction."[86] Mitchell mirrors that sentiment: "The conviction emerges that the explanations heretofore accepted contain unnoticed discrepancies, that some new ideas simply don't fit into the old schema, that once-forbidden feelings unaccountably surface when they seem least appropriate."[87] Wilber puts this dissonance into a larger context of a four-stage change process:[88]

- *Fulfillment*: individual has generally fulfilled the basic tasks of a given stage or wave.

- *Dissonance*: individual feels torn, pulled in several directions, a sort of profound dissatisfaction with present level.

- *Insight*: individual discovers what he or she really wants.

- *Opening*: it becomes possible to demonstrate or act on the new value.

An important point to keep in mind is that it is very difficult for outside groups to change an individual's values. They may be able to create the trigger event that leads to rethinking, but the actual change process is an inside job, an educational process that takes time. Williams notes that "attitudes can be changed by persuasion, whereas values need to be changed by education."[89] Attending a motivational speech, for example, may be successful in jarring people to re-examine their values process, but it is not likely to create an on-the-spot change in values. While there may be occasional "burning bush" conversion experiences, for the most part, values changes are a gradual process.

Values change slowly and gradually—and they can be reversed

Values can change. This is being stated simply because there is an alternative viewpoint that they don't. Mitchell asserts that "the popular notion that a person's psychological structure is formed and fixed at eighteen—or at any other age—is simply in error."[90] And Rokeach argues that "all such experimental work suggests that values can be affected, and that value changes can persist and can lead to related and persisting changes in attitudes and behavior."[91]

"Typical" progress along the values continuum over time

Fast

Rate

Slow

| Traditional | Modern | Postmodern | Integral |

The approach here suggests values are central to identity, and both tend to change relatively slowly and gradually. It was noted earlier that the circumstances of one's upbringing and one's parents and peers has a big influence on values. The developmental approach suggests that change will be toward engaging a wider range of values. Mitchell suggests that "most [people] experience one or two shifts from one comprehensive pattern to another. Change is not random, but progresses step-by-step. People tend to settle into a values/lifestyle pattern where they feel most comfortable; they tend to gravitate to a 'home lifestyle.'"[92] The change is more like punctuated equilibrium than gradual evolution. That is, there are a few periods of fairly substantial change rather than incremental changes over a long period of time. This is because values tend to go together in patterns; a change in one value has ripple effects on the others. Thus, the whole set, or at least a substantial portion, tends to change. As the figure above suggests, there are a few periods of relatively rapid change, perhaps even small reversals, and longer periods of relative stability.

Values change slowly because the change process is difficult. It's more comfortable to stay where we are. Williams notes, "Resistance to change is strongest for beliefs and values that are most important (central). If a particular value or belief is changed, the more central it is, the more numerous will be changes in other beliefs and values."[93] Since values are central to identity, changing them brings one's identity into question, getting to the very question of who we are.

The developmental approach does not suggest that people are compelled to pursue the path to a greater range of choices. Inglehart notes that "while we find the metaphor of evolution useful in describing how social change works, we do not equate evolution with determinism."[94] Inertia is strong. Values are typically stable, and change is typically episodic. Change can persist over a period of time, but one will eventually settle back into a state of equilibrium.

In fact, people can regress to values previously held under certain circumstances. Inglehart's World Values Survey, for example, found that values in South

Africa regressed along the development path following apartheid. Adverse economic conditions will also tend to drive people back to more comfortable tried-and-true values. Inglehart found that "striking period effects are evident: there was a clear tendency for each cohort to dip toward the materialist pole during the recession of the mid-1970s, and again during the recessions of the early 1980s and the early 1990s."[95] Mitchell reinforces this notion: "Progress can be reversed under adverse social conditions."[96] It is important to consider the regressive tendency under adverse conditions as it suggests that when those conditions are gone, the development tendency resumes, which is what the data shows. It fits with Beck's idea that values tend to match life conditions. Changing is perceived as more difficult by most people than staying the same. Thus, a challenging context can slow or reverse the change process, but when it is safe again, that process can resume.

As noted in the beginning of the work, the impact of the current Great Recession appears to be having the opposite of the predicted effect, at least among those with postmodern and integral values. Rather than reverting to more comfortable values of their past, their movement into the new terrain of postmodern values is reinforced by the Great Recession. The movement away from emphasis on material goods dovetails with economic constraints to make the new lifestyle more palatable, if not appealing. The postmodern values holder is thus in a stage where economic achievement is deemed less of a priority at the same time that economic realities make it less achievable in the first place.

Values changes oscillate between inner (individual) and outer (community)

Beck's Spiral Dynamics uses a spiral metaphor to convey the idea of worldviews and values evolving in an oscillating pattern: "The overall spiral is forged by a pendulum-like alternation between the self-expressive (agency) and the self-sacrificing (communion)."[97] The developmental approach suggests that individuals will confront challenges to their inner sense of self and adjust those inner-oriented values. When those challenges are met and the new values adopted, the next set of challenges will typically involve one's relationship with others and the community; or vice-versa. This pattern alternates in a consistent pattern over time. Some people with a strong orientation toward either being inner-directed or outer-directed may "skimp" somewhat on their nonpreferred challenges and accompanying values. They may pass through that stage more quickly and back to their preferred orientation. On average, though, the pattern among large groups of people is to alternate their focus.

Values change is largely age-independent

While the data suggests that younger people are more inclined to adopt new values and older people tend to eventually settle into a pattern, this is not a hard-and-fast rule. The slight bias toward young people adopting newer values owes to changes in the conditions of their upbringing, as noted by the Theory of Intergenerational Value Change above. As societies develop economically over time, greater options for change are available, and thus younger generations will often develop different value priorities than previous generations. This is especially true for societies going through rapid economic development. South Korea, for example, went through rapid economic development and as a result has large generational differences in values.

Inglehart asserts that "intergenerational [values] differences reflect socio-economic changes rather than anything inherent in the human life cycle."[98] Essentially, this means that people don't necessarily get more modern or postmodern as they age. Similarly, Inglehart notes that "there is no tendency for given birth cohorts to become more materialistic as they age."[99]

Values change can take place at any time in life and has more to do with changes in life conditions and a sense of identity than chronological age.

Values change is developmental/directional

A key assumption informing this work is that values change follows a developmental approach in a direction towards greater complexity, defined here as having greater choices or access to a wider range of options in terms of values. Beck suggests that "the emergence of thinking systems along the spiral is from lesser to greater complexity."[100] This is not intended to suggest values at the higher level are "better" than the preceding levels. It does not mean "better" in a general sense but simply better suited to evolving life conditions. As life becomes more complex, new values emerge to suit this complexity.

> ### A note on hierarchies of values
>
> Hierarchies imply that the higher entities are "better" or "more advanced" than the lower ones. While this may be a natural inference, it is not binding and can even be offensive to those whose values are "less advanced." The view is that values ought to be seen through a lens of appropriateness to the life conditions in which people find themselves. Spiral Dynamics makes this case particularly well. Nonetheless, an emerging set of values, integral, adopts just that stance, so one could argue it is more advanced. (Beck would call it "second-tier.")
>
> ### More complex ≠ better
>
> "The continuum of being nonetheless shows gradation, for various emergents appear in some dimensions that don't appear in others, e.g., wolves can run, rocks can't." Wilber, K. (2000, 2nd Ed.). *Sex, Ecology and Spirituality: The Spirit of Evolution*. Boston,: Shambhala,8.

The parallel is that if life conditions remain the same, there is less need to evolve to greater complexity. Take the Middles Ages, for example. That was a period of time in which life conditions didn't change much, and as a result, there was little change in values. Current times, in contrast, are characterized by great change and thus suggest a need for values to adjust appropriately.

The progression is a subordination of older, lower-order values and a prioritization of newer, higher-order values. Mitchell offers a way to think about it: "The total array is thus a nested model, with all preceding steps buried within each existing stage."[101] Wilber echoes this idea as "transcend and include"; that is, one can go beyond current values, but this does not mean that they lose access—they do not go away but become less of a priority.[102] He notes that moving into new stages involves both differentiation and integration (transcendence and inclusion); one differentiates from the lower level, identifies with the next higher level, and then integrates the two.[103] In other words, one does not forget what one has learned or immediately abandon all previous values but builds upon them in moving to greater levels of learning.

From Constraint to Choice

"The core of the human development sequence is the expansion of human choice and autonomy."

Inglehart, R., & Welzel, C. (2005). Modernization, Cultural Change, and Democracy: The Human Development Sequence. Cambridge, UK: Cambridge University Press, 2.

As socioeconomic development takes place, people are confronted with more choices that in turn create pressure on them to adjust their values to handle those choices. Inglehart notes, "Economic growth, rising levels of education and information, and diversifying human interacts increase people's material, cognitive, and social resources, making them materially, intellectually, and socially more independent."[104]

Traditional societies, found primarily among the poor W3 nations today, are characterized by clearly defined roles assigned at birth and the expectation that a person's job in life is to fulfill that role. In traditional societies, there are not a lot of values choices to be made. As socioeconomic development takes place and societies modernize, people encounter both more obligations and more opportunities to make values choices. Thus, modern values emerge focused on the need to meet the changing conditions resulting from economic growth.

In a modern society, economic progress eventually faces its own challenges and a third major transition in values takes place toward postmodern values. The costs of economic growth and progress become increasingly apparent, and modern values prove insufficient to meet them. Thus, postmodern values emerge in those societies most economically developed. For example, the pursuit of economic achievement leads to a neglect of community life and concerns—there is simply not enough time. Postmodern value holders feel this neglect and seek a reconnection with their communities, which manifests in part as the localization trend (described in Chapter 5).

Finally, integral values will emerge in response to the insufficiencies of postmodern values in confronting yet a further expansion of choices. Beck cites this transition to what he calls the Integral worldview as being a "second-tier"[xix] change compared to the previous ones (traditional to modern and modern to postmodern) in that integral values adopt a much more nuanced and sophisticated approach that requires a flexibility in adopting whatever values best fit the particular situation. He cites the integral worldview as beginning a transition to second-tier worldviews/values that is a revolutionary shift in consciousness. The key distinction is that traditional, modern, and postmodern values holders each assume that their particular values are the best solution to any situation while integral values holder adopt a flexible, "it depends" approach characterized by drawing upon the best of each type that fits the challenge at hand.

The changes are structural: culture still matters

The evidence suggests the world is not heading toward a global village of cultural convergence. In fact, global trends are moving in exactly the opposite direction. As Inglehart observes, "The values of rich countries are changing rapidly, while poor countries' values are changing slowly or not at all."[105] The key distinction to keep in mind is that while the values changes are structurally similar across countries in similar stages of development, the specific interpretation of the values is heavily influenced by culture. For example, self-expression is a key value across the postmodern populations, but self-expression in the United States is different than it is in Denmark and than it is in Japan. Different cultures shape how the values get expressed. We should not worry too much about a homogenization of values as there will continue to be structural differences in values, as well as differences in how structurally similar values are expressed in different cultures.

---

xix   The first six worldviews of Spiral Dynamics are first-tier. Integral, the seventh, is considered second-tier in that it, and the other two identified (turquoise and coral), does not hold that their value system is the "right" one that others adopt. First-tier worldview holders tend to view their worldview as the "right" one that all should hold.

How values changes manifest over the long term

When looking at aggregate changes across whole societies, Inglehart suggests that values changes go hand in hand with economic development, political change, and other cultural changes in a mutually reinforcing relationship. This 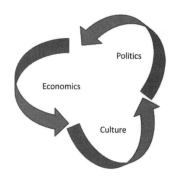 pattern is part of a larger human development sequence. Economic development is perhaps the principal driver as greater economic freedom provides the opportunity for greater options in other areas. He suggests that the core of the human development sequence is the expansion of human choice and autonomy. Along those same lines, values preferences follow a similar directionality in that they move away from constraints and toward having greater choices.

Inglehart offers the Theory of Intergenerational Value Change, based on two key hypotheses:[106]

- *A scarcity hypothesis*, in which material sustenance and physical security are the first requirements for survival. Thus, under conditions of scarcity, people give top priority to materialistic goals, whereas under conditions of prosperity, they become more likely to emphasize post-materialist goals.

- *A socialization hypothesis*, the relationship between material scarcity and value priorities is not primarily one of immediate adjustment as a substantial time lag is involved because people's basic values to a large extent reflect the conditions that prevailed during their preadult years.

It is important to keep in mind that it is the subjective sense of security, rather than the objective economic conditions per se, that dictate the presence of postmodern values. If people feel more secure, that is the important factor. This sense of security during childhood makes it easier to choose different values than our parents (raised under condition of lesser security). Again, this is based on the assumption that change is difficult, and in times of insecurity or great challenges, it is safer to retain our current values. In times of relative security, it is less risky to venture out and experiment with change.

As noted above, Inglehart suggests that socioeconomic development drives changes in values, which come in clusters dubbed traditional, modern, and postmodern. This work adds Integral as the fourth cluster. These clusters are present everywhere globally to greater and lesser extents. Postmodern values, for instance, are high in Northern Europe, Japan, and the United States. Modern values are increasingly predominant in the high-growth emerging markets, such as China and India, while traditional values are predominant in less-developed nations. As countries move through socioeconomic development, they move from traditional to modern to postmodern, and the forecast is eventually to integral values. Societies, as well as individuals, can hold a mix of values from the four types. The United States, for example, has a relatively high percentage of individuals with postmodern values—perhaps 25%—but it also has a relatively high percentage of traditional values in comparison with Northern Europe. This can be explained by differences in cultural heritage—the United States having its roots in religious separatism, with religious orientation being a characteristic of traditional values. And modern values are still predominant in the United States, as can be evidenced by the continued strong support for economic development. The difference between the United States and Europe was wisely characterized by former U.S. Labor Secretary Robert Reich when he asked whether the United States wanted to be a society or an economy. It can be argued that most of Europe has opted to focus on being a better society—with its emphasis on social programs—while the United States is still focused on being a better economy.

As more people adopt a new set of values, these eventually reach a critical mass and become the prevailing system. Mumford's *The Transformations of Man* (1956) suggests that there have not been more than four or five transformations in which a society goes through a fundamental change involving its values, institutions, and culture in the entire history of Western civilization, with the most recent one marking the end of the Middle Ages. Along those lines, Harman notes that "these transformations rest on a new metaphysical and ideological base and form a new picture of the cosmos and the nature of man."[107] Many other works—Toffler's *Third Wave*, Roszak's *Person-Planet*, Capra's *The Turning Point*, Ferguson's *Aquarian Conspiracy*, to name a few—have suggested that there are a just a few large-scale transformations. These ideas fit with the view here that **there have been just two major values transformations (traditional to modern and modern to postmodern), and that a third may be on the cusp of emerging (postmodern to integral).**

THE SHIFT TO POSTMODERN AND INTEGRAL VALUES

The postmodern shift

Postmodern values are focused on the search for meaning in our lives, with priorities such as self-expression and an emphasis on individual responsibility as well as choice, imagination, tolerance, life balance and satisfaction, environmentalism, wellness, and leisure. This shift away from modern values is a course-correction from modernism's emphasis on achievement, growth, and success. It finds that these values are no longer satisfactory and engender a sense of emptiness such that success on those terms no longer provides satisfaction or well-being. There is disillusionment with the accumulation of material goods and growth at all costs. The costs begin to be recognized as serious and perhaps not worth the victory.

Alongside this questioning of the modern values priorities, new concerns begin to emerge. For instance, economic growth is highly prized by modern values, with environmental consequences a secondary concern and viewed as a cost of doing business. Postmodern values seek to redress this balance and bring environmental issues to a level of equal concern. Thus, concepts such as the triple bottom line emerge, in which economic, environmental, and social concerns are weighted equally. Similarly, the accumulation of material goods comes into question.

source: UofAweb.ualberta.ca

Postmodern values see experiences of equal or perhaps greater values. For example, instead of buying a boat, motorcycle, or second car, the postmodern values holder may instead take a family trip or perhaps volunteer to build a home for the disadvantaged with Habitat for Humanity. They find the camaraderie and personal relationships and friendships from these experiences to provide a greater sense of satisfaction or well-being than acquiring yet another possession.

As described above, changes in life conditions can spur a questioning of values. While the initial trigger event might focus on a particular value or two, the interconnectedness of the values will gradually bring more and more values into question. More anachronisms will begin to emerge. If someone becomes a firm believer in sustainability—that is, showing a growing concern for stewardship of the planet—it may raise similar questions about is caring for one's own body. This may lead to a shift from the concept of health as the absence of disease to wellness, which expands the range of health concerns beyond the physical to include the mental and spiritual conditions as well. There is something of a domino effect that takes place, as one value after another is questioned, and over time the locus of emphasis shifts from modern to postmodern.

There are two types of changes that take place. First, as described above, some values morph into a counterpart at the next level: materialism gives way to experiences, health gives way to wellness, and so on. Table 6 below shows how the vast majority of modern values have morphed to a postmodern counterpart.

Table 8. From modern to postmodern

Modern	MORPHS TO	Postmodern
Achievement, accomplishment of something noteworthy	MORPHS TO	*Enjoyment*, experiencing satisfaction or delight in an activity
Action, making things happen	MORPHS TO	*Experimentation*, trying out a new procedure, idea, or activity
Adventure, exciting or remarkable experience	MORPHS TO	*Thrill seeking*, searching for a feeling of great excitement and pleasure
Affordability, availability within one's financial means	MORPHS TO	*Access*, freedom or ability to obtain or make use of something
Attractiveness, arousing interest or pleasure	MORPHS TO	*Cool*, fashionably attractive or impressive
Belonging, being part of and enjoying status within a group	MORPHS TO	*Self-expression*, expression or assertion of one's own personality
Challenge, task or other activity requiring special effort or dedication	MORPHS TO	*Discovery*, pursuit of and deep interest in the unknown
Change, experience or bring about alteration or transformation	MORPHS TO	*Appropriateness*, suitably designed for the task at hand and user capabilities
Choice, options or alternatives	MORPHS TO	*Freedom*, power to determine action without restraint
Competition, contest for some prize, honor, or advantage	MORPHS TO	*Collaboration*, working jointly with others
Confidence, belief in oneself and one's powers or abilities	MORPHS TO	*Authenticity*, state of being genuine; not false or an imitation
Control, to have authority over oneself or another person, or to direct the course of a situation	MORPHS TO	*Spontaneity*, acting on natural feeling or impulse, without effort or premeditation
Convenience, freedom from effort or difficulty	MORPHS TO	*Customization*, to build, fit, or alter according to individual specifications
Curiosity, desire to know	MORPHS TO	*Passion*, deep motivating interest in a topic
Determination, quality of being resolute, with firmness of purpose	MORPHS TO	*Understanding*, showing a sympathetic or tolerant attitude toward something
Do-it-yourself, of or designed for construction or use by amateurs without special training	MORPHS TO	*Smartness*, innovations that increasingly shift information and decision-making burdens from the user to a device or service
Efficiency, ability to do more with less	MORPHS TO	*Novelty*, something new or unusual
Energy, capacity for vigorous activity	MORPHS TO	*Fitness*, state of being physically fit
Equality, corresponding in quantity, degree, value, rank, or ability	MORPHS TO	*Diversity*, inclusion of different types of people, styles, and ideas

Modern	MORPHS TO	Postmodern
Flexibility, capable of adapting to a situation as needed	MORPHS TO	*Open-mindedness*, freedom from prejudice, bigotry, or partiality
Growth, increasing capacity of an economy to produce goods and services	MORPHS TO	*Sustainability*, reducing the human footprint on the environment while maintaining quality of life
Health, soundness of body or mind	MORPHS TO	*Wellness*, advanced state of physical, emotional, and spiritual well-being
Independence, freedom from the control, influence, support, aid, or the like, of others	MORPHS TO	*Uniqueness*, having no like or equal
Individuality, being true to one's unique self	MORPHS TO	*Community*, group of people with a common characteristic or interest living together within a larger society
Luxury, indulgence in something that provides pleasure, satisfaction, or ease	MORPHS TO	*Simplicity*, freedom from intricacy or complexity
Materialism, preoccupation with or emphasis on material objects, comforts, and considerations, with a disinterest in or rejection of spiritual, intellectual, or cultural values.	MORPHS TO	*Experiences*, collecting memorable activities instead of or along with material goods
Practicality, focus on getting results	MORPHS TO	*Creativity*, ability to come up with new and interesting ideas
Quality, superiority, excellence	MORPHS TO	*Design*, objects and environments thoughtfully constructed according to an aesthetic ideal
Realism, viewing or representing things as they really are	MORPHS TO	*Skepticism*, attitude of doubt or a disposition to incredulity either in general or toward a particular object
Resourcefulness, ability to devise ways and means	MORPHS TO	*Empowerment*, acquiring the tools, resources, and authority to get a task done
Secularism, belief that religion should not be involved with the ordinary social and political activities of a country	MORPHS TO	*Spirituality*, interest in and pursuit of the meaning and purpose of life
Style, distinctive manner or custom of behaving or conducting oneself	MORPHS TO	*Sophistication*, process or result of becoming more complex, developed, or subtle
Subversion, undermining the power and authority of an established system or institution	MORPHS TO	*Nonconformity*, refusal to adhere to an established or conventional creed, rule, or practice

Alongside the morphing, the second type of change is the emergence of new values without a predecessor from the previous level. This is clearly the case with the transition from traditional to modern values where the number of values doubled from 19 traditional values to 40 modern values. That transition is fairly mature, and modern values are the dominant segment globally today. There are eight modern values—ambition, performance, prestige, pride, recognition, speed, technology orientation, and time—that do not yet have a clear postmodern counterpart.

Yet my research has so far identified 36 postmodern values. One explanation could be that postmodern values are still in their emerging phase, and more will emerge over time. Another, and perhaps more likely explanation, is that the speed of these transitions is greatly accelerating and thus there is less time available for new values to emerge within a particular level—what happens instead is that a new level emerges. Thus, integral values are emerging fairly quickly alongside the maturing of the postmodern values. To bring the timescale into perspective, one could argue that traditional values were dominant for centuries; modern values began their emergence with the Enlightenment in the 19th century, while postmodern values emerged in the late 1960s and over the course of a generation made significant inroads. The length of each stage is much shorter, matching the more rapid changes in life conditions.

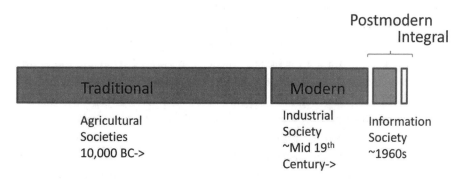

Figure 9. Timescale of values: how long they have been present

The logic of the developmental approach is toward greater complexity, options, and choices. The postmodern values holders will have access to a greater range of possibilities for meeting the greater range of outer dimension changes they are encountering. Of course, modern values holders may encounter exactly the same outer dimension changes but feel that their modern values system is sufficient to the task and not feel the need for more options. Others will encounter these new conditions and feel the modern value system wanting, and thus begin the transition to postmodern values.

As noted earlier, these transitions are difficult. People going through the transition, while they are questioning their values and hence their sense of identity, may be jealous of the modern values holders who appear content with their situation and are not faced with the dilemma of whether to change.

The emergence of integral values

Integral values appear to be emerging as the next wave of values behind postmodern values. I recall many times in the last decade talking about values changes and postmodern values and confronting the inevitable Q and A query, "So, what's after postmodern?" For several years, my answer was "I don't know." But subsequent research and the analysis of Beck's Spiral Dynamics have provided an answer. The Spiral worldviews overlapped with the World Values Survey value types. Spiral Dynamics, however, went a step further and included an Integral worldview. Subsequent research suggested that emergence of a new set of values synched up well with the integral worldview, thus the New Dimensions system calls them integral values.

A key facet of integral values is a more practical and functional approach to employing values that best fit a particular situation. Since postmodern values—and the accompanying Communitarian worldview—have an outer orientation, the prediction would be to alternate to inner orientation, which is indeed the case. Integral values are focused around one pursuing personal growth, but with an understanding and sensitivity to larger systemic considerations. Integral values holders are very much independent spirits who think carefully about doing the right thing in terms of their inner sense of right and wrong. They are thoughtful about the consequences of their actions, of how those consequences sync up with their personal code. This typically includes a global orientation; that is, they are attuned to how their individual actions influence the greater good, and they weigh this as an important consideration. Still, it will be the match to the inner self that is predominant. Beck suggests that the next evolution of worldviews, which he calls planetary (turquoise), will bring that global emphasis front and center. This worldview is, of course, even more nascent than integral, and thus beyond the timeframe of this work.

Beck estimates that the percentage of the global population with an integral worldview is perhaps 1–2%. They are most likely to be found in the affluent nations. Since this worldview is still in the emerging stage, it is speculative to assign values to it. Nonetheless, research suggests some ten values that would seem to fit this orientation. Table 7 below shows the evolution from postmodern to modern values that will gain strength moving forward.

Table 9. From postmodern to integral

Postmodern	MORPHS TO	Integral
Appropriateness, suitably designed for the task at hand and user capabilities	MORPHS TO	*Functional*, serving an intended or useful purpose
Collaboration, working jointly with others	MORPHS TO	*Interdependence*, sensitivity to how things depend on each other
Community, group of people with a common characteristic or interest living or working together within a larger society	MORPHS TO	*Connectivity*, ability to reach and communicate with others as desired
Creativity, ability to come up with new and interesting ideas	MORPHS TO	*Integration*, combining elements into a coherent whole
Customization, to build, fit, or alter according to individual specifications	MORPHS TO	*Personalization*, alteration for the preferences of the individual
Design, objects and environments thoughtfully constructed according to an aesthetic ideal	MORPHS TO	*Co-creation*, collaboration in the creation or augmentation of design and content, and sharing these creations with peers
Empowerment, acquiring the tools, resources, and authority to get a task done	MORPHS TO	*Influential*, ability to make a difference in an outcome
Enjoyment, experiencing satisfaction or delight in an activity	MORPHS TO	*Contentment*, comfortable sense of well-being over time
Experiences, collecting memorable activities instead of or along with material goods	MORPHS TO	*Transcendence*, ability to rise above a particular circumstance in allegiance to a higher principle or principles
Nonconformity, refusal to adhere to an established or conventional creed, rule, or practice	MORPHS TO	*Questioning*, characterized by or indicating intellectual curiosity
Open-mindedness, freedom from prejudice, bigotry, or partiality	MORPHS TO	*Systematic*, methodical; given to having or following a plan
Passion, deep motivating interest in a topic	MORPHS TO	*Commitment*, state of being bound emotionally or intellectually to a course of action or to another person or persons
Skepticism, attitude of doubt or a disposition to incredulity either in general or toward a particular object	MORPHS TO	*Vision*, ability to see how events or circumstances fit into the bigger picture
Smartness, innovations that increasingly shift information and decision-making burdens from the user to a device or service	MORPHS TO	*Assistance*, seeking technological help in keeping up with increasing mental and physical demands

Postmodern	MORPHS TO	Integral
Sophistication, process or result of becoming more complex, developed, or subtle	MORPHS TO	*Thoughtfulness*, characterized by careful reasoned thinking
Understanding, showing a sympathetic or tolerant attitude toward something	MORPHS TO	*Tolerance*, possessing a fair, objective, and permissive attitude toward opinions and practices that differ from one's own

Key points

- The research behind the creation of the *New Dimensions Values Inventory* is described, including reference to 20 systems touching on the subject of classifying values, with key insights highlighted. The exciting point from a research perspective is that despite being carried out by different researchers at different points in time and often with different objectives, they reach striking similar conclusions. Even in cases where the resulting system had a different orientation, it was still not difficult to identify the overlap and thus come up with a very robust system.

- The *New Dimensions Values Inventory* of 110 values is classified into four types: traditional, modern, postmodern, and integral. This clustering into four types enables a convenient shorthand that makes the system relatively easy to describe to a novice audience. The basic model can be described and grasped at a high-level by most audiences in 15 minutes or so (and this almost always whets their appetite for more).

- The link between values and needs and worldviews is made, creating a powerful argument for a developmental model of relatively predictable change over time. A developmental model suggests a consistent change over time. Each of these three units, described by different systems and researchers, reaches similar conclusions about how they change over time in a way that overlaps amazingly well.

- Characteristics of values and patterns and how they evolve are identified. A key principle is that people do not simply replace values in the form of one in and one out. Rather, newer values gain greater priority as older ones recede in importance. Older values also tend to morph into new incarnations, such as religion morphing into secularism, which in turn morphs into spirituality. The change process is more fluid than lockstep.

5

HOW CATALYSTS OF CHANGE ARE SHAPING AND BEING SHAPED BY CONSUMERS

C hanges in consumer life are the product of inner- and outer-dimension changes. The inner-dimension changes were covered in the previous three chapters. This chapter covers changes in the outer dimension. As noted previously, values changes most often come about in response to some external stimulus or challenge. The life conditions change and present a challenge to values, sometimes dramatically and other times nudging along changes that have been brewing internally.

Whole books can be and have been written about emerging trends and changes anticipated over the next decade. For this work, the choice is to synthesize the changes in the form of 13 "catalysts" or forces of change that represent the interplay between multiple trends and values that could tip (using Gladwell's "tipping point"[xx]) in the future. They are also variously called change drivers, driving forces, drivers, or macro trends, among others. The term "catalyst" was chosen to distinguish it from the existing terms that often have a particular interpretation depending on the organizations or people involved.

Catalysts are the building blocks upon which the need states and personas in the subsequent chapters are based. They in turn are derived from the values inventory (described in the previous chapter) and trend research. The primary selection criterion was "importance to consumer life in the next decade." The catalysts were crafted by a creative problem-solving approach that identified patterns among the various trends and values and clustered them together into themes. Several dozen initial themes emerged. They were then combined, consolidated, pruned, and repurposed to get to the 13 covered in this chapter. To further aid high-level understanding—long lists tend to challenge recall—the catalysts are grouped into three sets:

Table 10. Three sets of catalysts influencing consumer life		
Engaged Consumers	**Blurring Boundaries**	**Bounded Consumption**
Consumers shifting from a passive to an active orientation	Consumers facing new challenges and opportunities in navigating the emerging virtual world	Consumers confronting new limits to their lifestyle choices
• Empowered individuals	• Ubiquitous connection	• Enoughness
• Emerging market rise	• Life-shifting	• Living within limits
• Consumer co-creation	• Truth and truthiness	• Sustainable consumption
• Consumer augmentation	• Integration of virtual and real	• Relocalization
	• Continuum of ownership	

---

xx   See Gladwell, M. (2002). *The Tipping Point: How Little Things Can Make a Big Difference.* Back Bay Books.

Each of the 13 catalysts is analyzed with a consistent approach:

- The catalyst is introduced and described.

- The key drivers behind it are identified.

- Examples of what it looks like in the present are provided.

ENGAGED CONSUMERS

The set of "Engaged Consumers" catalysts is about the shifting balance of power between consumers and the organizations they do business with—with the shift in power being from organizations toward consumers. Growing numbers of consumers are becoming more engaged with their product and service providers, both because it is now easier to do and because the values shifts toward individuality and self-expression encourage it. In effect, their orientation is shifting from passive to active.

A key factor driving this shift is the growing amount of information at the disposal of consumers. Not only is more information available, but the trend toward transparency is enabling more and more information to be disclosed. Consumers are demanding more information, owing in large part to the shifts in values described earlier. At the same time, new technologies are providing more capabilities for generating, accessing, and storing information. These two factors are coming together to empower consumers. This increased power is sometimes expressed as a consumer desire for greater influence in the design and manufacture of their products and services. This sometimes extends to actually participating in product and service design.

Another important factor is growing affluence. In emerging markets, large new groups of people are attaining consumer lifestyles for the first time. They will challenge existing businesses as they bring new tastes and expectations to the table. While emerging market consumers will often have different values priorities— typically modern values—than will postmodern/integral W1 consumers, their sheer numbers will influence the consumer landscape.

Consumer demand for power is not only expressed vis-à-vis organizations, but many are aiming at themselves in exploring or adapting augmentation technologies. Self-expression, for instance, can be aimed at the peer group or the organizations with which an individual interacts. For the consumers interested in augmentation, they are expressing themselves, in part at least, by seeking to stretch the limits of the performance and extend their capabilities.

Empowered Individuals

Consumers have the free will to choose one product or brand over another, but their ability to make decisions has at times been hampered by a lack of information. With vehicles, for example, before the Internet, potential car buyers were at the mercy of monthly publishing cycles to get information from *Consumer Reports* about the most reliable models—a problem for anyone who wanted to buy immediately. Consumers also didn't have the ability to aggregate information from other consumers. They might ask their friends and neighbors for advice, but there was no easy way to leverage the experience of thousands of other people who had real-life experience with product X or Y.

The equation has been changing as consumers gain power in the buyer-seller negotiation. Vocal consumers can broadcast in real-time their enthusiasm (or anger) about products and brands. Product reviews, once the work of newspaper and magazine writers, are more frequently being written by knowledgeable amateurs who, as independent agents, are not beholden to the companies they are reviewing. Organizations who try to game the system risk damage to their product if they are caught, and chances are, they will be. And whether the sentiment is positive or negative, and whether it is broadcast on Epinions.com or Twitter, consumers are very much in control of the conversation.

There is also a host of new tools giving people access to timely, useful information that lets them compare prices and leverage the experience of their peers before making purchases. All these things empower consumers; with this newfound power, consumers seem to be acting with greater confidence and asserting themselves in new ways.

For example, a few years ago Tropicana spent an estimated $35 million to launch a redesigned package for its Pure Premium orange juice carton. After a barrage of phone calls, letters, and e-mails—and generally unwanted attention on blogs about the design—they dumped the new design and went back to the old package layout and brand symbol (the orange with the straw in it).

Drivers of empowered individuals

The phenomenon of empowered individuals is being driven by a variety of factors:

- *The Internet and broadband.* Perhaps the primary drivers of the empowered consumer, the Internet and broadband, have changed the dynamics of information access and distribution.

- *Mobile devices.* "Smartphones" and other personal devices such as the iPad are upping the ante and creating the consumer expectation for anywhere, anytime information. Consumers are now empowered anywhere, anytime.

- *Web 2.0.* This second phase of Internet usage—two-way interaction—has refocused the Internet experience from being primarily about simply finding information to sharing and collaboration. Social networks create communities of trust online and increasingly are used—often instead of search engines— to filter for and find information. Flickr lets users post and share photosets documenting instances of poor service. Video-sharing sites and wikis allow people to share their perspective and reach audiences in the millions.

- *Transparency.* The increasing ability to gather, store, and share information is making it easier to learn about people, products, companies, and governments, propelling the world toward at least the perception of transparency.

What it looks like

So what does the phenomenon of empowered consumers look like today, and who's doing it? Consider these examples:

- *Online consumer opinion.* Consumers can broadcast their praise (or scorn) for brands with the click of a mouse. Whether posting on Epinions.com to praise the cleaning power of a new washing machine or tweeting about the poor presentations at a professional conference, online consumer feedback is powerful—apparently more powerful than other forms of media. A 2009 Nielsen study found that globally 70% of people trusted consumer opinions posted online, compared to 33% who said they trusted online banner ads and just 24% who trust ads on mobile phones.[108]

- *Lendingtree.com.* It makes great sense from a consumers' perspective: they submit a single loan request, and multiple lenders compete for their business. Information plus competition turned the power equation for consumer loans on its head.

- *Retail comparison apps.* Scan the barcode or type in the product number of something at Home Depot or any other store, and price comparison apps like Save Benjis for the iPhone will find if the in-store price can be beat. This kind of pricing transparency empowers consumers to make smarter shopping decisions.

- *Global citizen activism.* The ability of social media to empower individuals was made clear during post-election protests in Iran in 2009. The Iranian public got their message out to the world—with dramatic Twitter messages and compelling videos—despite attempts by Iranian authorities to shut down the flow of information. While conventional, centralized media outlets can be silenced or ejected, individuals using global social networks could not be.

Empowering individuals is really all about the shift and decentralization of power, and with it the rise of a much more savvy, information-hungry, and knowledgeable class of consumers. In the next decade, several additional factors will coalesce to further the empowered consumer ethos. A new set of technologies—distributed sensors, next generation smartphones, location-based services, etc.—will combine to give consumers new types of information. Additionally, Gen-Y consumers in the United States will enter into a new life stage focused around family formation and major consumption decisions such as buying a home. As digital natives, their expectations for transparency will be even more intense and will force brands to open their operations even further to general scrutiny.

Emerging market rise

Emerging market countries such as China, India, South Africa, and Brazil continue to increase their economic and cultural power and boost their prominence in the world. This is clear by any number of measures from GDP growth rates and expanding scientific capabilities to the rise of emerging market brands such as Haier, Lenovo, or Tata Motors, which now compete on a global scale. The rise of emerging markets is also instantly clear to anyone who has stood on a busy street in Bangalore, Shanghai, Rio, or Johannesburg and sensed the "electricity" and optimism of areas in the midst of rapid socioeconomic development. As these areas undergo their own sweeping geopolitical and economic changes, they will increasingly gain and assert their influence on the rest of the world.

The rise of emerging markets has been decades in the making, but the bright economic future for emerging markets has gained more attention in recent years. It was especially brought to light in a 2003 Goldman Sachs report entitled *Dreaming with BRICs*, which detailed the economic prospects of Brazil, Russia, India, and China (a.k.a. the BRIC nations). This piece of research helped mainstream the idea that a major power shift is under way on the economic and political stage and focused investors and corporations on figuring out how to take part in this future growth. Goldman Sachs forecast that the economies of the BRIC nations would grow larger than traditionally dominant countries like Italy, France, the United Kingdom, and Germany—and that in 2050, the six largest economies would be China ($44.4 trillion GDP), the United States ($35.1 trillion), India ($27.8 trillion), Japan ($6.6 trillion), Brazil ($6.0 trillion), and Russia ($5.8 trillion).[109]

Always hungry for the next opportunity, investors and brands are now looking for the next set of hot emerging markets to invest in and develop as consumer markets. Some are now talking about the growth potential of the STICs—South Africa, Turkey, Indonesia, and Columbia. Others are talking about "The Ten"—a group of ten non-BRIC middle-income nations that includes Mexico, Poland, Saudi Arabia, Thailand, and Argentina, and others. This group of ten countries collectively had a nominal GDP of $5.6 trillion in 2008, larger than either Japan or China, according to IMF data.[110]

Regardless of how the next big markets are defined, it's clear that a new set of global players is emerging and becoming more important to the future of the global economy and consumerism.

Drivers of emerging market rise

The rise of emerging markets is being driven by a variety of factors:

- *Aging of W1.* Aging is expected to have a downward effect on GDP in W1 as workers retire and spend less. This puts more focus on the opportunities that can be found in emerging markets. Indeed, even before the Great Recession, the U.S. Bureau of Labor Statistics estimated that U.S. GDP would decline from 3.1% (1996–2006) to an average annual rate of 2.8% (2006–2016) because "as the 77 million baby boomers begin to retire, the pace of labor force growth will slow down."[111] McKinsey put it this way: "As the Boomers grow older, they will work and spend less, slowing real U.S. GDP growth to a more modest pace than in recent decades: from the 3.2% average annual rate enjoyed since 1965 to 2.4% over the coming three decades."[112]

- *Positive demographics.* In contrast to the low birth rates and consequential aging of W1, emerging markets have more positive demographic profiles to support economic growth. Emerging markets are becoming more important as consumer markets as incomes rise—and are no longer seen as the makers of inexpensive exports for W1 consumers. As an official from the investment firm Aberdeen Asset Management said, "Four billion people around the world live in emerging markets and they tend to be very young populations, so they are the workers and consumers of the future."[113]

- *Investment and modernization.* Domestic and international investment and outsourcing have helped modernize the economies of emerging markets. Countries such as China and India have also been focusing heavily on developing domestic scientific and technological capabilities, which has already shown signs of success. Already in 2003, China was ranked third in the world in nanotechnology publication and patents, after the United States and Japan.[114] Brazil is already a global leader in the production of ethanol and is aggressively investing in new feedstock and processing technologies.

- *Stage of socioeconomic development.* Emerging markets are in what would be considered to be the modern phase in societal development while developed markets are shifting from the modern to the postmodern phase. This implies that these countries will be focused on values such as modernization, achievement, growth, material acquisition, etc., whereas consumers in the increasingly postmodern countries of W1 will be more focused on sustainability and quality of life rather than pure growth.

What it looks like

So what are some of the signs of the rise and modernization of emerging markets? And how are these changes playing out at the consumer level? Consider these examples:

- *Emerging market elites.* While there have always been tiny segments of ultra-rich consumers in developing markets, modernization and booming business are creating a new, larger class of wealthy emerging market consumers. India provides a stunning—if not totally representative— example of the potential for the future. A McKinsey Global Institute study estimates that the number of consumers in India's wealthiest class will rise from 6 million in 2005 to 23 million in 2025—more than the current population of Australia.

- *A grocery revolution.* Formal grocery-store chains are spreading rapidly in the emerging markets, with formats ranging from tiny convenience stores to large-scale supermarkets. This shift from traditional food sellers such as stalls and street vendors to chains is having significant impacts on consumers and businesses alike: often reducing food costs, expanding product diversity, pushing traditional retailers to modernize their operations, and in some cases pushing small retailers and farmers out of business.

- *Emerging market brands.* New brands are appearing on the world stage— in apparel, electronics, appliance, media, and even the automotive sector. These emerging market companies are developing their international brand presence and globalizing their products. Li-Ning, a Chinese sports apparel company with clear global ambitions, has opened an R & D center and flagship retail location in Portland, Oregon—the home of Nike. India's Tata Motors, which arguably launched the market for ultra-low-cost cars with its $2,500 Nano, has plans to sell in Africa, Latin America, and Southeast Asia. It also is pursuing the U.S. and European consumers—and the Nano passed the EU safety tests for front and side impact in July 2009, an important step toward exporting the Nano to W1 markets.[115]

The rise of emerging markets and the resultant increase in consumer income will be a primary driver of lifestyle changes for W2 consumers in the next 20 to 30 years. Even modest increases in income will enable the purchase of goods previously out of reach, such as appliances, scooters, or low-cost cars such as the Tata Nano. Rising income will also open the door to new experiences and opportunities, including access to credit, higher education, and leisure pursuits such as foreign travel. Ultimately, higher income leads to changes in values and attitudes.

As emerging markets develop, they will increasingly challenge established W1 powers like the United States, Germany, the United Kingdom, and Japan more directly in areas as diverse as media, product design, and scientific and technological innovation, and thus influence W1 consumer life as well.

Consumer co-creation

Co-creation involves consumers in the design or development of a product or service. This participation ranges from simple customization of product options in its weak form to direct participation in product design in its stronger form. This catalyst reflects the fact that product purchasing is increasingly a form of self-expression and a means to forge or express identity. It is one of many outlets for consumers to express themselves. Spending on products and services is seen by these consumers as a form of "voting" or expressing their approval for the way an organization does business. It also takes the form of avoiding organizations that do not share their values. In making their choices about who to do business with, these consumers apply the yardstick of shared values—favoring those who share their values and avoiding those who do not.

Co-creation reflects the ongoing shift of power to consumers. As they have more information about their products, services, and the organizations they interact with, they can make more informed choices about who to do business with. This is not to say that every consumer wants to co-create every product. They focus on those products and services that have a deeper meaning to consumers. Since it is a time-intensive commitment, this participation will be selective, at least until it becomes simple enough to do on a mass scale.

Product and service providers benefit as well. It shifts some labor and development costs onto consumers. It often requires an investment in a web-based platform that can provide consumers with the tools and templates they need. This fits well with organizations that are always looking for ways to reduce their production costs.

Drivers of co-creation

Co-creation is still in its infancy, but it is being driven forward by a variety of factors:

- *Identity expression.* W1 consumers are increasingly seeking opportunities to express their identity through the products and services they purchase and the choice of companies to do business with.

- *Digitization and the rise of virtual worlds.* Digitization and user-friendly software are enabling consumers to express their desires more easily and to participate in the design of products they really care about. This is both a driver and a result of the move toward creativity in design as a key differentiator—with quality taken for granted. Co-creation will take place in varied venues, whether in the showroom, via web-based software, or in a virtual world format. As virtual worlds improve, this will lead to increased demands by consumers to obtain a real-world equivalent of their virtual world products. Virtual worlds can also provide a form to test various options that they might like to see in their real world products.

- *Open source.* A model for co-creation is found in the Open-source software movement. Participants in open source typically care deeply about these products that they freely share their innovations with the rest of the community. This creates a mutually reinforcing feedback loop—as more people share, the more benefits accrue for all, and the more the community learns from others. This sense of commitment has been great enough to overcome the "free rider" problem (those who simply take and don't contribute).

- *Product lifestyle acceleration.* The time it takes for an idea or a trend to go from fringe to mainstream is decreasing, and businesses need solid strategies to stay ahead of the curve and craft innovative, unique experiences and solutions for consumers. The pace of mainstream innovation has begun to accelerate dramatically. As social media forums expand on the Internet, more and more everyday consumers are being introduced to the new fads and trends emerging at the fringes of our culture. This can now occur almost instantaneously since the life cycle of mainstream trends has declined dramatically.

What it looks like

Co-creation is playing out with many kinds of consumers in many different sectors. Consider these examples:

- *Prius and other hybrids.* While these are not directly involved in co-creation, these vehicles are symbols of products that speak to identity expression—badge products that are symbols of people's commitment to environmentalism and to a sustainability ethos. Not only do they express people's values, but they serve as symbols or reminders to others about the importance of environmentally friendly vehicles. In some cases, or in some areas, they create peer pressure on others to join in and do their part in environmentalism. That said, actual adoption is still largely among those consumers with a strong environmental ethos and has not quite "mainstreamed." A potential boost in the United States might come from the Obama administration's pledge in March 2009 to have 1 million PHEVs (plug-in hybrid electric vehicles) on the road by 2015, backed up by a series of supporting federal programs.[116]

- *Linux and open-source software.* Linux is an open-source software package that has become a serious player among established manufacturers. It provides its source code for users to tweak and share and incorporates the best innovations into future releases. There are now a wide range of applications that run on Linux, and it can be used by anyone irrespective of computer knowledge.[xxi] Over time, the open-source movement has been integrating more closely with conventional commercial approaches. Gartner predicts that "by 2011, growing diversity among open-source adopters will result in three distinct categories of OSS (open source software): (1) community projects, with broad developer networks; (2) vendor-centric projects controlled by commercial technology providers; and (3) commercial community projects, which have vendor-independent support channels."[117]

- *Consumer-generated content.* Consumer-generated content has contributed to the success of many "Web 2.0" websites, like Flickr, YouTube, and Delicious (a.k.a. del.icio.us). Some companies are experimenting with using consumer-generated content to promote their brands on the Web. The confectioner Mars, Incorporated, snack foods is promoting its Skittles candies on the Skittles.com website by featuring consumer-generated content produced by enthusiastic Skittles fans. In one example, they featured postings about Skittles that were found on Twitter. As a result of the attention, the term "skittles" became one of the most discussed terms on Twitter for a short period of time.

Consumers are increasingly becoming content providers and producers, blurring the distinction between consumers and organizations. It raises questions of whether or how consumer-generated content should be compensated. Goodwill is important but may not be enough to move co-creation beyond the

---

xxi   For more information, see http://www.linux.org/info/

fringe. It is likely that compensatory mechanisms will need to be developed to mainstream this phenomenon.

Consumer augmentation

Significant technological advances—from increasingly sophisticated mechanical implants to chemical, genetic, and nanotechnology-enabled approaches—will enable augmentation of human capabilities, both physical and mental.

Physical augmentation is taking several forms. Most of it today is simple substitution, replacing old, injured, or worn-out body parts with synthetic components, such as hips and knees. Most replacements are still not quite as good as an original in working order, but things get interesting when the replacement exceeds the capabilities of the original (see Blade Runner example below).

Physical performance enhancement reached popular attention with the performance-enhancing drugs such as steroids and the debate about what effect these drugs have on the validity of records. While the usage has long tarnished professional baseball, steroid usage has been an issue in most if not all competitive sports. Affluent societies, where more people have the wherewithal to pursue augmentation, are beginning to confront this as a public health issue. In sports, new rules, regulations, and oversights have emerged, and in the vast majority of cases the governing bodies have ruled against allowing enhancement, perceiving it as cheating. Moving forward, however, it may be that views on enhancement will evolve. There may also be societies that view enhancement as acceptable, and they may perhaps encourage it as a means of competitive advantage, which may force those societies currently against it to reevaluate their position.

Mental performance enhancement is not as far along, but some pharmaceuticals provide a preview of what's to come. Prozac®, for example, was the first widely used antidepressant, and its popularity made it more socially acceptable to use drugs to enhance mood. As brain science research advances, a whole new realm of mental performance options is likely to emerge.

Advances in genetics and biotechnology suggest the potential for a new approach to both physical and mental performance. Gene therapy techniques, for example, may offer new options for enhancement, although it is likely that initial push would be to fix disorders or conditions before enhancement.

Drivers of consumer augmentation

While augmentation is still early in its development, several advances are driving toward its eventual adoption.

- *Cosmetic surgery, implants, and bionics.* At a mundane level, cosmetic surgery is thriving, and it sets a precedent for "improving" people's natural endowments. It exposes a mass audience to this idea and has become more socially accepted over time, perhaps providing a precedent for more serious interventions. For instance, an implantable telescope used for the treatment of macular degeneration, a disease that causes visual impairment and blindness in millions of elderly, received FDA approval in mid-2009. Cochlear implants are widely used by those who are profoundly deaf or severely hard-of-hearing; these use an array of electrodes to directly stimulate the auditory nerve. More than 100,000 people worldwide have had the implants.

- *Military research on performance enhancement.* The military is an important source of enhancement technologies since it could be argued that there are fewer ethical concerns in terms of providing soldiers the best chance to survive and perform. In the United States, for example, DARPA has funded research to improve digestion so soldiers can digest cellulose, making it possible for them to eat grass, leaves, and otherwise inedible materials. Other DARPA research has investigated "pain vaccines" that can block the transmission of pain-signaling biochemicals in the human body, temporarily reducing pain sensitivity. The anti-narcolepsy drug Provigil® has been in use since the early 2000s to help soldiers stay awake and alert for as much as 40 hours straight.

- *Pharmaceutical research.* Pharmaceutical companies continually search for the next blockbuster drug and may find the cognitive enhancement realm to be a potentially rich hunting ground. On a less intense but more widespread scale, there has been an increase in the number of students using ADHD drugs such as Ritalin® and Adderall® to boost their mental stamina and focus when studying and test taking. A wide range of supplements is available claiming to boost memory and focus. While these are not yet validated, many people believe they deliver useful results. "Smart Bars" have also emerged that offer these types of options in a public, retail setting.

What it looks like

The seeds of future controversy are already being sown in the present. For example:

- *Blade Runner.* The International Association of Athletics Federations, the sport's ruling body, ruled against the participation in the Beijing Olympics by a runner with two amputated legs who uses Cheetah flex-foot carbon fiber blades. That ruling was overturned on appeal, but generated a storm of controversy, with experts divided over whether they unfairly enhanced his performance. Critics claim the elongated blades allowed him and other runners to cover more distance per stride and protected them from lactic acid buildup, and that by springing back into shape, they restore 95% of the energy expended in sprinting.[118]

- *Transhumanism.* This movement has a value system that promotes human enhancement and augmentation. They don't fear augmentation but rather seek to promote it. They view advances in nanotechnology and biotechnology as phenomenal achievements that have the potential to be leveraged for life extension, the replacement or upgrading of biological components, and tight integration of man and machine. Longer-term possibilities include the enhancement of human thinking and memory and upgrading the base DNA for humans.

- *The singularity.* While its occurrence is forecast to be further into the future, the discussion is already here. The singularity is the concept that machine intelligence will surpass human biological intelligence. Its most popular advocate, Ray Kurzweil, puts the date of this event around 2045. He suggests that "the singularity is an event in which the pace of technological change will be so rapid, its impact so deep, that human life will be irreversibly transformed."[119]

Innovations will challenge norms of what is desirable, permissible, and normal. They will raise questions that will challenge values and may open a host of new business opportunities. For instance, who might volunteer for a brain implant that would enable them to do a "dump" of all available information around a subject they are researching so that it would become instantly available? Who might take Provigil® to stay awake for 40 straight hours to meet a critical deadline? The quest for competitive advantage will raise these kinds of issues and require thinking through values and policies.

BLURRING BOUNDARIES

The set of "Blurring Boundaries" catalysts is about how consumers are confronting the challenges of an increasingly virtual world. The boundaries between the physical and the virtual world are becoming blurred as the two increasingly integrate. There will be fewer distinctions between the two as virtual technology improves and consumers become increasingly comfortable with it. There is growing evidence of increasing interplay between the two "worlds" as virtual products and services have their physical world equivalents. For instance, Webkinz® for kids popularized the idea of having a physical equivalent of an online avatar. Similarly, physical things are increasingly represented in the virtual world. Many organizations have a virtual workspace that mirrors, complements, or substitutes for the physical office. This will present challenges to relationship dynamics as people learn how to relate to people they rarely or never meet in person.

The virtual world will not be seen as a separate destination as it is always on and always available. People won't have to "go online"—they will always have instantaneous access to the online or virtual world. Access to the virtual world will be increasingly taken for granted, much as electricity is now, and simply assumed to be there.

As these worlds integrate, they present opportunities for consumers to reinvent how they spend their time. This enables flexibility with traditional schedules. With DVR and on-demand services, for example, it becomes possible for people to watch their favorite television shows whenever it is convenient rather than adhering to a network programming schedule. Work schedules are also becoming more flexible, particularly as virtual employment enables workers to choose when to perform actual work and when to attend to other matters. Technology increasingly enables more collaboration options such that far-flung participants can cooperate on global projects through conference calls, on-line meetings, etc., irrespective of state, country, and time zone boundaries.

The growing importance of the virtual world also presents opportunities to re-think traditional business models. Consumers facing economic and resource limitations may take the opportunity to reexamine what they need to physically own and what can be shared. The long-accepted model of owning software programs is increasingly being challenged by online applications. Virtual worlds make sharing or barter-type services much easier to manage. Local currencies and goods-and-services-sharing approaches are examples of the many social experiments likely to emerge as technology makes these more convenient to manage.

Ubiquitous connection

Ubiquitous connection is making information access more constant, whether at home or on the go. It has created an expectation that we can stay in contact with family, friends, or colleagues around the clock. As a result, the distinctions between home and work are eroding. This is viewed as both a blessing and a curse since it makes it much easier for work time to encroach on personal time, and vice-versa. For many workers, particularly knowledge workers, easy electronic access makes it easier to connect globally with colleagues and customers. While this is a boon to productivity, it often creates a need for conference calls that cross time zones and cut into what used to be personal time.

In addition to the work-related information, media content is becoming available any time, any place, on demand. This helps free people from the constraints of time schedules as people can access the media they like when it is convenient for them.

This catalyst is found particularly among younger cohorts. The futures consulting firm Social Technologies (now Innovaro) did a large study on the *Future of Youth Happiness* in 2007 that identified "lack of access to technology" as a key stressor of youth aged 12 to 24.[xxii] Young people are comforted by the fact that they have access, even when they don't need to use it. This contrasts with older generations who often cite the desirability of being unreachable at certain times as a goal.

Drivers of ubiquitous connection

- *Media platform convergence.* The traditional model of a family or a group of friends sitting down in front of the TV in the living room or family room at regular times is giving way to video and other information access anytime and anywhere. It is not unusual for the television to be on, with laptops running and the smartphone being used at the same time. As digital displays proliferate, it further blurs the distinctions among devices that display, from televisions to computers to iPads.

- *Social networking booming.* Social networking tools enable friends, family, colleagues, and acquaintances to stay in touch and communicate online. They have given people a new platform for unmediated communication with whoever wants to "listen." Social networking has spread beyond youth markets and has been quickly adopted by Baby Boomers, corporate employees, and even retirees. Social networking meets the consumer need for connection. It is geared to quick bursts of communication that enable users to quickly touch base and feel connected. It also greatly expands the range of the connections available.

- *Time and place shifting.* In an age in which consumers increasingly want everything at the touch of a finger, functions and features of infotech and communication devices, and the once-distinct lines between different forms of entertainment, are all converging. Communication and entertainment systems and devices are becoming increasingly smart and interrelated, taking on a rapidly growing number of functions and features, many overlapping with very dissimilar devices and technologies for use in homes, vehicles, and on the go—creating a need for new kinds of communication services. At the same time, entertainment forms—from games and movies to music and DVDs—are also converging.

---

xxii   Study is available for download at http://www.mtv.com/thinkmtv/research/

- *Wi-Fi expanding*. The increasing availability of Wi-Fi in a wide range of venues has increased the options for consumers to stay connected. As access has expanded, the trend is toward making it free. For instance, Starbucks finally switched from fee to free Wi-Fi in all its outlets. McDonald's has done so for all its U.S. outlets.[120] The free trend is reaching across other outlets as well, with Amtrak and many bus services in the United States providing free service, and some municipalities—for example, Sunnyvale, California; and Minneapolis, Minnesota—doing so as well. In May, 2010, London Mayor Boris Johnson pledged London-wide Wi-Fi by 2012.[121]

What it looks like

- *Work-life balance under pressure*. Workers are blurring the lines between home and work with increased telecommuting and using PDA-phones such as the Blackberry® to check business e-mail constantly. Conversely, workers are mixing work time with leisure time at the workplace, checking Facebook pages, IMing, and catching up on news and shopping via the Internet during "work" hours. Portability and rapidly expanding wireless reach and broadband penetration allow more people to carry screens with them wherever they go. Even schools are being "invaded," and some teachers struggling to maintain the attention of their students have had to ban the devices from the classroom. Over the long term, it is likely that classrooms will evolve to accommodate this connectivity and multitasking and convert it to a benefit to improve instruction—at least most of the time.

- *An on-demand world*. The DVR, popularized by TiVo®, enabled consumers to record programs and watch them at their convenience. On-demand programming is now emerging as the next step in that evolution. An Infonetics Research study found that spending for video-on-demand and associated infrastructure components and devices by providers held steady at $625 million in the fourth quarter of 2009, though spending was down for the year overall due to the Great Recession.[122] High-definition programming should further drive investment, and consumer comfort with the technology will increase over time as well. It is not inconceivable that scheduled programming, except perhaps for news or live events, could almost completely disappear at some point.

- *A socially networked world*. Nielsen data shows that three of the world's most popular brands online involve social media—Facebook, YouTube, and Wikipedia. The world spent over 110 billion minutes in 2010 on social networks and blogs, equating to 22% percent of all time online—and they are visited by 75% of global consumers who go online. The average visitor spent almost six hours on social media sites in April 2010 compared with 3:31 hours the previous year.[123]

Ubiquitous connection is quietly, or perhaps not so quietly, revolutionizing many aspects of consumers' daily lives. It brings a new capability to consumers—access to the virtual world at one's fingertips. Consumers are proceeding along the learning curve and trying to make sense of how to use this capability. As comfort with the technology grows, new and unanticipated applications will emerge.

Life-shifting

Traditional life stages and schedules are becoming increasingly obsolescent as new technologies enable consumer autonomy and erode boundaries and limitations. The changes are rippling across family, work and recreation. The nuclear family, which became the dominant model during the 18th century, is becoming less dominant again as the long-term trend toward diversity in family structure continues. The decline in the percentage of nuclear-family households has been mirrored increasing diversity in traditions in general. The empowerment of individuals has often come at the expense of tradition, although there is no value judgment implied here: some traditions falling by the wayside include no longer having to wait for stores to open to shop, thanks to e-commerce, and setting aside particular times each week to watch favorite television shows thanks to DVRs.

Life-stage shifts have led to the paradox of delayed adulthood and teen sophistication; that is, kids are mimicking grown-ups sooner, and adults are mimicking children longer. Children are exposed to more adult behaviors and lifestyles through their exposure to a wide array of media channels, and thus they often adopt the attitudes, behaviors, and values of the adult world sooner than have previous generations. At the same time, many adults who "kept their nose to the grindstone" and worked and studied hard in order to succeed feel they've missed out on their childhood and are seeking to relive it to some extent. One recent example is the emergence of adult kickball leagues and other types of "kid activities" increasingly being taken on by adults.

Many university classrooms provide a window on this phenomenon; the traditional 18-to-22-year-old college students now share the lecture halls with adults of all ages, including seniors who are going back to school not to retrain for work but simply because they enjoy learning. In essence, consumers no longer feel bound to convention and are seeking to do what they want to do, even if it is not "age-appropriate."

Driver of life-shifting

- *Nonnuclear families and household composition.* Affluent W1 countries in particular are experiencing dramatic changes in the so-called "traditional family," a configuration that has slipped into the minority. The traditional values that seemed to demand homogeneity have also given way to modern and postmodern views on race, religion, household roles, ethnic background, and sexual orientation; these all span a broad range of market and workforce segments. Individuals identify with one or more of these segments and expect to be recognized and tailored to in that context. They reject consumer messages and marketing that stereotypes them into unrealistic one-size-fits-all nuclear family models.

- *Age bending.* Conventional notions of age are blurring—and age is becoming an increasingly poor predictor of life stage, circumstance, income, attitudes, aspirations, or behaviors. Adults of all ages are behaving in new and surprising ways. Internet users over age 45, for example, account for 33% of YouTube hits and 27% of Myspace users. Aging baby boomers are healthier than previous generations, and survey data suggests that about 75% are not planning to retire. Adults in their 20s, 30s, and 40s are meanwhile carrying on activities traditionally associated with adolescence—e.g., prolonging college years, wearing younger clothing styles, driving flashier cars, buying the latest gadgets, having more fun—rejecting conventional concepts of what adults can and cannot do. At the same time, children are acting older, developing more mature and sophisticated tastes, behaviors, and affiliations at younger ages and consuming products and services (e.g., coffee, cosmetic surgery) traditionally associated with older consumers.

- *Technologies of "freedom."* A whole array of technologies—e-commerce, DVRS, on-demand, smartphones, social networking, GPS, etc.—introduced for a special purpose are being used in ways that enable life-shifting. As consumers experiment and learn with new technologies, they become comfortable with them and begin to innovate and use them in ways that were not originally anticipated. In this case, a common theme among the technologies is the ability to free consumers from the constraints of time and space. Of course, it can be argued that this freedom comes at a price, as the idea that people can stay in touch everywhere and get things done from anywhere can cause them to feel constant pressure to perform and find it difficult to simply relax. Constant connection is a personal choice; however, you don't have to answer your phone, respond instantly to e-mails or instant messages, or go online.

What it looks like

- *Print media in flux.* Traditional schedules are under fire with the advent of 24/7 technologies combined with consumer demands for up-to-the minute information. Print media circulations and revenues have dropped, and many print publications have gone out of business. In the United States, many daily newspapers have consolidated, reduced, gone away, or gone completely electronic. For example, the Detroit Free Press and the Detroit News just scaled back home delivery to three days a week. Two big-city dailies, the Rocky Mountain News in Denver and the Seattle Post-Intelligencer, have closed and gone exclusively online. The San Francisco Chronicle and the Boston Globe have also recently received threats of closure from their parent companies.[124] And so on. Their efforts to adapt to the digital world have proven difficult, as they compete with information that is free and often just as good. They continue to search for a value proposition that works. Many are experimenting with different pay-to-play schemes.

- *Just-in-time life*. Infotech is enabling people to live in the moment. This "just-in-time" lifestyle, which is enabled in large part by new social networking tools, will reshape the way people socialize, work, and shop. From GPS for navigation to "flash mobs," mobile communications make it easier to coordinate with friends and do things on the spur of the moment instead of making plans. It enables one to adjust schedules on a moment's notice. Deciding where to go, what to eat, and what to do can be based on real-time information, including input from friends, family, and co-workers. Some of this is just for fun. For example, Worldwide Pillow Fight Day was a flash mob attracting more than 5,000 participants that took place on March 22, 2008, in over 25 cities globally. Word spread via social networking sites, such as Facebook, Myspace, blogs, websites, text, e-mail, and word of mouth.[125] More serious applications include organizing protests against corporations or even governments.

- *People tracking*. Foursquare is one of many location-based social networking services that have recently emerged. Users check in at various locations, from parks to retail shops to restaurants, letting their friends know where they are, and in the process being awarded points and badges for doing so. A user who checks in the most from a location becomes the "mayor." Variations on this service will emerge as users become more comfortable with them. For instance, Trackdropper is an Android application that lets users "drop" songs from their phone's music collection in physical locations. Then, other users can go on treasure hunts to find and play the dropped songs.[126]

Life-shifting will intensify as information resources proliferate, mobile data flows increase, location based services multiply, and more people and things are tracked in real time. Consumers want things when they need them, according to their schedules, not the schedules of goods and service providers. This will push organizations into delivering via unconventional formats at unconventional times. Information may need to be customized for PDAs or iPhones instead of for desktop or even laptop computers—and it may need to be done before a 9 p.m. conference call with Singapore.

Truth and truthiness

Social media, search engines, and blogs are changing the way people communicate and consume information. These tools have made it simultaneously easier and more difficult to manipulate the truth, allowing misinformation to spread just as easily—and quickly—as the genuine article but also enabling widespread peer review. The new media environment diminishes the power of authoritative media sources and enables the spread of misinformation. In the new age of information, transparency and democratization, consumers, companies, and governments alike are learning to adapt to the blurring line between fact and fiction, reliable and unreliable, and its implications for the future of truth.

Digital tools help spread truth but also enable deception. Changes in how people consume info (blogs, social media, Google) create more opportunities for "deciding" what the truth is. It is not often a case of outright fraud but a fine distinction between opinion/fact, self-promotion/deception, and public/private blurring. Mechanisms to enable trust by verifying virtual information lag behind.

Drivers of truth and truthiness

Three important factors will have a significant impact on the future of truth.

- *Transparency.* Consumers now expect access to a whole range of information resources about people, places, and organizations—including status, history, location, ideology, social connection. They have unprecedented access to information, but it is often subject to manipulation and management by vested interests. Technology enables transparency, but these same tools make it easier than ever to manufacture misinformation. Technology reduces inhibitions to lying—people feel anonymous and therefore freer to deceive. Polls have found that lying via technology produces less guilt to the extent that some people even question whether it is really wrong to embellish one's profile on match.com or other dating sites.

- *Identity management.* Managing online identity is becoming more important, and sometimes this includes manipulating the truth. Nearly half of all teens say they doctor their social network profiles with false information to protect their privacy. According to Pew data, 10% of adult Americans claim to have a job that requires them to manage their online reputation, and 6% of online adults have asked someone to remove information about them, such as a photo or video, which was posted online. Companies also know that online reputation and identity is critical. One controversial but popular marketing tactic—now illegal—involved companies paying bloggers and websites to post favorable, apparently independent, reviews of their products without disclosing their financial relationship to the reviewer. Sony and Wal-Mart both made headlines when they were caught paying freelance writers to maintain fake blogs on their behalf, and both ultimately apologized for their actions.

- *User-generated media.* User-generated content enables people to "crowdsource" the truth. The case for this is suggested in works such as James Surowiecki's *The Wisdom of Crowds*, which makes the case for large numbers or aggregations of people being better at making decisions than any single individual.[127] Nonetheless, aggregations contain a combination of fact and opinion that can be challenging to sift through. Wikipedia is an example of a tremendously successful application of user-generated media, but it is not without challenges to its credibility. In a user-generated content world, the traditional brokers who provided the authoritative—and often biased—view of what's true and what's not are finding themselves cut out, or at least competing for attention. Thus consumers assume the burden of determining what is and isn't true for themselves. There remains a potential gap for consumers in terms of finding expertise when they need it.

What it looks like

- *Reputation systems.* Reputation systems are becoming increasingly important for commerce, with credit rating systems underpinning the lending system and buyer rating services supporting the evolution of e-commerce companies like eBay. The Internet has driven a shift from the passive creation of reputation—an entry in a phone book, an address in a newsletter, or a listing in a court record, all generated without active intervention from the subject— to active creation. More and more, people maintain, groom, and polish their online reputations.

- *Future of truth.* Online dating sites are among the most popular services on the Web, yet polling by MIT found that 90% of users felt that other site members lied to them on a regular basis, and 20% admitted misrepresenting themselves to other users. An increasing number of people feel the need to manage their online reputations, sometimes altering the truth for reasons of privacy and security and sometimes for reasons of self-aggrandizement and selfishness. As the Wal-Mart and Sony examples show, companies fall prey to this, too.

- *Personal transparency.* New genetic research is undermining the notion that humans are born as a blank slate. Personal genetic screening, gene surveys, and the identification of links between genes and behaviors are revealing new insights into the nature-versus-nurture debate. Over the next decade, people will have to confront the new reality of genetic heritability, renewing debates over the role of free will and the extent to which "human nature" can be changed by environmental interventions.

- *Social polarization.* Societies are dividing into cultural, social, ethnic, and economic subgroups. The proliferation of specialized media reinforces the fragmentation of identity. People can increasingly get cable channels and websites that cater to their specific interests and outlooks, from politics to obscure hobbies. No matter what your interest, you can find others on the Web who share it.

Increasingly, truth will derive from a combination of sources including both old media (professionally vetted, comparatively authoritative) and new media (user-generated, blending fact and opinion, lacking citations). Trust will gain in importance as a brand asset, yet it is becoming increasingly hard to manage. In an era in which trust has to be earned, building and keeping it has tangible value. Moreover, being trusted enables a company to fight more effectively against misinformation. But trust will be difficult to manage, and businesses will be as vulnerable as consumers, if not more so, to having the tools for altering others' online reputations turned against them. Reputation cleaners may become a fact of life for corporations as well as for individuals.

Integration of virtual and real

In the early days of the Internet, the digital world was a separate place unto itself. Digital text, images, sounds, etc., lived there—but didn't really intersect with "real world" information and objects. This was even clear in how people talked about accessing this other place—saying they were going to "go online" as though they were traveling to somewhere different than an actual place in the real world.

This is changing. Today, the virtual and the real worlds are increasingly intertwined. The boundaries between the "real" and the virtual are becoming porous as new digital technologies emerge and they become increasingly sophisticated.

Virtual worlds such as Second Life and the launch of "mixed reality" events—where a concert or lecture happens at a physical venue and also in the virtual world simultaneously—have emerged. Family communication patterns are changing and increasingly rely on digital technologies such as text messages, Skype calls, and virtual reunions. Real-world professional success is likely to increasingly depend on having an aptitude to navigate and network in virtual environments.

This blurring of the virtual and the real worlds is a natural progression—the next logical step for the Internet. The virtual is becoming less of a separate destination and more of an always-on, location- and context-aware component of everyday life. As this transition gets under way, it's already started to change the way people think about a range of issues associated with personal property. For instance, is income in a virtual world taxable? And, what does it mean for relationship dynamics that many people have never met their best friends or work colleagues face-to-face?

Drivers of virtual-real integration

The integration of the real and the virtual worlds is being driven by a variety of factors:

- *Connectivity.* Broadband and always-on connectivity via mobile devices have changed how people experience the digital world. It's shifting from access in bursts—sitting down, logging in, reading and replying to 20 messages, doing a few searches on Google—to an experience that is more fluid, constant, and integrated with real-world experiences. The barriers to engaging in digital behavior are lower than they used to be.

- *Consumer expectations.* People are creating and using more virtual objects, and there is growing interest in finding ways to bring such items into reality. It will not be long before consumers will expect a digital counterpart to anything that appears in the physical world—and vice versa. This will be especially true for future generations, the people who spent their childhood years playing with toys like the Webkinz® that integrated the physical experience of a stuffed animal with an online/virtual world experience.

- *Location-based technologies.* A range of location-based technologies is helping to stitch together the real and virtual worlds. Geotagging adds geographical metadata to digital objects (photos, videos, etc.), allowing users find photos based on location rather than subject/keyword tags on photo-sharing sites like Flickr. GPS is becoming ubiquitous, and as it's added to personal devices, people have constant access to precision geolocation data. People are just starting to experiment with what this means through location-based social networking services such as Foursquare, which enables users to "check in" and broadcast their location to their network.

What it looks like

Examples of how the real and virtual are being integrated are becoming easier to find every day. It's all around and in nearly everything people do. Consider these examples:

- *Virtual goods market.* The market for virtual goods emerged with online virtual worlds, and now also extends into social network sites, where users can adorn their profile pages and send items to friends. Investment bank Piper Jaffray estimates that the U.S. market for virtual goods will rise from $265 million in 2008 to nearly $2.5 billion by 2013. Worldwide virtual goods could be worth $6 billion that same year.[128]

- *The Wii.* The Wii was revolutionary when it was released because it provided something that previous gaming consoles didn't—a way to bridge the virtual and the real. Its innovative controllers allowed players to use the real-life motions they knew from bowling or tennis to control their virtual characters. There is no need to be adept with a joystick or other multibutton controller to take part, which makes the Wii accessible to everyone from toddlers to grandparents; it also means that game-play happens both on-screen and face-to-face as people can square off against family and friends as though they have bowling alleys or tennis courts in their own living rooms. In other words, it provides a more balanced experience: real and virtual.

- *Visual search.* New visual search technologies are letting people access the vast amounts of information in the digital world by taking pictures of the real world and using them as a search "question." For example, with the Google Goggles application, people can take photos with their phones of a book on a store shelf and receive reviews, information about the author, pricing info from other merchants, and more.

- *AR Drone.* Augmented reality (AR) overlays data and virtual imagery on the real world—giving users a view of the world that is… well, augmented. AR technology is advancing and will quickly make its way to consumer applications in coming years. One example is the AR Drone, a flying robotic toy that users control with their iPhones. Onboard cameras feed footage back to the iPhone screen—images can be "re-skinned" as enemy planes or obstacles. As such this game is half in the real world—and subject to real world effects like gusts of wind—but also half in the digital world.[129]

These examples offer a glimpse of how products and services and consumers' day-to-day experiences are bridging the gap between the real and the virtual worlds. New interfaces and technologies will aid the integration and lead to more immersive mixed reality experiences. And some even foresee the day when one can "print" products at home on 3-D printers using digital plans purchased over the Internet.

The next generation of consumers who are currently age ten and younger will never know a world where the real and the digital were not closely related. They're already being raised with stuffed animals that have online lives like WebKinz®, and they will likely welcome a wide array of sophisticated virtual products.

Continuum of ownership

Modern consumerism and ownership go hand in hand. Consumers are used to buying the things they want and need. In recent years, though, new business models and legal structures have emerged that blur the lines of ownership. It is more helpful to think in terms of a "continuum of ownership" that applies to physical goods as well as elements of the digital world.

The continuum of ownership gives people the opportunity take advantage of goods and services without having to actually own them in the traditional sense. Examples range from fractional ownership models—where an individual might own a share in a Ferrari and get to drive it a few weeks a year—to innovations such as the Creative Commons licensing system, which lets people share, remix, and even commercially use other people's professional and creative works with certain stipulations.

From a consumer point of view, the continuum of ownership is attractive because it offers the benefits of ownership without some of the costs that often accompany it. It provides access to what a person needs when they need it, which in many consumers' minds can be preferable to outright ownership. This message of access over ownership is a powerful message in consumers' minds—especially during a recession—and it could be a very powerful way of going forward as consumers rethink their consumption patterns.

Drivers of the continuum of ownership

The continuum of ownership is being driven by a variety of factors:

- *The Internet.* The Internet provides the infrastructure that enables many innovative ownership and business models. For example, without the Internet, there would be no way for Netflix to manage its business and serve its 12 million subscribers.

- *Democratization of luxury.* Expectations and aspirations for luxury products have risen around the world. This can drive interest in fractional ownership because it allows aspirational middle-class consumers—who can't afford the full cost of luxury ownership—to indulge in the high life. Want a Jimmy Choo bag for that big date? A small monthly membership fee to one of the many handbag clubs will deliver it to your door. It's temporary luxury on a budget.

- *The Great Recession.* Economic disruptions can force consumers to try new things—and as such, the recession has driven interest in the idea of a continuum of ownership because it gives people a way to maintain access to what they want, even if they don't necessarily own the item. For example, Victoria Godfrey, CMO of the car-sharing service Zipcar®, told AdAge.com that the recession and the renewed consumer focus on saving money is one of the primary trends behind her company's growth.[130]

- *Simplicity and post-materialist values.* Some of the interest in the new continuum of ownership model is driven by the desire to simplify and de-clutter one's life. With this transition to a post-materialist outlook come new priorities and consumer values, specifically a shift toward simplicity, quality of life, sustainability, and less of a focus on acquiring "things." It's not that people lose their desire to be consumers—but simply that their consumption choices are refocused. For example, rather than creating a collection of hundreds of DVDs, movie buffs will be content to know that the movies they want are available in the cloud (on a network) and are conveniently available whenever they want them.

What it looks like

Including the timeshare concept for resort vacations that sprang up in the 1960s, there are numerous examples of the continuum of ownership, giving consumers access to everything from art to airplanes.

- *ZipCar®.* Perhaps one of the most easily recognizable continuums of ownership businesses is ZipCar®, which gives customers access to a car—plus gas and insurance—for an hourly fee. In doing so, it provides a compelling alternative to car ownership for, as the company's website puts it, "savvy city residents and businesses looking for an alternative to the high costs and hassles of owning a car in the city."

- *Art ownership services.* Fractional art services—such as Artlab—give people access to art that might otherwise be out of their reach. A $200 monthly fee can get a subscriber five works of art for their home or office and let them swap them for new items several times per year.

- *Creative Commons.* The Creative Commons licensing system lets people share, remix, and/or even use commercially other people's professional and creative works—from music and photographs to newscasts, scientific journal articles, or even whole books. As of March 2010, there were over 125 million images on the photo sharing site Flickr licensed under Creative Commons licenses.[131]

- *Fractional jet ownership.* Business people can get the private jet experience without actually owning a jet, with fractional jet services such as NetJets and XOJET. These systems can be consistent with sustainability efforts, because they maximize the use of an asset. The Federal Aviation Administration estimates that fractionally owned aircraft average 1,200 annual hours in the air, compared to just 350 hours for the typical business jet.[132]

These examples offer a glimpse of what the continuum of ownership looks like. In coming years, there will continue to be innovation and experimentation around these concepts, as organizations look for ways to make money and serve consumer needs without actually selling them more "stuff." In some cases, this will raise new issues and challenges related to the ownership of intellectual property—as has already been the case with file sharing, mashups, and other areas related to digital media. But the drive toward consumers valuing access without ownership is likely to continue and the obstacles that emerge will be dealt with, no doubt in unimaginably creative ways.

BOUNDED CONSUMPTION

Consumers are confronting new limits to their lifestyle choices. Boundaries are emerging, or at least being considered around consumption. The sense of never-ending growth and abundance, while perhaps not ever a realistic view, nonetheless could be seen as an accurate characterization of the mindset of many W1 consumers. The Great Recession in particular has raised questions about this view in the minds of many consumers. It provides a focal issue around which other questions about limits, such as energy and environmental issues, get lumped in and have given consumers pause and a sense of concern. This pause has led many to rethink their consumption patterns and lifestyle choices, with some in turn making adjustments to streamline their consumption habits. The interesting question for the future, then, is if economic conditions improve sufficiently, will consumers go back to their old ways, or are some, most, or all of these changes permanent? The values shifts outlined in Chapter 3 provide reasonable evidence that these "streamlining" changes may be more long-lasting than previous responses to a resumption of good economic times.

The economic difficulties are not the whole story. Alongside it is a growing sense that the commitment to high-consumption lifestyles has other lifestyle consequences, primarily in cutting into personal time. Many consumers feel that they have lost control of their lives and their time, and are seeking to regain control it. And if that means working less, and consuming less, some are willing to accept that tradeoff.

A sense of living within limits dovetails with long-brewing concerns about sustainability to bring the consumption issue front and center. There is a growing sense that nature's bounty is not unlimited and that lifestyle changes will have to be made to preserve it. Sustainability has emerged as a solution for the limits problem. It is not as if consumption needs to stop, but it needs to be reconsidered in light of limits. While some proposed changes are merely cosmetic in nature, others take a more serious approach. Many businesses are responding with products and services that address this emerging sensibility.

Limits are also being considered with respect to the impact of globalization. While there is not yet a strong anti-globalization ethos emerging—at least in the mainstream—there is a growing sense of preference for things local. It's not a rejection of globalization, but a renewed emphasis on the local. It ties in with the point about consumers feeling out of control. While globalization brings many benefits, one of the costs is an increasing disconnection with goods and services. Values shifts are moving toward a growing desire for connection between identity and consumption, with local products and services providing a means to connect. Spending locally allows people to see how they contribute to the well-being of the community and makes consumption feel like an investment in "connection."

Enoughness[xxiii]

GATEWAY
ENTER
SIX
http://bit.ly/oQPGhl

Many consumers have become fed up with the current state of their lives. Again, they feel that loss of control; they see themselves caught up in a lifestyle or consumption treadmill, and they want to get off. This doesn't mean that they don't want to consume at all, but rather it signals a decision to re-prioritize their consumption habits. Buying decisions are no longer instantaneous; now they include pause, deliberation. These consumers were perhaps already skeptical of the link between material acquisition and happiness. Now they are more interested in experiences—they would rather take an ecotourist vacation than buy new furniture.

They are looking for ways to simplify their lives in general. This can mean fewer possessions, working fewer hours, and even de-cluttering social and activities calendars. This group includes and expands upon those who have already been practicing voluntary simplicity. For the newer entrants, while there is a motivation to simplify, it is not entirely voluntary, but a recognition of necessity.

---

xxiii Thanks to Australian futurist Marcus Barber for bringing the "enoughness" concept to my attention

Drivers of enoughness

Enoughness was catalyzed by the Great Recession, but momentum building toward it has been gaining for several years.

- *The Great Recession.* This was an influential trigger event. It forced many to cut back or at least think about their consumption habits. Economic limits may have catalyzed a larger sense of ecological and environmental limits. High-energy prices reignited discussions about peak oil. Environmental issues that may have once escaped notice caught people's attention in a vicious circle of challenging news about limits. This in turn created an opportunity to reexamine priorities, with many realizing a need to accept some limits on their aspirations and spending.

- *Voluntary simplicity.* A growing segment of consumers adheres to some version of voluntary simplicity. Some of the characteristics are a disenchantment with owning more stuff and shifts from hedonism to spirituality, from cynicism to caring, and from overtime to family time. They reject opulence or flashiness and a "me-first" attitude. They are downsizing their lifestyles and taking themselves out of the luxury market, even though many are quite well-off financially. These consumers may switch to buying used goods, have greater willingness to repair or replace items, or even forego purchases of big ticket items (e.g., homes, cars, appliances).

- *Post-materialism.* Many consumers in developed economies have household incomes that easily cover basic necessities, leading to diminishing satisfaction with increased goods consumption, and the emergence of new post-material needs. Some of these new post-material needs include a greater interest in experiential commerce and recreation as well as a greater desire to make consumer choices that meaningfully express individual values and self-identity. It is pointing toward a certain "chic" emerging for having fewer possessions.

What it looks like

Enoughness is a current phenomenon poised to gain strength. As more consumers go in this direction, it creates a positive feedback loop that brings others on board. Some examples include these:

- *The "experience" economy.* Pine and Gilmore brought this trend to popular attention a decade ago, pointing out the phenomena of coffee moving from a cheap commodity to a more expensive experience with the advent of Starbucks.[133] More and more consumers are opting to collect experiences rather than material goods. The integration of experiences with material goods is proceeding alongside this development. Consumers are interested in the story behind some of the goods they consider important to them. They like being able to tell guests, for example, that their dining room table was crafted by hand by an artisan in some village or community and how their expenditure helped that local economy. They are seeking a deeper meaning in life and that is reflected in the products, services, and experiences they consume.

- *Gross National Happiness.* Increasingly, governments are adopting efforts to monitor their people's happiness as a gauge of the effectiveness of national policies. As happiness wins higher priority at the societal level, more and more nations will fine-tune their studies of what makes their people happy. Bhutan, in the early 1970s, adopted the idea of GNH (Gross National Happiness) to signal a commitment to building an economy that would serve Bhutan's unique culture. It dovetails with many expert analysts' calls for rethinking Gross Domestic Product (GDP) as a chief economic measure, on the grounds that it misses many important factors such as environmental protection and the well-being of citizens. In 2009, the 5th International Conference on Gross National Happiness attracted more than 800 participants.[134] Brazil and France are among several nations exploring this concept in greater depth. French President Sarkozy has proposed a measure to seriously consider factoring in measurements of national happiness into the calculation of national GNP and growth targets.

- *Economics of cheap and easy.* Consumers are increasingly adopting "just good enough" solutions for computers, entertainment devices, and computing software. In TV, it is the low-definition and ubiquitously available online video with surging popularity, not HDTV. In music, MP3s of average quality dominate digital audio, leaving behind technically superior and higher fidelity alternative audio formats. Software is increasingly threatened by free online services like Google Docs, which offer basic functionality or the ability to create and share online documents as a free software service. Products in this market niche can potentially deliver 80% of the functionality for only 20% of the cost or the complexity. Many consumers are increasingly finding that the price and convenience are right, thus threatening more established and mainstream industry players.

These examples suggest a potentially dramatic shift in the consumer mindset. The acquisition of material goods was once seen by many as a sure route to success and happiness. That assumption has come under question, and alternative routes to happiness are being pursued. This has obvious implications for consumer goods companies and suggests a shift in emphasis from quantity to quality, and from goods to experiences.

Living within limits

Pick up a paper any day of the week and there are stories about experts raising red flags about fading long-term prospects for natural resources, including oil, potable water, certain commodities, arable land, etc. While there are dissenting voices, there is a growing perception that the planet is reaching some limits and that societies may be constrained in the future by shortages of natural resources. The Great Recession only added to concerns by raising the possibility that future limits could extend to the availability of financial resources and jobs.

Taken together, these emerging limits could impede future growth and may constrain certain consumer behaviors in the future. Some have even suggested that future resource shortages will be the provocation for future armed conflicts. Though this sounds dire, these limits could also be the catalysts that spark new forms of innovation, from clean energy and transportation, to new approaches to health and medicine, to creative new business models.

Drivers of living within limits

These potential limits are being driven by a variety of factors:

- *Population growth.* At the most basic level, the rise in the global population is putting increased pressure on finite resources. Exacerbating this is the fact that almost all population growth continues to occur in W2 and W3 where there is often already pressure on limited resources.

- *Development and modernization.* As countries modernize and develop their industrial capacity, their use of natural resources goes up. Factories need water for processing and cooling and constant energy to operate. Increased trade usually means export of natural resources such as timber and minerals, as well as increased energy use for transport, and all this typically increases environmental stress and pollution.

- *Changing consumer patterns.* As development occurs and incomes rise, aspiring consumers gain new consumption options. Diet is one of the first areas where people spend their newfound income—and they begin to substitute meat and poultry for grains and vegetables. This is already happening in much of the developing world and will intensify. Consider that per capita meat consumption is expected to rise from 10 to 12 kg today to some 18 kg in 2020.[135] Leisure habits also change. There are already 100 golf courses in and around Beijing and 12 ski resorts making their own snow. Both of these are huge users of water.[136]

- *The Great Recession.* The recession has brought home to many the idea of living within limits. It put a financial spin on the issue and brought it into sharper focus for the average person in the affluent W1 after years of debt-fueled spending.

What it looks like

So what kinds of limits are emerging in the future? Consider these examples:

- *"Rare earth" element shortages.* Concerns about the availability of potable water have been raised for many years. Starting around 2005, newspapers and other media have been inundated with reports of "peak oil." Recently, a new potential shortage has been grabbing the press—"rare earth" elements such as europium, lanthanum, and neodymium. These rare minerals are proving crucial to green technologies, from hybrid car batteries to the magnets in wind turbines and also for many advanced consumer products like flat-panel TV displays.[137] The problem is, China produces 93% of the world's rare earths—and has recently started to limit production and export, in effect ensuring supplies for its burgeoning high-tech and green industries.[138]

- *Low-cost cars and a coming gas crunch.* Petroleum production is peaking. While the precise date of peak oil is subject to debate, there is a broad consensus that the production of petroleum will peak by 2025 (if it hasn't already). Compounding the problem are the changing consumer consumption patterns noted above. In India and China, for example, rising incomes and the emergence of low-cost cars like the Tata Nano are opening the door for millions of new cars to flood the roads. W2 automakers will expand out of their home markets into other W2 countries, looking toward Africa and Latin America—further increasing the overall global demand for oil, even if W1 takes measures to improve national fuel efficiency and fuel security.

- *A debt hangover.* Many W1 consumers overspent and undersaved during the housing bubble years of 2003–2008. Many homeowners cashed out their equity during moves or refinancing, and much of that equity was channeled into consumer spending. With housing prices in correction and unprecedented levels of unemployment, consumers are gradually trying to fix their personal balance sheets by curbing spending. In the United States, for example, a longstanding decline in the savings rate has actually reversed from a previous negative savings rate to one that is slightly positive and slowly increasing.

- *And a reset of priorities.* Many consumers have adapted to recession not only by learning to live with less, but also by developing a genuine sense that less is more. Whether through choice or forced by economic necessity, consumers have been reassessing priorities in the way they live as well as in the way they spend. Living with less has prompted many consumers to recognize the enjoyment, fulfillment, and sense of purpose found in a renewed focus on family and community, rather than in professional achievement and material acquisition.[139] For example, just over half (53%) of U.S. consumers say that the recession "has made me appreciate the simple things in life."[140]

These examples offer a glimpse of some of the potential limits that may intensify and shape the business environment and consumer behavior in the coming decade. But we shouldn't get fixated on this as some sort of situation that has never been dealt with or seen before; it's important to recognize that there have always been limits that consumers and businesses have had to manage and cope with. The difference is that today there are signs of potential limits on things that consumers have long taken for granted as being abundant, especially in W1—oil, water, land, growth, and even the desire and ability of consumers to spend freely.

Limits or restrictions that keep consumers from behaving in established ways aren't inherently bad; they are often the kernels that spark innovation. So if one steps back and looks at these so-called limits, they may well lead to some of the more interesting innovation opportunities in the next decade.

Sustainable consumption

Consumers increasingly are seeking out products and companies that are aligned with their personal values. Sustainability is one of those values that consumers are increasingly subscribing to. The concept of sustainability was coined back in 1987 as "development that meets the needs of the present without compromising the ability of future generations to meet their own needs."[141] The concept has provided a unifying theme around which to gather various environmental causes and issues. More recently, the triple bottom line concept has emerged as a next-generation view of sustainability.[142] It expands the scope of sustainability beyond just the environment to include social and economic concerns as well.

Together, these concepts have come to serve as an umbrella for a wide variety of environmental, social, and economic concerns, from local production to organic food to labor practices to carbon footprints to corporate social responsibility, among others.

Drivers of sustainable consumption

- *Climate change awareness.* Awareness has been steadily increasing globally. A September 1988 poll found that 58% of Americans recalled having heard or read about the greenhouse effect. This was a big jump from the 38% in 1981. Polls in the 1990s found that roughly half of Americans thought global climate change was already here and many of the rest thought it was coming. Al Gore's *An Inconvenient Truth* had the third-highest box office receipts of any documentary in history, and the book reached the top of the bestseller list. International polling found that almost everywhere in the world, a majority of the population had heard of global climate change. Educated people in most developing nations expressed more concern about climate change than their counterparts in the industrialized world and more commitment to action. The United States lagged behind most of the world in expressing a need to do something about it, as skepticism is strong there.[143]

- *Conscientious consumption.* Labels on food and other products are supplementing information content with text and symbols that make it easier for consumers to select products that accord with their personal values. Research shows that 67% of consumers in the United States and the EU have boycotted a food, beverage, or personal-care product on ethical grounds.

- *Corporate social responsibility.* A 2007 study conducted by Deloitte Consulting found that 85% of U.S. consumer business companies had "active sustainability initiatives," of which the most common were recycling and energy conservation. In determining the primary drivers behind these initiatives, the study found that 60% of the companies cited internal motivations such as cost reduction, mitigation of regulatory risk, and concerns over deficient commodity inputs.

What it looks like
- *Natural is better.* Natural ingredients, foods, and practices—for instance, those that are free from pesticides or the modern scientific process—are increasingly perceived as wiser choices for both consumers and the planet at large. People in developed and emerging economies are feeling the effects of modernization and increasingly crave the therapeutic powers of the natural world. This in turn creates awareness that nature is fragile and ought to be protected.

- *Environmental footprints.* Over the last decade, the concept of an environmental footprint has become a prominent tool in simplifying the presentation of product environmental impacts. Conceptually, these footprints calculate the quantity of resources used over the entirety of the production process, theoretically capturing the use of natural resources at every stage of the supply chain. These incremental uses added together comprise a total footprint for an individual or product. The footprint concept has been expanded to focus on a variety of natural resources: carbon footprints measure emissions of greenhouse gases, ecological footprints measure impacts on nature, and water footprints measure water use in production and distribution. A related concept is food miles, which measures the distance that crops travel from field to table and the locality of food resources.

- *Fair Trade.* Coffee was the first product that TransFair USA certified (starting in 1998) and remains the mainstay of the fair trade movement.[xxiv] Fair Trade Certified™ coffee imports have been growing by an average of 50% annually for the last decade. TransFair USA certified 110 million pounds of coffee in 2009. Since 1998, U.S. imports of Fair Trade Certified coffee have generated $220 million in additional revenue (measured against the market price for coffee) and premium funds for coffee producers.[144]

- *Personal Carbon Trading: CRAGs.* Various schemes have been proposed to implement carbon trading at the personal level. The early manifestations are in CRAGs (Carbon Rationing Action Groups). They first surfaced in the United Kingdom in 2006, have gone international and today some 30 groups—active and in the process of forming—exist in the United States, the United Kingdom, and Canada. CRAG members voluntarily agree to live within an annual specific carbon allowance. They track and report activities involving carbon use, such as home energy consumption, autos, plane travel—and they have their carbon allowance debited accordingly. At the end of the year, those with a carbon deficit must pay into a fund for "over-emitters."[145]

The footprint examples above may be harbingers of a stampede when combined with the many other causes that fit under the broad sustainability umbrella. Momentum toward sustainability has been growing for some time and may reach a critical mass where it moves from a secondary to a primary concern. In essence, the fringe has been infiltrating the core, and if this continues, at some point the core itself will be transformed. Organizations that have been keeping pace with these changes should be able to adapt, but those playing a wait-and-see game may find themselves unable to catch up should these changes catalyze faster than anticipated.

Re-localization

For every trend there is a counter trend, as the foresight truism goes. It may take time for it to surface, or it may be hard to pin down at first, but this axiom seems to hold true and the pendulum eventually swings back at some point. So it is with relocalization, the counter trend to what has been the dominant characteristic of economic change in the 20th century: the integration of national economies, which has come to be generically called globalization.

---

xxiv   According to Wikipedia, fair trade is an organized social movement and market-based approach that aims to help producers in developing countries achieve better trading conditions and promote sustainability.

Relocalization is the idea that there is a new and growing focus on local economic activity (manufacturing, agriculture, services, etc.), rather than an unquestioning acceptance of items produced by globalized economic actors. It's about a growing consumer desire to link up with local merchants, artisans, manufacturers, farmers, and have a stronger connection to the people that are making the stuff they're buying.

Sometimes this happens directly—e.g., buying beer at one of the thousands of microbreweries now in the United States. Sometimes this happens indirectly through an established retail channel, e.g., shopping in the "locals" aisle at a chain grocery store or eating where a chef features food harvested within 50 miles of the restaurant.

While it's true that globalization provides distinct advantages such as giving people access to products that were previously unavailable, perhaps the most compelling thing it brought consumers in the last century was low prices. In rich countries, a smaller percentage of incomes was required for necessities, in effect freeing up money for "luxuries" such as entertainment and recreation. In developing countries, the percentage of income allocated to necessities has also decreased, enabling increasing numbers to participate in the consumer economy.[146]

But changes in the market are in some cases reducing the price advantages of globalization and values shifts are causing consumers to look *beyond* price alone and causing them to base their consumption choices on a wider set of criteria/ attributes, especially place of origin. So now both businesses and consumers are experimenting—and in some cases embracing—the idea of relocalization, finding that it can provide them with both tangible and emotional benefits.

Drivers of re-localization

Re-localization is being driven by a variety of factors:

- *Energy costs.* Globalization has been enabled by cheap oil, but uncertainty about the future price and availability of oil will put more focus on all things local. Already during the late 2000s, some businesses were adopting "near-sourcing" strategies to protect against spikes in oil prices. The attraction of shortening one's supply chain isn't surprising, considering it only cost $3,000 to ship a 40-foot container from Shanghai to the U.S. East Coast in 2000, but cost $8,000 in 2008 as the price of oil rose.[147] One manufacturer who pursued this strategy was IKEA, which opened its first U.S. manufacturing facility in May 2008 to get production closer to consumers. It also provides a way to reduce risk for operations in an increasingly volatile world.

- *Carbon/environmental concerns.* Concerns about carbon emissions and the impact of transporting goods thousands of miles are refocusing some consumers and businesses on local production options. Buying locally produced goods gives them a tangible way to reduce their personal carbon footprint and feel that they're contributing to fighting climate change.

- *Desire for jobs and regional development.* After decades of job losses to overseas workers, state governments in the United States are keen on the idea of re-localization of manufacturing as a way to create jobs and build strong local and regional economies. Some see green technology manufacturing as the next great opportunity area and a way to bolster the U.S. job market.

- *Need for flexibility and customization.* Local production can improve speed, flexibility, and customization. American Apparel, which has integrated critical steps of its operation (design, manufacturing, marketing) into a central facility in Los Angeles, claims that this allows them to be more flexible and react to market trends more quickly than their competitors. (See below for more on American Apparel's approach to re-localization.)

What it looks like

So what does re-localization look like today, and who's doing it? Consider these examples:

- *American Apparel.* Most clothes are made in places like China, Vietnam, Honduras, or Bangladesh. Yet a shirt might have been designed in Europe but made in China with cotton imported from the United States. American Apparel has grown its business from using a totally different business model that exemplifies re-localization. There are some 5,000 American Apparel employees (about half its total workforce) working at its headquarters in the heart of Los Angeles where they do almost everything: clothing design, marketing, knitting, dyeing, and sewing. This has made them one of the largest employers in Los Angeles and the largest clothing manufacturer in the United States.

- *Purveyors of local food.* One of the first signals of re-localization at the consumer level came via the local food movement, a trend emerging since the early 2000s. The global flow of food and industrial agriculture continues to make the process by which food gets from farm to table a real mystery to the average consumer. But at the same time—and perhaps in reaction to this—a growing number of people are paying more attention to food origins and seeking alternatives to the modern food system. Some Americans are replacing lettuce grown 3,000 miles away in California with local food from CSA (community-supported agriculture) operators who offer seasonal shares of the produce they grow on their farms. The number of farmers' markets in the United States has been growing in recent years, and restaurants are featuring local ingredients on their menus. Google has even gotten into the act, with the launch of Café 150, which sources everything within 150 miles of the Google corporate campus.

- *Local currencies.* Cities and towns in the United States, United Kingdom, Germany, and elsewhere around the world are experimenting with local currencies that can only be used in the community of issue. While this is not a scalable solution, that seems to be the point. It's more about building relationships and keeping capital flowing locally than just about making a sale. Paul Glover founded Ithaca HOURS, a local currency in 1991, a concept that has been flourishing ever since. He shares his insights with large multinationals and has been featured in national news and in the print media. The city of Ithaca, New York, issues this currency, and it is accepted around town for goods and services. In this way, the city can keep the money from flowing out of the area and toward places and purposes that may not be supported by or supportive of the Ithaca community. Ithaca HOURS can be used for many things. One user, Margaret, uses HOURS as rent payment, for flea control, phone calling, food, movies, engineering consulting, books and gifts. People can choose whether to accept payment in dollars or Ithaca HOURS. Says Margaret, "Because HOURS can be used both for goods and services [that] are not always part of the formal economy, as well as for retail and professional transactions, the local economy gets a boost every time HOURS are earned. That's what any money is all about, facilitating exchanges among people."[148]

- *Smart growth.* Though by no means the dominant form of development, there is clearly an interest in growth that fosters community livability. Often referred to as new urbanism, this school of thought focuses on building more compact cities and neighborhoods that offer people a rich mix of retail, residential, commercial spaces and options for pedestrian, bike, and public transport. It's about refocusing architecture and urban planning to give people everything they need to work and live locally—right at their fingertips. Portland, Oregon, is a pioneer in this area, and has followed smart growth policies for the last several decades focused on containing urban sprawl and its consequences.[149]

These examples offer a glimpse of how some innovative organizations and communities are re-localizing their operations and how consumers are re-localizing their lifestyles. While this clearly won't take root in all sectors or product categories, re-localization will be a more important aspect of the business and consumer landscape in the future, as consumers re-prioritize what they want out of products.

Key points

- The outer dimension of consumer life is described in the form of catalysts: groups of trends and related consumer values driving change in a particular direction. These catalysts work hand in hand with the values changes in that they influence and reinforce one another. The catalysts are in part manifestations of the values changes, and in part they help enable the values changes.

- There are 13 catalysts identified as the key drivers of change, grouped into three sets with a common theme:

  o *Engaged consumers*: Consumers shifting from a passive to an active orientation.

  o *Blurring boundaries*: Consumers facing new challenges and opportunities in navigating the emerging virtual world.

  o *Bounded consumption*: Consumers confronting new limits to their lifestyle choices.

These themes in turn have a common theme of consumers facing challenges to their current lifestyles. While one could argue there are always some kinds of challenges, there are two important differences: (1) here, the nature of the challenges is unprecedented, e.g., the emergence of a virtual world, reaching the limits to key resources, etc., and (2) these consumers will not passively accept change but take an active stance and work toward what they want.

- Each of the 13 catalysts is analyzed with a consistent approach: they are introduced and described, the key drivers behind them are identified, and examples of what they look like in the present are provided. So, all of these catalysts are in existence to some extent today, but on a small scale. They will be increasingly influential in the future.

PART TWO

WHAT THE CHANGING CONSUMER LANDSCAPE WILL LOOK LIKE

Part One provided an understanding of why the consumer landscape is changing. Part Two builds on that understanding to describe what the changed landscape will look like. The first part is much more of a classical research work that provides data, references, and support for the proposed theories and concepts. The intent is to provide support for this more speculative second part of the work.

Now that you've learned all about how and why the consumer landscape is changing in Part One, it's time to put all that knowledge into action. Part Two describes what tomorrow's consumers will look like and what they'll want. It provides a preview of the future consumer landscape.

Part Two thus takes a different approach. One difference is that there is no direct data and references. There are no future facts to cite but rather a descriptive analysis of how the consumer life model, with its related values and catalysts, is likely to play out in the future. The future consumer landscape is described in two formats: need states and personas. The processes for deriving the future need states and personas will be described in each chapter. They are established tools used by futurists, even though different firms will have somewhat different approaches. But the general practice of deriving a forecast of future states based upon a conceptual model and research is routine for futurists. A key difference is that the need states and personas are derived using qualitative approaches relying on interpretation.

6

CONSUMER SWEET SPOTS: IDENTIFYING EMERGING NEED STATES

Threpe inner dimensions of the *New Dimensions of Consumer Life Model* were laid out in Chapters 2 and 3. Values were focused on in Chapter 4. Changes in the outer dimensions were covered in Chapter 5. This chapter describes how these changes come together in the form of emerging need states. The next chapter will then take the need states a step further and bring them to life in the form of future personas.

ABOUT NEED STATES AND THE PROCESS

Why need states

Need states are used as the primary mechanism for illustrating the changes in consumer life, as they—along with the personas in the next chapter—provide a good target for market researchers, new product and business developers, and strategists to aim at as they anticipate and plan for the future. The descriptor "emerging" was carefully chosen to signify that these need states are already appearing in consumer life to some degree. They do not represent totally new needs that will come into being at some point in the future—that could be the subject of another book. Rather, the idea was to provide help for today's researchers, students, and businesspeople in developing futures-centric ideas that can be applied in the present. Certainly timing issues are of paramount importance. For example, one does not necessarily want to "bet the farm" on an emerging need state being full-blown in the next 18 months. A safer approach would be to perhaps aim at understanding the leading edge of consumers with this need state in order to ramp up efforts as the need state gains momentum over time. At this point, it may be that running small-scale experiments is the proper approach. That said, the relative maturity of the following need states will differ—some will be "more emerged" than others, and it could be that one or more are closer to emerging in the present rather than in the future.

Emphasis on the newly emerging

An important caveat is that the emphasis here is on "new" need states, not all need states. There are lots and lots of need states in existence today that can provide excellent opportunities. As consumers and nations move through the development process, need states that once provided great business opportunities in one geographic area are likely to emerge in new areas with new groups of consumers. Modern values were instrumental in driving the economic growth of affluent W1 countries. Now they are transitioning to postmodern values. Modern values are gaining strength in emerging market W2 countries as they go through their growth stage. While the modern values of W2 today may be interpreted somewhat differently than the modern values of say, Japan, during its high-growth phase, in a sense it is not really news—it's happened before. There is no similar precedent for postmodern and integral values, thus their manifestation in need states is the topic of interest here.

Similarly, there may be incremental changes in existing need states that could open up new opportunities. This work, however, aims at the new. Accordingly, there will be a bias toward consumers and nations further along the developmental curve, primarily the nations in W1. To recap, it would be silly to claim that all of the new opportunities of the future are in W1, with billions of consumers in W2 poised to enter consumer life on a large scale. The distinction being made is that these W1 opportunities will tend to be newer to the world, and if the development process continues, these opportunities will eventually reach W2 on a large scale as well.

Where the need states come from

The inner dimensions piece of the consumer life model briefly introduced the concept of needs. To recap briefly, Maslow's hierarchy is used as the primary source of universal human needs; in the model, these needs are linked up with values and worldviews where appropriate to form the core explanation of inner dimension change. Maslow's Hierarchy of Human Needs has been the most widely used system for categorizing needs. One of the "benefits" of a system's being popular is that it will be analyzed, criticized, and picked apart. This is perfectly reasonable, as the dominant ideas in any discipline or perspective are typically the starting point for a discussion of ideas. While this system may have flaws, one should not toss out the baby with the bathwater. The overall scheme hangs together well on its own and it also syncs up with the World Values Survey and the Spiral Dynamics Worldviews, the other primary inputs into the New Dimensions approach, as well as the other systems analyzed.

There are two other needs systems that are incorporated with Maslow's to form the list of universal needs used for this work. Manfred Max-Neef developed an excellent system of Human Scale Development needs in support of his work on behalf of promoting the development needs of emerging markets, particularly in Latin America. "We have organized human needs into two categories: existential and axiological,[xxv] which we have combined and displayed in a matrix. This allows us to demonstrate the interaction of, on the one hand, the needs of Being, Having, Doing, and Interacting; and, on the other hand, the needs of subsistence, protection, affection, understanding, participation, idleness, creation, identity and freedom."[150] His system of nine fundamental needs in four categories produces what he refers to as 120 "satisfiers"—"an ultimate sense the way in which a need is

---

xxv   Pertaining to values

expressed."[151] Max-Neef explains that "from the classification proposed it follows that, for instance, food and shelter must not be seen as needs, but as satisfiers of the fundamental need for Subsistence."[152]

Reiss has derived a system of 16 empirically tested basic desires (power, curiosity, independence, status, social contact, vengeance, honor, idealism, physical exercise, romance, family, order, eating, acceptance, tranquility, and saving). His findings suggest that the desires are largely unrelated and may have different evolutionary histories.[153] He draws upon the work of social psychologists studying intrinsic motives and does an admirable review of the literature in support of his theory and subsequent psychometric research and behavior validation, developing a self-report instrument called the Reiss Profile of Fundamental Goals and Motivational Instruments. He asserts that the satiation of these 16 desires leads to an intrinsic joy.[154] This system syncs up less directly with Maslow's needs and overlaps into values, as defined here. Nonetheless, there was some overlap and some of his desires are incorporated into the New Dimensions list of universal needs.

While both these systems approach needs from conceptual frameworks different from Maslow's, they reach similar conclusions. A key advantage of Maslow's system is that it suggests a progressive development over time, which fits with the views here on the evolutionary nature of values and worldviews. For convenience's sake, the choice was to fold the ideas of Max-Neef and Reiss into Maslow's structure, but it is acknowledged that both are in their own right commendable and deserving of attention. The incorporation makes the *New Dimensions Values Inventory* more robust. For example, Max-Neef suggested that "it is likely that in the future the need for Transcendence, which is not included in our proposal, as we do not yet consider it universal, will become as universal as the other needs."[155] This syncs with the observations and futures-oriented perspective of this work, and this need was included in the *New Dimensions Values Inventory*.

Table 9 organizes the universal needs using Maslow's structure and notes how the categories overlap with the New Dimensions values: survival needs–traditional values; belonging needs–modern values; self-actualizing needs–postmodern values; self-transcending needs–integral values. The needs are further organized into three subcategories: self-related, other-related, and existential. By reading across the rows, one can get a sense of how needs evolved over time as an individual matures. Here is a scenario using the self-related needs as an example:

- First, one eats, drinks, and seeks security, etc.

- When those needs are met, self-respect is the next quest.

- When that need is met, it is on to independence, creativity, etc.

- Finally, it's on to fulfilling one's purpose.

Real life, of course, does not proceed that linearly or sequentially but iterates, starts, and stops. The point is that the overall directionality holds, and it gives a sense of how priorities shift over time. The satisfied needs don't go away but become less of a focus as new needs challenges emerge.

Table 11. Universal needs			
Survival needs (fit with traditional values)	Belonging needs (fit with modern values)	Self-actualizing needs (fit with postmodern values)	Self-transcending needs (fit with integral values)
Self-related needs			
Physiological (breathing, drinking, eating, excretion, sexual activity), health and safety (physical), financial, employment, moral, psychological, and property security	Self-respect	Independence, identity, creativity, reaching fullest potential, leisure, idealism, freedom	Fulfilling purpose
Others-related needs			
Family security, ability to save, sense of order	Love needs (friendship, affection, sexual intimacy, supportive family, participation), esteem needs (acceptance, respect of others, recognition/status)	Closeness to other people	Planetary connection
Existential needs			
God/religion/ supreme authority (otherworldly)	Secularism (this worldly)	Appreciate life, system of morality, personal spirituality	Planetary connection

Crafting the need states

The universal needs provide the foundation for creating the need states. Each need state has one to three core needs, supplemented by three to five related values (the inner-dimension component), and intersects with two to four catalysts (the outer-dimension component). Need states differ from universal needs in that they are needs within a specific context, situation, or set of activities. For understanding consumer life, this specificity is essential. If one is making breakfast cereal, for example, there are interested in specific needs around the breakfast situation. To simplify: need + situation = need states.

Several steps were taken to create the need states. While the research team may have had top-down intuitions about potential need states beforehand, these were kept aside and the bottom-up approach described below was followed. In most cases, the top-down hunches were largely confirmed.

First, the team assembled the raw list of the key components of the inner and outer dimensions—the 39 universal needs, 34 postmodern values, 16 integral values, and 13 catalysts—into a spreadsheet. For each of these entities, the team brainstormed potential future need states (existing need states were screened out) that might derive from each. For some entities, no ideas were generated; in other cases, there were multiple ideas. This led to a list of 120 raw and generic potential emerging need states.

Next the team created a generic framework of situations to bring specificity to the potential emerging need states. They selected the framework from John Robinson's Time Diary studies, as reported in his excellent book, *Time for Life*,[156] in which he tracked Americans' time use via diaries and broke down daily activities into several categories (work, household/family care, shopping, personal/ biological necessities), learning, leisure (entertainment/recreation), affiliation, and communications). The team compared the generic needs with Robinson's categories using a simple matrix, with more specific need states being identified at the intersections where appropriate. This led a list of literally hundreds of potential specific need states.

Table 12. Situational needs	
Committed time	**Free time**
Work	Learning
Household/family care	Leisure (entertainment/recreation)
Shopping	Affiliation
Personal/biological necessities	Communications

The next task was to look for patterns in the matrix. This rather painstaking process involved combining, consolidating, and pruning the large list. After several iterations, 37 rough draft need states emerged.

After that, the team began "beefing" up the candidate need states by adding related values and catalysts. After completing this process, the team carried out one final consolidation: they identified the 23 need states to highlight in this work and further refined them by identifying one to three core needs for each of the need states.

The team felt that a list of 23 was too long to be useful and once again analyzed this list for themes; they came up with 7 overarching meta-needs. These 23 emerging need states organized into 7 meta-needs are judged to be useful as starting points for market researchers, new product and business developers, and strategists as targets for identifying opportunities to better serve consumers in the future. Chapter 8, "Customizing the Personas: Persona Construction Kit," provides advice on how to customize the need states for the specific needs of an industry or topical area and/or an organization.

<u>**FORMULA**</u>

39 Universal Needs + 33 Postmodern Values +15 Integral Values + 13 Catalysts

=

23 Need States in 7 Meta-Needs

THE 23 NEED STATES IN SEVEN META-NEEDS

This section highlights the key ideas of the 7 meta-needs and the 23 individual need states written from the perspective of consumers who are, or eventually will be, making them a priority in their lives. The clusters represent meta-needs in bold with related need states bulleted underneath them.

Keeping it Real: Preference for the Straight Story
- The Authenticity Premium

- Au Naturel

- The Simplicity Premium

- Less Is More

Pushing the Envelope: Challenging Performance Boundaries
- Performance Enhancement

- Getting Real with the Virtual

Every Moment Matters: Taking Back Control of One's Time

- Whenever, Wherever, Whatever

- Investing Time Like Money

- Living in Real-Time

The [Relentless] Pursuit of Happiness: Taking Responsibility for One's Well-Being

- Help Me Help Myself

- Identity Products, Services, and Experiences

- Systematic and Consistent

- Reinventing the Self

- I'm Not a Consumer

- Pursuit of Happiness, a.k.a. Well-Being

Community First: Preference for Things Local

- Local Preferences

- Community Support

- Trust the Network

We [Really] Are the World: Feeling Responsible for the Well-Being of the Planet

- Global Citizens

- Making a Difference

Glass Houses: Everyone is Watching

- Trusted Partners for the New Insecurity

- The Truth, Whole Truth, and Nothing but the Truth

- Expanding Accountabilities

For each cluster, the meta-need is briefly characterized and then the supporting need states are described. Each need state is introduced, with an accompanying representative image and a table that highlights the core needs, supporting values, and related catalysts. The needs are assumed to be self-defining, the values are explicitly defined, and the catalysts are described in detail in the previous chapter. Each individual need state is characterized, then examples are provided on "how it shows up" and the implications are explored in "what it means."

KEEPING IT REAL

The key word for these consumers is authenticity. It is the core value driving consumers to this meta-need. They are asking organizations to give it to them straight and trust them to be able to handle the truth. They will reject any paternalistic "for your own good" kind of sugarcoating. Their view is "treat me as an adult, as an equal, and as someone with a brain. Don't manage me."

The four need states at the core of "keeping it real" are these:

- *The authenticity premium*. Pursuing the pure and unadulterated, not tainted by marketing spin and packaging.

- *Au naturel*. Preferring natural solutions where available.

- *The simplicity premium*. Appreciating the extra work and elegance that goes into simple offerings.

- *Less is more*. Valuing the chic of pushing the envelope towards more sustainable lifestyles.

The authenticity premium

Pursuing the pure and unadulterated, not tainted by marketing spin and packaging.

These consumers have a core need of realism complemented by an avid curiosity about how things work. They want to know what's really going on, "warts and all" and are confident in their ability to handle the truth. Their curiosity drives them to probe beneath the surface of the obvious. They feel it is better to understand, even if that understanding is unpleasant, than to be blissfully ignorant.

Table 13. The authenticity premium		
Needs	**Values**	**Catalysts**
Realism Curiosity	Authenticity: State of being genuine; not false or an imitation. Experiences: Collecting memorable activities instead of or along with material goods.	Enoughness Truth and truthiness

They are reacting against an overly managed world. "Delighting the customer" has gone to an extreme. As management of consumer experiences has gotten increasingly sophisticated, it has created a situation where every aspect of the experience is micromanaged, and these consumers sense that, and feel that they are being manipulated. The micromanagement of consumers manifests in several ways:

- Individuals are bombarded with more and more marketing and advertising messages, with no opportunity passed up in pursuit of a potential new opportunity to reach more eyeballs.

- Spin control dominates politics, and this is now increasingly true of organizations as well. Everyone is trained to be on message. Particularly in large organizations, individuals must check with the public affairs people before saying anything publicly. Conference presentations are sanitized to fit with the corporate image. It is rare to hear the unvarnished truth.

- Event planning has risen to the level of a science, such that every aspect of the experience is carefully thought through to create the intended impression. One of the unfortunate byproducts of the so-called experience economy is that the experiences have become increasingly managed over time.

- As networking becomes increasingly important to business and professional success, every meeting or encounter becomes a potential to get one's message across—it could be that down the road this person could provide a referral or business, so the presentation of self needs to be in line with the intended messaging.

- Everything seems staged and for the camera. Reality television, YouTube clips, and social media have made everyone a potential "star" and thus increasingly conscious of image. As production technologies have filtered to the masses, the "on camera" mind-set has accompanied it.

It is increasingly difficult to distinguish "truth" from messaging. And consumers are getting tired of it. Thus, there is a craving for plain speaking.

These consumers seek authenticity in dealing with organizations. They have an innate curiosity about how things really are. They seek more of a human touch in dealing with organizations. They want the straight story and are capable of handling the truth. They feel disrespected when they are dealt with on an impersonal basis that lumps them in with some market research segment and follows a script. This desire is related to their growing interest in real experiences. They see encounters with other people and relationships as one of many experiences in their life, and they want these to be positive and meaningful. They value their time and expect those they deal with to reciprocate.

How it shows up

Tourism is an industry experiencing both the drive for authenticity and experiences. Here, growing numbers of tourists are avoiding the conventional tourist experience. These consumers will even object to being called tourists—they see the label conjuring up a negative association as people in floppy hats and Bermuda shorts snapping photos and being "fed" a totally staged experience. Rather, they want to really experience what life is about in the places they visit. They don't want to follow tour guides to all the "regular" spots but want to deviate off the route and get the experience of what life is really like. Some of the options they are pursuing, for example, are ecotourism. In contrast to say, a safari, where the experience is a carefully managed experience at a distance, they want to roll up their sleeves and do something. Ecotourism provides the opportunity to not only experience the situation but to contribute to it. It's like learning by doing rather than learning by observing at a safe distance before moving to the next exhibit in a timely manner.

What it means

Responding to these consumers will challenge two key orthodoxies. One is "being on message." Most organizations have spent years training their people to understand the company message and be able to follow the script. This need state does not suggest abandoning a company's point of view—one could argue it makes the need for alignment even more important. It does mean, however, that the alignment with company purpose and values is internalized, felt, and bought into. It's not about being able to repeat the five company values in the hallway when quizzed. It's about internalizing that message. Thus, when dealing with these consumers, there is no need for being on message, as employees simply act on their deep understanding of what the company stands for. They respond as human beings, not as actors who can parrot a script.

A second orthodoxy that will be challenged is around not saying anything that reflects negatively on the organization. There is good reason this orthodoxy exists. Who can forget President Jimmy Carter's famous malaise talk that "told the truth" and was critical of citizens' attitudes. One could argue that that talk was a key factor in his not being re-elected. He was defeated by Ronald Reagan and his vibrant, upbeat message of "It's morning again in America." There is plenty of evidence that being forthright and not telling people what they want to hear can get one in trouble. But these consumers know that "stuff happens." No organization is perfect, and it is irritating to hear evasive denials or skirting around the truth. They will appreciate a frank discussion of an organization's mistakes. In most cases, this will strengthen their commitment to the organization over the long term. Trust is built when an organization admits its mistakes and seeks to make things right—this shows the human element that these consumers are looking for.

Au naturel

Preferring natural solutions where available.

The core need for these consumers is an appreciation of the beauty and wisdom of nature. It is not totally an aesthetic appreciation but a sense that the evolution of nature contains within it some lessons that people would do well to pay attention to. They are getting back in touch with nature and natural approaches, bringing that sensibility with them into consumer situations.

Table 14. Au naturel		
Needs	**Values**	**Catalysts**
Appreciate nature	*Authenticity*: State of being genuine; not false or an imitation. *Simplicity*: Freedom from intricacy or complexity. *Skepticism*: Attitude of doubt or a disposition to incredulity either in general or toward a particular object. *Sustainability*: Reducing the human footprint on the environment while maintaining quality of life.	Sustainable consumption Enoughness Living within limits

This need state, like "the authenticity premium," also is motivated in part on perceived excesses of the modern world. It crystallizes around the sense that technology, while a valuable tool in enabling growth and progress during modernization, has consequences that bring its value proposition into question. They have become skeptical about the benefits of technology and feel that the technology cure is in some cases worse than the disease. It is not necessarily an inherently anti-technology sentiment but one that raises questions about it. *Is it really necessary? Does it make things better? Are there harmful consequences?* These types of questions were rarely asked during the modernizing phase, where the focus was on economic growth. This can perhaps be summed up best by former President Bill Clinton's campaign slogan, "It's the economy, stupid!"

These consumers see hubris in the modernizing world. The sense that man reigns supreme over nature—that nature was to be conquered by the superior intelligence of humans—was a largely unquestioned assumption during modernization. Technological approaches are seen as inherently superior to natural ones. Efficiency is a key value in the modern world, which often runs counter to nature's messy approach of resiliency and redundancy. These consumers see wisdom in this inefficiency in terms of creating systems that are more robust over the long term. In the past, for example wetlands, were often done away with to suit the desire for more development space, despite the knowledge that wetlands play important roles in the ecosystem, such as providing filtration and outlets for flooding. The damage inflicted by Hurricane Katrina in New Orleans highlights the differing approaches. Instead of relying on wetlands and natural approaches to flood management, a system of dikes and barriers was engineered as a more "efficient" approach. Critics suggest that a more natural approach might have spared New Orleans from such severe damage. The consumers in this need state will have a bias toward natural approaches, and will be skeptical of totally engineered ones—though not averse to combining the best of both.

How it shows up

Sustainability is a core value for these consumers, and they see that technological approaches have often had adverse effects on the environment. Their appreciation for nature leads them to favor natural approaches over technological ones, unless there is evidence to the contrary. Thus, there has been a flourishing of natural approaches from food to clothing to cosmetics and even pest control. Sales of natural products, while still relatively small in comparison to overall product sales, have reached the hundreds of billions of dollars and often sales rates are growing faster than for conventional products. Some of these consumers are willing to pay a premium for a natural approach. There are positive and negative motivations. On the positive side, they feel that purchasing natural promotes sustainability; on the negative side, they see natural approaches as reducing the chances for unforeseen side effects.

In food, for example, natural and organic product sales growth rates have been outpacing conventional products for the last decade, though they still represent a small percentage of overall food sales. Organic products in particular have benefited from certification approaches that provide some assurance to these consumers that their food has been handled in a natural way. Even noncertified whole and natural foods have flourished. An emerging trend likely to capture the interest of these consumers is the growing body of knowledge revealing that single-nutrient approaches—often via fortification—fail to achieve desired aims because food is an inherently holistic entity. In simpler terms, engineering more of a desired ingredient doesn't work as intended because it upsets the natural balance of the food. The combinations of ingredients in whole foods often make a difference. This kind of evidence confirms the suspicions that these consumers have had about high-tech approaches and reinforces their bias toward natural approaches, even with a lack of compelling evidence.

What it means

For some industries and organizations, reaching these consumers will present a strategic issue. If an organization has long produced its products relying on technology and engineering approaches, shifting to a different natural approach could be seen as undermining the organization's view on what works best or is really the right way. Internally, it could be seen as challenging an organization's mission or core competency. There could also be a lot of internal skepticism about natural approaches.

The good news is that indications are that these consumers, with perhaps the exception of a hard-core fringe, do not see an inherent contradiction in producing things both ways. In other words, an organization does not have to ditch its established approaches in order to add natural ones. They can be clearly distinguished and branded as such. The challenge for the organization, however, will be to maintain strict adherence to its natural credentials. If these consumers sense that organizations are cutting corners and paying only lip service to the natural approach, they will find will spread the word that the organization is not to be trusted. It is best to keep the lines clear. With that said, as consumers build trust in the organization, it may be possible for the organization to make a case for a hybrid approach that combines the natural and the technological, but the plans will have to be authentically communicated and involve a participatory listening approach—for example, "We can produce product xx at this cost naturally, but by adding this 'un-natural' product or ingredient, we could increase its effectiveness and reduce its cost—what do you think about that?"

The simplicity premium

Appreciating the extra work and elegance that goes into simple offerings.

The core needs of freedom and a sense of order for these consumers hearken back to traditional values even though they are embraced by the postmodern consumer. Those exposed to the values shift often remark at first glance that there appears to be a cyclicality in that postmodern values to some degree mark a return to traditional values. While there is some truth in this, the common thread between traditional and postmodern values is that they are both anti-modern and thus appear similar. And in some cases, a postmodern value is simply a reinterpretation of a traditional value. The value of simplicity, for example, can be thought of as evolving from the traditional value of thrift, and both of these are at odds with the modern value of luxury.

Table 15. The simplicity premium		
Needs	**Values**	**Catalysts**
Freedom Order	*Design*: State of being genuine; not false or an imitation. *Functionality*: Attitude of doubt or a disposition to incredulity either in general or toward a particular object. *Simplicity*: Freedom from intricacy or complexity.	Life-shifting Enoughness Living within limits

As with the previous two need states, this one also is a reaction against a sense of an overly managed and complex world. There is the sense that humankind has gotten too smart for its own good and has introduced as many problems as it has solved. Technology is often seen as a culprit in making life more complex than it needs to be. Thus, simplicity emerges as a core value for these consumers. They recognize how easy it is to get caught up in gadgetry and lose touch with the purpose that the gadgets are intended to serve. They are thus being more thoughtful about the technologies they choose to invest in, and they will ask the question whether there is a simpler way.

How it shows up

The poster children of overcomplexity are the thick user manuals that once accompanied every technological device. The long-running jokes about people not being able to program their VCRs reflected a sense of haplessness, of being overwhelmed by technological complexity. For these consumers, this haplessness has morphed into a sense of resentment against the purveyors of such devices and manuals. The value proposition of investing time to learn how to program a VCR was not seen as worth the payoff. Clay Christenson of The Innovator's Dilemma fame pointed out the tendency of innovations to eventually reach "performance overshoot," in which the innovation delivers far more capability than the consumer really needs, and thus a simpler, less elegant disruptive innovation often emerges to supplant it.

What it means

This leads to an appreciation for products or services that lessen this sense of being overwhelmed; simpler solutions are seen as elegant. Where the modern fascination with growth tends to see more as better, the opposite holds true here. More features on a device, for example, are seen as wasting one's precious time. There is an appreciation for an organization or a product that knows what's essential and what's not or provides a mechanism for consumers to make their own choices.

These consumers will appreciate a sophisticated but simple way to use a product or service over one that has an amazing amount of cutting-edge features. The test might be as simple as how long it takes to explain how to use a new feature or offering. If it is not readily intuitive or easily grasped within a short period of time, it is not likely to be used, and this raises the question of "Why am I paying for things I don't use, don't know how to use, and will never use?" This may challenge the organizational culture of continually trying to improve performance by "adding"—for these consumers, the challenge may be how to improve performance by subtracting. It's looking for what can be sacrificed, streamlined, and simplified in terms of consumer interaction. What goes into the black box may be highly sophisticated, but it shows up in a user-friendly experience for the consumer.

Less is more

Valuing the chic of pushing the envelope toward more sustainable lifestyles.

These consumers also relate to the sense of a world that has gotten too complex and overly managed. The feeling of powerlessness and being overwhelmed is not one that people enjoy, and these consumers have reached a point where they are ready to do something about it. Their core needs of recognition and idealism suggest they want to do something about it and tell the world. They are proud of their new lifestyle, and they feel that others should adopt it as well. But it is more subtle than evangelical proselytizing; it's more about being a role model—demonstrating a new approach, often through the products, services and relationships one chooses—as a way to attract others.

Table 16. Less is more		
Needs	**Values**	**Catalysts**
Recognition Idealism	*Appropriateness*: Suitably designed for the task at hand and user capabilities. *Cool*: Fashionably attractive or impressive. Functional: Serving an intended or useful purpose. *Self-expression*: Expression or assertion of one's own personality.	Continuum of ownership Sustainable consumption Enoughness Living within limits

They see themselves as trendsetters and opinion leaders and prefer to lead by example. They may do with fewer overall possessions but are not afraid to spend money for the right cause. They are willing to spend more for a green product, and they want their friends and colleagues to know about it. They are not above applying peer pressure in service of their goal of spreading the word. They enjoy the attention, if not admiration, they get for adopting this new lifestyle.

How it shows up

A classic example of a green badge product is the Prius (recent issues notwithstanding). This purchase is a visible symbol of being enviro-chic. These consumers will typically be pleased to tell others the story about why they bought a Prius and how it fits into their overall green approach. They might share how they recently converted to green power sources in their home, how they have streamlined their consumption habits, and perhaps how they bought carbon offsets on their last business trip. They may come across as a bit naïve in their idealism about the impact of their actions, but they believe change starts at the grassroots, and the way to change the world is one step at a time.

What it means

Products and services that provide the opportunity to be seen by others are well suited to appeal to this group. They are looking for badge products. It may be possible to stimulate word-of-mouth marketing campaigns, potentially using social media to create a buzz around the chic of a particular offering. It may help to get celebrity endorsements, but only from those whose credentials in the area are established. If it is known that a particular celebrity is "green," then getting their endorsement and/or usage of a particular offering may help to ignite the buzz around it. The potential trap to avoid is forcing this kind of approach in a situation where the energy is not really there. This is about tapping a latent or emerging phenomenon and helping it to grow.

PUSHING THE ENVELOPE

These consumers are all about being the best they can be. There is a competitive aspect to this need state, but it is primarily about competing with oneself rather than competing with others. To illustrate, the modern values holder seeks to be number 1 and to emerge victorious over the competition. The postmodern/integral values holder enjoys competition with others and sees it as a means help them improve their own performance. They will be happier achieving their personal best rather than besting the competition. Whereas today, one expects to hear athletes happy that their team won, even though they may have themselves played poorly; in the future athletes will rather play to their maximum potential, even if they lose the competition.

In its extreme manifestation, pushing the envelope can be achieved by any means necessary. These consumers are intrigued by possibilities and enjoy experimentation. They take what they view as well considered risks, even though others may question their sanity.

The two need states at the core of "Pushing the envelope" are these:

- *Performance enhancement.* Applying science and technology to improve performance.

- *Getting real with the virtual.* Seeking assistance in incorporating the growing presence of the virtual into one's life.

Performance enhancement

Applying science and technology to improve performance.

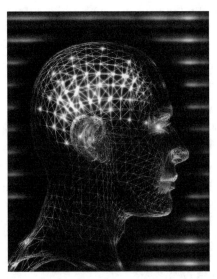

These consumers see life as providing challenges and opportunities for personal growth. Their core need is to reach their full potential in the areas they deem of interest to them. It is not necessarily an across-the-board phenomenon, though in some cases it could be. In most cases, there will be particular activities or areas of people's lives where this need state expresses itself. In other areas, people will be content with just getting by. An important distinction needs to be made between the postmodern-integral approach to performance enhancement and the modern approach. The former is motivated by personal improvement, while the latter is more inclined to the "beat-the-competition" ethos.

Table 17. Performance enhancement		
Needs	**Values**	**Catalysts**
Reaching fullest potential	*Empowerment*: Acquiring the tools, resources, and authority to get a task done. *Experimentation*: Trying out a new procedure, idea, or activity. *Self-expression*: Expression or assertion of one's own personality.	Consumer augmentation

These consumers find joy in the pursuit of perfection, a good feeling in seeing progress, while recognizing that there may not be a particular end point where they are fully satisfied. As they grow, their expectations grow with them. There is a search for an edge or a means to push themselves beyond conventional limits. A sense of experimentation, even a hint of playfulness, accompanies this pursuit. There is a constant quest for new concepts, techniques, and approaches. Limits are seen as conventions to be pushed beyond, as long as others are not harmed along the way. They want to be empowered to make their own decisions and they resent intrusions by regulatory groups into the personal domain.

There is an element of risk-taking behavior, but it is carefully thought through, not a reckless pursuit that disregards consequences. Rather, it is a decision to try the experiment, gathering as much information as possible and making an informed choice. The risk factor is accepted as a necessary evil in pursuit of the greater good of making the breakthrough to enhanced performance. It is about self-expression, not necessarily to persuade others to adopt a similar approach, but to live one's own life to its fullest potential.

How it shows up

The performance enhancers, for example, may have fitness as an area of interest. They will research and experiment with what are at present seen as fringe approaches or therapies—for example, trying an approach that includes large quantities of supplements, even though this may involves substances not approved as safe by the appropriate regulatory body (e.g., the U.S. Food and Drug Administration). They acknowledge the risks involved but see them as being outweighed by potential performance gains. They are likely to be the first to try new technological approaches, such as, an implant that monitors vital health functions in order to improve their personal fitness. They may travel overseas to try an experimental procedure that is not approved for use in their home country.

The leading edge of this emerging need state is evidenced today by the controversy over the use of performance drugs by professional athletes. This example, however, misses the larger trend that reaches into the ranks of amateurs and hobbyists. Professional athletes have the clear motivation of fame and fortune. What is less clear but no less powerful is the motivation of "weekend warriors" seeking to improve their performance—for example, shortening their time in a road race, even though it moves them from 350th to 345th place. For these individuals, the motivation is not fame and fortune but rather the challenge of pushing oneself beyond expectations.

The larger public is somewhat fearful of those choosing this path. And they are outraged by those seen to be cheating, regardless of the users' rationalizations, when this breaks the rules. The challenge to conventions is bound to invoke a reaction, as well as a deep-seated fear about how one can keep up with those willing to push beyond the norms. This may puzzle those who are taking the enhancement approach as they are not motivated by a desire to beat others, only themselves. They don't feel they are threatening anyone. Public pressure against performance enhancement could indeed be a barrier to its expansion.

What it means

These consumers seek to be empowered by the organizations they choose to engage with. They are likely to be demanding in the sense of asking lots of questions and wanting access to as much information as possible. But they will reward an organization that is patient with them and invests in the relationship. They are happy to invest their time and money in their performance improvement and in organizations that assist them in their quest.

There could be legal issues involved as these consumers push the organizations. While the consumers may be willing to sign waivers or give consent, organizations must still protect themselves. While this may seem to be a lot of hassle for a relatively small group, these early adopters may well portend developments that will eventually reach the mainstream. Of course, this needs to be carefully assessed on a case-by-case basis.

Getting real with the virtual

Seeking assistance in incorporating the growing presence of the virtual into one's life.

Those pushing the envelope will often see the virtual world as a rich playground to expand their capabilities. They will embrace the novelty and look for ways to add it to their repertoire of tools for improving personal performance. They may try on different personalities in the virtual world as a means to better empathize with others in the real world. The virtual world will be viewed as a new frontier full of enticing possibilities.

Table 18. Getting real with the virtual		
Needs	**Values**	**Catalysts**
Identity

Creation | *Collaboration*: Working jointly with others.

Experimentation: Trying out new procedure, ideas, or activities.

Integration: Combining elements into a coherent whole. | Virtual-real—digital tribes

Life-shifting

Ubiquitous connection |

These consumers will seek assistance in how to integrate these possibilities into their lives, and be the first to try the latest innovations in the virtual space. They will not be overly concerned with the practical applications, at least in the beginning, but will enjoy the experience of something new. At some point, however, the enthusiasm will wear off if there is no longer a sense of how it can add to one's capabilities. Their thirst for novelty will push those providing offerings in this area.

How it shows up

They may experiment with software or tools that enable virtual offices, conferences, or meeting rooms. They would see these as potential mechanisms to improve productivity. They will often be the first to volunteer inside an organization that wants to experiment in this area. Their quest goes beyond just the workplace and is all-pervasive. They will often report on their nonwork activities and urge their organizations to get involved with what they see as the next big thing. They may visit virtual worlds to experiment with products and services or even with their identity. They may take on the personae of the opposite gender or other races or try to experience the world from a different cultural viewpoint.

The virtual world will provide myriad opportunities for try-before-you-buy, including the opportunity to personalize or even co-create—that is, to participate in the actual design of products. Indicators of this are starting to appear, with hundreds of millions of people inhabiting virtual spaces. Virtual economies are growing, with hundreds of millions of dollars being exchanged for virtual goods and services. More people are making their living selling virtual dresses or running virtual nightclubs. Things will get really interesting as advances in 3-D printing will eventually make it cost-effective to create physical versions of objects that are created in the digital world.

What it means

Organizations seeking to tap into this consumer base will need to establish a presence in virtual space. It may require running small experiments and trying different approaches to establish this presence in a way that catches the interest of this group. The Toyota Scion, for example, has established a presence in several virtual worlds. They are careful to align with the ethos of the worlds they enter as they seek to establish credibility and trust with the participants. It is most likely a patient investment in terms of taking time to build credibility and discover ways to monetize the participation. But as the growth trends continue to accelerate in this space, these consumers present an enticing target as they are like to play a trendsetting and opinion-leading role as they seek to push their capabilities and spread their word among their colleagues and networks.

EVERY MOMENT MATTERS

These consumers are taking back control of their lives. This might seem a pipe dream to those currently feeling overwhelmed with responsibility. These consumers have felt this pain and have finally decided to do something about it. They are rethinking their priorities on how they invest or spend their most precious asset—time. They are going to be purposeful about this investment, weighing it along the lines of making a financial investment. They are rebelling against the sense of being in the rat race or on the treadmill and hitting the stop button, rethinking what is important in life, and exploring how to reorganize their lives in that pursuit.

They are actively seeking ways to save time in some areas so they can invest it in others. They have a wide range of interests but recognize that there isn't time for everything and see the need for trade-offs. They are looking for organizational partners that can both save them time and help them be more productive in the areas where they do want to invest more of their time.

The three need states at the core of "every moment matters" are these:

- *Wherever, whenever, whatever*: Going beyond traditional schedules and timing to being available when needed.

- *Investing time like money*: Valuing time as more precious than money is approached with an investment mentality.

- *Living in real time*: Opening up to spontaneously take advantage of opportunities as they arise.

Wherever, whenever, whatever

Going beyond traditional schedules and timing to being available when needed.

These consumers are rebelling against the constraints of schedules and seek to better manage their time and commitments. It's part of taking back control of their lives. They have a core need for freedom and at the same time seek respect for their time in their dealings with other people and organizations. They are a tech-savvy group and see technology as a tool for empowerment and for helping them better manage time and life. They expect others to be technically capable as well and will often be impatient with those who are not.

Table 19. Wherever, whenever, whatever		
Needs	**Values**	**Catalysts**
Freedom Respect	*Connectivity*: Ability to reach and communicate with others as desired. *Personalization*: Alteration for the preferences of the individual. *Spontaneity*: Acting on natural feeling or impulse, without effort or premeditation.	Life-shifting Ubiquitous connection

While there is an element of simplifying, a stronger theme is better management and a consequent search for technologies and solutions that can enable it. They stay connected to the world of information, networks, and people and are at the ready to deal with opportunities as they arise. They are less intimidated by obstacles and have the sense that they can take charge of any situation and navigate through obstacles as they arise.

They can be very demanding, but they are not necessarily prima donnas. They are driven by a strong sense of practicality. Their view is that there are tools to make life more manageable, so why not take advantage of them? They see an abundance of solutions and are impatient with organizations, products, services, and even people lacking this same vision. They reject the tyranny of the schedule. They prefer, and even demand, that things be done on their time whenever possible.

How it shows up

If flexible solutions are possible, why not do it? These consumers are likely to be fans of flextime, telecommuting, and virtual work. They are responsible enough to manage this responsibility and in their view it enables them to work when they are most productive. There is a strong sense of self-awareness driving them. They are tuned in to what they want and what works best for them. If they are night people, they'll seek to work at night.

They value personal digital assistants or smartphones that can enable them to follow up or act on the spur of the moment. They are typically multitaskers who don't take kindly to waiting or wasting time. They'll make the best of it and may be checking in with Facebook and chatting as they wait their turn. At the same time, they recognize that technologies can facilitate overload if one allows this to happen. They are ratcheting up their expectations of technology, in particular being focused on how technology can work for them—instead of finding themselves working for technology.

What it means

Organizations will need to be tech savvy to reach these consumers. This could mean bringing on people who possess the necessary skills but who may be at odds with the current organizational culture. While this may be exactly what the organization needs, it nonetheless could be challenging. These consumers will tend to skew younger, particularly those having a heavy tech emphasis, so another strategy for bringing some of them into the organization is a reverse mentoring program—in which the younger, tech-savvy intern gets needed work experience, but they can mentor the staff on understanding the culture of these consumers and the technology and can help devise approaches for the organization to better reach them.

Investing time like money

Time is valued as more precious than money and is approached with an investment mentality.

Time is the precious commodity for these consumers. They feel they have enough money, even if they could use more, and are likely to use their money to buy time. For example, instead of saving money by cutting their own lawn, they see the time involved in this task as more valuable and will hire it out. In the time-money trade-off, they increasingly favor saving time.

Table 20. Investing time like money		
Needs	**Values**	**Catalysts**
Appreciate life Reaching fullest potential	*Empowerment*: Acquiring the tools, resources, and authority to get a task done. *Nonconformity*: Refusal to adhere to an established or conventional creed, rule, or practice. *Transcendence*: Ability to rise above a particular circumstance in allegiance to a higher principle or principles.	Enoughness Empowered individual Life-shifting Continuum of ownership

They pay greater attention to how they are spending their time. If time is more precious than money, and people typically pay attention to how their money is invested, then a similar if not greater commitment should be made with time investment. Sent a meeting request, for example, they will weigh the time costs and benefits. They would not refuse out of laziness or because they would prefer to do nothing, but rather because they see other, more worthwhile uses of that time. They are continuously thinking in terms of options. They have a portfolio of activities waiting for the next available time slot, creating a competitive aspect around which option gets the time. At the same time, they recognize the value of free time and will be mindful of not falling into the trap of busyness.

How it shows up

A variety of service occupations have sprung up around this need for saving the time of busy people who have the financial means to buy time. These range from traditional services such as lawn care to dog walkers to a more sophisticated range of personal concierge offerings. One research firm estimates that revenue from online outsourcing websites will grow from $250 million in 2007 to $2 billion in 2015. Websites like AskSunday.com, GetFriday.com, YourManInIndia. com, Elance.com, and Guru.com offer these time-strapped consumers a chance to pay others to run their personal errands. The sites offer pay-as-you go or monthly plans.[157]

What it means

The spirit of these consumers as they interact with organizations, products, and other people is that they need to prove they are worth the time investment. They are not bound by conventions but use the value of time investment as their yardstick. They despise unsolicited intrusions into their time. They will be ardent opponents of any intrusive marketing and advertising approach. They recoil from the aggressive salesperson who tries the hard sell when they walk into a retail establishment. If they are interested in something new, they will do their own homework and ask questions when they are ready. In other words, "I won't waste your time if you don't waste mine."

<u>Living in real time</u>

Opening up to spontaneously take advantage of opportunities as they arise.

These consumers are seeking to live in the moment. Their core needs are being creative, spontaneous, and reaching their fullest potential. They see life as an adventure and filled with possibilities. They feel it is up to individuals to discover their passion and pursue their dreams. They prefer to keep an open and flexible schedule and avoid getting tied down by too many commitments. They abhor monotonous routine and will struggle in these situations.

Table 21. Living in real time		
Needs	**Values**	**Catalysts**
Creation Spontaneity Reaching fullest potential	*Co-creation*: Collaboration in the creation or augmentation of design and content and sharing these creations with peers. *Discovery*: Pursuit of and deep interest in the unknown. *Open-mindedness*: Freedom from prejudice, bigotry, or partiality. *Spontaneity*: Acting on natural feeling or impulse without effort or premeditation.	Life-shifting Empowered individual Co-creation

This may be a reaction to previously feeling that they missed out on the simple pleasures of life in dogged pursuit of some goal or dream—or just being caught up in the struggle to keep up with an overload of responsibilities. Their spontaneity may be viewed by others as impulsiveness. If a mood or idea strikes them and they want to do something about it, they would rather go for it in that moment and not wait for the "proper" time. They resist convention and expectations about what they are supposed to do. If today seems like a good day to go to the beach, they arrange it and go, confident that they will make up for any lost time and keep their commitments.

How it shows up

When they are interested in something, they go for it with gusto. They trust their passion. They may say that they are listening to what life is telling them, and they are not afraid to act on their intuition. Their open-mindedness may lead others to see them as gullible, but they are typically highly attuned to signals of change or the possibility of new options. If they become interested in virtual worlds, they will likely spend long hours in them—as long as their interest lasts. They will likely seek to play an active role in the community. If they become interested in a cause, they are likely to become active participants. They seek to personalize their experience but to co-create it where possible. For example, Grouper provides services to those interested in mashing: a place to post and share their own video content with friends, family, and the world at large, plus access to user-generated content created by others.

What it means

They cherish the chance to express their creativity and enjoy working with organizations, products, or people that enable this. When they are particularly passionate about something, they will seek to actively participate. It may be possible for organizations to tap their creativity for its benefit as well as for its larger customer base. Lego Robots, for example, now issues a hacker's license that allows users to innovate with the software and share their innovations with the user community. It is the same spirit one sees with open source software, where people contribute to the common good because of the passion they share around having the best possible product.

THE [RELENTLESS] PURSUIT OF HAPPINESS

The values shifts described in Chapter 3 have a major theme of consumers rethinking the purpose of their lives. The pursuit of happiness is a purpose shared by many. It reflects the growing range of choices enjoyed by postmodern consumers who enjoy relative economic security.

Traditional values do not leave much room for the pursuit of happiness, as people's role is ascribed largely at birth by the powers that be. This is not to say that traditional values holders are not happy but that the range of options available for their pursuit of happiness is constrained, and the definition of happiness itself may be different than for those with modern, postmodern, or integral values. The modern values holder has greater freedom and availability of choices, as economic development provides the opportunity to improve one's status through hard work. Their pursuit of happiness tends to focus around economic achievement and material prosperity. Again, this does not suggest that economics is the only route, but that it tends to be the dominant one. Still, even here the range is more limited than it is for the postmodern values holder. The postmodern values holder, with relative economic security, has the freedom to consider a wider range of routes to happiness. Ironically, the modern-to-postmodern transition is often accompanied by a sense of angst. Many have experienced a sense of emptiness from the material prosperity route and call the meaning of their lives into question. The resultant search for meaning in life is not always easy or pleasant. Happiness becomes something that has to be achieved—it does not necessarily arrive on its own for the postmodern consumer.

There is a relentless aspect to this pursuit among some, reflecting a seriousness of purpose: "What makes me happy, and what do I have to do to get there?"

The six need states at the core of "the [relentless] pursuit of happiness" are these:

- *Help me help myself.* Looking for opportunities for co-creation with tools, templates, and advice in product and service offerings.

- *Identity products, services, and experiences.* Investing great time, attention, and money in offerings viewed as important to one's identity while price shopping on others.

- *Systematic and consistent.* Looking to fit products and services into larger lifestyles, values, and sense of purpose.

- *Reinventing the self.* Continuing desire to expand one's skills, capabilities, and purposes.

- *I'm not a consumer.* Demanding to be treated as a whole person, not just a statistic that makes purchases.

- *Pursuit of happiness, a.k.a. well-being.* Evaluating product, service, and experiences offerings in terms of how they contribute to my—and in many cases, my community's—happiness and well-being.

Help me help myself

Looking for opportunities for co-creation with tools, templates, and advice in product and service offerings.

These consumers are active participants in their pursuit of happiness. It is a personal quest. Their core needs of participation and creation lead them to be pioneers in the trend toward co-creation. They are highly self-aware and will often be involved in some form of self-help. They see this more as helping them to reach their potential rather than as a negative view of fixing problems.

Table 22. Help me help myself		
Needs	**Values**	**Catalysts**
Participation Creation	*Collaboration*: Working jointly with others. *Creativity*: Ability to come up with new and interesting ideas. *Self-expression*: Expression or assertion of one's own personality.	Co-creation Consumer augmentation

They enjoy the self-discovery process. They feel they have lots to contribute to life and are eager to share their contributions with others. They want to be treated with the respect they feel they deserve. They enjoy challenging themselves, learning, and gaining new experiences. For interests or pursuits they deem worthy of their time, they prefer to be actively involved. In extreme form, the concept of helping oneself is found in the consumer augmentation and pushing the envelope.

How it shows up

Current evidence of this trend is seen in part in approaches to healthcare, particularly the pursuit of wellness. These consumers do their own research and approach health professionals with questions. They do not passively accept the judgment of authorities but probe for answers and understanding. They are inclined to self-diagnosis, the use of home test kits, and are likely to be open to alternative medicine. They prefer approaches in which they can take an active role in their pursuit of wellness. This includes emotional and spiritual aspects as well as the physical. They are likely to be involved in some form of self-help and are likely to hire personal trainers or life coaches to help them achieve their goals. They like DIY and guided software such as TurboTax®. In this case, as in many others, basic tasks are off-loaded to consumers who want the control—and the cost savings—and the experts play a consultative role of helping with tough questions and providing advice.

What it means

They prefer to be taught how to fish rather than to be handed a bucket of fish and bring that sensibility to the organizations they choose to patronize. They enjoy the experience of participation and find it fulfilling. They cherish the creative process. It is about the journey rather than the destination.

They are looking for organizations that see them as creative individuals who bring something to the table. The organization moves into providing services around a basic offering that can be easily handled by the consumers. These consumers could become valuable assets to the organization beyond a particular sale in that they will spread the word about the organization to those in their network. Their decisions about whether or not to engage with a product, service, or organization will often be weighed against whether it serves a goal or purpose they have. For decisions or activities not seen as integral to happiness, they make take a more passive role, seeking instead to invest their time in activities that serve the larger purpose. It is helpful for organizations to understand their particular motivation around an offering—is it one they care a lot about and want to be actively involved with, or is it one they don't care about and bring a functional sensibility to?

Identity products, services, and experiences

Investing great time, attention, and money in offerings seen to be important to one's identity while price shopping on others.

These consumers see their choice of products, services, and experiences as making fundamental statements about their identity, which is a core need for them. The choice of whom to do business with or which products to buy helps express their sense of self. Thus, these decisions are thoughtful ones.

Table 23. Identity products, services, and experiences		
Needs	Values	Catalysts
Identity	*Commitment*: State of being bound emotionally or intellectually to a course of action or to another person or persons.

Passion: Deep motivating interest in a topic.

Self-expression: Expression or assertion of one's own personality.

Uniqueness: Having no like or equal. | Truth and truthiness

Co-creation

Empowered individual |

Buying a hybrid vehicle, for instance, is an expression of a person's environmental values. While this expression is fundamentally directed at people's sense of self, there is an element of wanting to share their identity with others: "This is who I am and what I'm about." It is not necessarily about converting others to a particular cause but letting others know who you are and what you stand for.

How it shows up

These consumers will investigate before they buy. They see it as a form of voting with their dollars. They will search out what an organization stands for and determine whether it aligns with their personal values. There may be particular values or causes that are the equivalent of a litmus test. Individuals with strong environmental values may be committed to reducing their carbon footprints, and therefore check out organizations' stance vis-à-vis carbon footprints. If the organization is clearly at odds with the consumer's values, this is likely going to cost them the business. If the organization is otherwise found lacking, the consumer may well go elsewhere, even at the expense of losing out on a better deal.

What it means

These consumers informally sort their purchasing decisions along a commodity-identity continuum. The commodity pole is for those offerings that are not viewed as important to identity. The identity pole is the opposite in which the offerings are seen as fundamental to identity. Products, services, and even relationships that mean a lot to people are seen as part of their identity—thus they invest their time and money on those (e.g., they buy a hybrid vehicle because they are environmentally conscious). For those products and service they don't care much about, they choose what is fastest, easiest, and cheapest. Thus, they may spend lots of time weighing a relatively inexpensive purchase, such as a coffee mug, because their choice of coffee is important to their identity. At the same time, a relatively high-dollar purchase, such as a new car, may be made rather quickly because to them, a car is simply a means of transportation. Similarly, these consumers may spend a lot of money on identity items and then scrimp on others; thus the phenomena of spending big money on a designer handbag and cutting costs on "essentials."

GATEWAY

ENTER

EIGHT

http://bit.ly/obuZPT

Systematic and consistent

Looking to fit products and services into larger lifestyle, values, and sense of purpose.

These consumers are extremely thoughtful and conscientious. Their core needs of spirituality and the search for meaning serve as guideposts for their decision making. They not only consider how their decisions and actions fit with their own values and sense of purpose but also how they affect others, ranging from immediate family to community to the planet as a whole. They typically have a highly developed environmental consciousness and are aware of how their actions affect the environment.

Table 24. Systematic and consistent		
Needs	**Values**	**Catalysts**
Spirituality Search for meaning	*Interdependence*: Sensitivity to how things depend on each other. *Spirituality*: Interest in and pursuit of the meaning and purpose of life. *Sustainability*: Reducing the human footprint on the environment while maintaining quality of life. *Systemic*: Methodical; given to having or following a plan.	Sustainable consumption Enoughness

They are systems thinkers, even though most will not have had any formal training in it, but it's a part of their style. They have a sense of the big picture and weigh individual decisions against the impact on the big picture. They are continually assessing their own performance in this regard. If they are committed to wellness, for example, they will be troubled by their daily consumption of donuts or other dietary habits at odds with this value.

They are patient and persistent in pursuit of their goals. They enjoy the process of getting to their goals—they are not in a hurry. They are willing to pause when necessary, even take a step backward, but they will resume their journey when practical. They may weigh a decision for quite some time before acting, but once they are "in," they are committed.

How it shows up

These consumers will often support a myriad of causes, such as fair trade products. They like the idea that their purchases can make a difference in someone's life. At the same time, they are seeking to avoid creating harm or worsening problems for their own peace of mind. In the era of sophisticated search engines, they will use these tools as screening mechanisms to help them decide with whom they should do business. The challenge for organizations is that they may be being screened out by these consumers without ever knowing it happened or why.

What it means

They will look to people and organizations they are thinking of associating with for their consistency. Is the organization talking "green" but acting otherwise? Such inconsistencies will be a turnoff to these consumers, who will scrutinize an organization's policies and practices to see if they share common values. If the organization does not offer Fair Trade products, for example, and they have the opportunity to do so, they will likely lose the business of these consumers, who will willingly accept a degree of personal inconvenience or spend a bit more of their money in support of their causes. They appreciate the intangible value in having made the world a slightly better place.

Reinventing the self

Continuing desire to expand one's skills, capabilities, and purposes.

The search for meaning and purpose does not necessarily follow a straight line. The discovery process has twists and turns that could lead to minor and perhaps major reinterpretations of one's identity. These consumers are prepared to redefine themselves as part of the discovery process. They have a core need for reaching their fullest potential and will leave no stone unturned in that pursuit.

Table 25. Reinventing the self		
Needs	**Values**	**Catalysts**
Reaching fullest potential	*Discovery*: Pursuit of and deep interest in the unknown. *Questioning*: Characterized by or indicating intellectual curiosity. *Transcendence*: Ability to rise above a particular circumstance in allegiance to a higher principle or principles.	Consumer augmentation Enoughness Integration of virtual-real

For instance, they may become more aware of environmental issues, perhaps seeing an image of the polar ice caps melting and be catalyzed into learning more. This investigation may lead them to fairly dramatic changes in behavior, in effect cleaning house around this issue: switching to a hybrid vehicle, buying energy-efficient windows, etc.

How it shows up

The reinvention process will likely involve symbolic gestures that express this new identity. If consumers become more environmentally attuned, as described above, they are likely to look for ways to express that new commitment, not only for themselves, but for others. Someone who makes a new commitment to animal rights, for example, joining PETA, may then go through the closet and throw away (or recycle) a leather jacket to solidify this new part of his or her identity. These moments could provide excellent opportunities for organizations to build lasting relationships. To contribute to someone's rethinking of identity forms a bond that is likely to endure.

What it means

As they scrutinize their consumption patterns, they will look to the behavior of the organizations they associate with as well. They will identify positively with the organizations they see as helping them reconceptualize their sense of self. Organizations may need to be patient with this group and listening skills will be at a premium. They are serious about being the best they can be and will honor the organizations that enable this pursuit. The reinvention process involves breaking new ground and will necessarily involve lots of questions. They will be hungry for information, and consequently, an organization may position itself as a broker that connects them to other users in a community of interest or social network.

I'm not a consumer

Demanding to be treated as a whole person, not just a statistic that makes purchases.

Some consumers resent the label of consumer. They are antagonistic to the importance of consuming, and find the notion of a consumer economy to be wrongheaded. They see it as a confusion of means and ends. The sentiment is that people don't live just to consume even though they must consume to live. They have core needs around acceptance and self-respect, and they feel that being labeled as consumers is disrespectful to their way of life.

Table 26. I'm not a consumer		
Needs	**Values**	**Catalysts**
Acceptance Self-respect	*Authenticity*: State of being genuine; not false or an imitation. *Connectivity*: Ability to reach and communicate with others as desired. *Understanding*: Showing a sympathetic or tolerant attitude toward something. *Uniqueness*: Having no like or equal.	Empowered individual Truth and truthiness Relocalization

They see themselves as having transcended or outgrown the consumer way of life. They will generally resist attempts at categorization or typecasting as they feel this misses the unique aspect of who they are. They expect, even demand, to be understood and appreciated.

How it shows up

This need state is in part a reaction against the materialism they may have abandoned earlier in their lives and a distaste for seeing it in action. The "anti-consumerism" sentiment was captured and popularized several years ago in the Cluetrain Manifesto, which made the point that markets are conversations. These consumers expect to engage in conversations and want prospective partners to invest time in getting to know who they are. These consumers were at the core of the no-branding movement. They will often buy generic brands or private label goods where available, not necessarily to save money but to make a statement against the notion of consumerism.

What it means

It is nearly impossible to escape consumerism completely, but nonetheless they see steps that can be taken to reduce the role or importance of consumption in their life. It would, however, be a mistake to write off this group as a consumer target. They will actually be quite thoughtful consumers and will consider purchases carefully. Referring to the above, they will place many purchases toward the commodity end of the spectrum but will be willing to invest time and money in those they judge to be identity purchases. They understand how their purchases have the effect of encouraging or rewarding good behavior on the part of organizations. For example, those with a strong environmental ethic are likely to be willing to spend more for green products. Similarly, they may spend more for "fair trade" products. In general, they will be willing to spend money to support the values and causes they support.

Pursuit of happiness, a.k.a. well-being

Evaluating product, service and experience offerings in terms of how they contribute to my—and in many cases my community's—happiness and well-being.

These consumers weigh choices in terms of how they add to or subtract from their overall sense of well-being. Their core needs are appreciating life, and they are often idealistic in this approach. They believe happiness is available to those willing to make the effort—it is not simply granted, but earned.

Table 27. Pursuit of happiness, a.k.a. well-being		
Needs	**Values**	**Catalysts**
Appreciating life Idealism	*Community*: Group of people with a common characteristic or interest living or working together within a larger society. *Contentment*: Comfortable sense of well-being over time. *Enjoyment*: Experiencing satisfaction or delight in an activity. *Wellness*: Advanced state of physical, emotion, and spiritual well-being.	Enoughness Living within limits Consumer augmentation

Their sense of happiness is perhaps different than the popular perception of being all laughs and smiles and more along the lines of contentment. They may not show outward signs of happiness but will exude an air of satisfaction. They appreciate life challenges and their ability to handle them. They are typically well connected to family, friends, and networks and are active members in the communities they belong to, whether physical or virtual.

How it shows up

They will ask whether they really need to make a purchase, and think about the impact it has on their lives and values. They may explicitly tie these decisions to their sense of wellness, looking for a physical, emotional, or spiritual benefit. They will consider the tradeoffs. For instance, in thinking about whether to purchase a home theater system, a positive would be the enjoyment it would bring to themselves and perhaps their family and friends. A negative could be that their current system is good enough, and perhaps this new purchase challenges their sense of "enoughness." They'll weigh these pros and cons against their overall sense of well-being and be favorably inclined toward those decisions with the most positive impact. They may seem self-indulgent or even dramatic to some, but this is because of their yardstick. They may take lots of times to make a decision on what may seem to be trivial decisions or purchases to others.

What it means

Products or organizations dealing with these consumers may have to patiently make their case and be sensitive to the consumer's dilemma. As stated earlier, a hard sell approach is likely to be a turnoff. While an appreciation of the dilemma may not get the immediate sale, it may build trust that will later pay off and may also build a relationship that goes beyond a single purchase to form a long-term relationship. And the seriousness of purpose that these consumers feel will often compel them to alert their network about an organization that either turns them off or turns them on. Imagine a Facebook post read by hundreds of friends that says "xyz organization really listened to me and gave me useful and helpful information" versus "xyz organization totally ignored me and gave me the hard sell."

COMMUNITY FIRST

The emerging values shifts described in Chapter 3 contain the theme of a preference of a shift in scale from large to small and in scope from mass to custom. This shows up most strongly in this emerging need state. It favors decentralized approaches. It is part of the sense, captured in other need states, that life has gotten too complex, moves too fast, and has become impersonal. It is this de-personalization in particular that drives the move to renewed interest in community as people seek to reconnect with their life and with one another. In the ascent up the growth curve in modern society, the frenetic pace is seen as worth the tradeoff for the economic reward. The postmodern consumer is more aware of the costs, has less need for economic security, and thus begins to reject this trade-off.

This desire for connection manifests in both the physical and the virtual worlds. These consumers question why they don't know their neighbors or even the mayor. They are looking for ways to get involved with what's going on directly around them as this helps to provide an anchor or security in what is seen as an increasingly chaotic world. The explosion of Facebook and other social networking sites is evidence of how the virtual world can serve as a mechanism for connection.

The three need states at the core of "Community first" are these:

- *Local preference.* Valuing local origins to support local community as well as reduce environmental impacts.

- *Community support.* Requiring that partners provide local distribution of benefits and/or are investing in the community.

- *Trust the network.* Placing trust in one's extended personal network or a "crowd sourced" community of interest over traditional institutional authority.

Local preference

Valuing local origins to support local community as well as reduce environmental impacts.

These consumers will demonstrate their community support by spending their time and money within the community, where possible. They put a great value on relationships, and their core needs are friendship, social contact, and closeness to people. They see spending money within the community and supporting local businesses as an investment. They also see it as a reward to their friends and colleagues, and expect that their support of local offerings will benefit the larger community. They may pay a bit extra for something at the local hardware store instead of saving money by shopping at the big national or multinational chain, particularly if that chain is seen as taking profits out of the local community and not doing enough to give back. Similarly, if they are inclined to do volunteer work, they will seek out local options where possible, again seeing this as an investment that will enhance the community and create a better life for themselves as well.

Table 28. Local preference

Needs	Values	Catalysts
Friendship/social contact Closeness to people	*Appropriateness*: Suitably designed for the task at hand and user capabilities. *Community*: Group of people with a common characteristic or interest living or working together within a larger society. *Influential*: Ability to make a difference in an outcome. *Interdependence*: Sensitivity to how things depend on each other.	Relocalization Living within limits

Another driver is a feeling of the global community and economy increasingly being at risk. A sense of limits to growth and expansion gives way to a sense of constraints and a personal need to scale back one's lifestyle. They are worried about the interdependence and fragility of the global economy and see it as a wise course to help develop local options. There is a slight retreat from participation in things global. This downsizing is also driven in part by the idea that shipping goods and services across the globe is an environmentally questionable practice. Buying locally is seen as better for the environment, even if there are instances where this is not the case.

How it shows up

These investments pay off in the sense of greater connection to daily life. They add an element of tangibility in an increasingly abstract world. There is an accompanying desire for increasing and enhancing one's relationships, which often were sacrificed in the modernizing phase of achievement. They will make choices such as patronizing the local coffee shops, local grocers, or other neighborhood or family-owned businesses. They also, rightly or wrongly, see the local options as more trustworthy—they feel they are more likely to get the straight story instead of some marketing-speak developed by a global headquarters somewhere across the country or even across the ocean. Some of these consumers will be virtual workers, and may use local coffee shops or cafes as full- or part-time workplaces, which provides an opportunity to interact with other locals and potentially to build new relationships.

What it means

They will enjoy getting to know local business people on a first-name basis. They will be interested in the origins and history of local businesses. They will tolerate a degree of lesser service or less efficiency if a relationship has been established. For large organizations or multinationals, while they are at a disadvantage, they have the opportunity to establish local credentials and demonstrate their commitment to the communities they serve. There are opportunities for them to develop truly local offerings and solutions. A clothing chain, for example, could offer space to local designers and feature them in their store. There may be opportunities to co-brand or form joint ventures with local partners that will bring a local flavor to their offerings, as well as building local credentials.

Community support

Requiring that partners provide local distribution of benefits and/or are investing in the community.

The local preference need state can extend beyond just the local community. These consumers will go a step further in supporting local options by extending it to communities quite distant from them. They would enjoy the chance to support a local community overseas as well as their own community.

Table 29. Community support		
Needs	**Values**	**Catalysts**
Participation Realism	*Collaboration*: Working jointly with others. *Community*: Group of people with a common characteristic or interest living or working together within a larger society. *Questioning*: Characterized by or indicating intellectual curiosity. *Sustainability*: Reducing the human footprint on the environment while maintaining quality of life.	Relocalization Sustainable consumption Emerging markets Empowered individual

They have core needs of participation and realism. They feel that by spending their money in their community, they further its well-being. They do not naïvely assume that their individual efforts are enough to save the day, but if it is necessary to "take on" organizations or issues they feel are wrong for the community, they are prepared to organize community support.

How it shows up

These consumers may support a small farmer across the country over a nearby agribusiness option. Knowing that an independent family farmer produced the corn they are having for dinner taps into this desire to reconnect. They appreciate knowing the story behind the origins of foods and services and will often pay a premium, whether for free-range chickens raised by local farmers or for handcrafted baskets made by local artisans. This sensibility can extend globally, with a preference for items that benefit poor villages. Knowing the story about the villagers involved and how their purchase helped it would be a strong selling point.

What it means

These kinds of purchases bring at least a small sense of connection that people don't get from dealing with large multinationals. This is not intended to suggest the coming demise of multinationals but rather indicates that they will need to invest and participate more in the communities they do business with if they want to earn the patronage of these consumers. This can range from sponsorship of local activities or teams to a commitment to reinvest a certain percentage of profits in the local community. One can envision some municipalities with a strong citizen base eventually requiring this of businesses in return for an operating license.

Trust the network

Placing trust in one's extended personal network or a "crowdsourced" community of interest over traditional institutional authority.

These consumers have a strong distrust of institutional authority. They tend to reject any information from an institution, however well intentioned and forthright the institution may be. Institutions may be puzzled over why consumers don't trust them when they have done nothing to suggest that trust is misplaced.

Table 30. Trust the network		
Needs	**Values**	**Catalysts**
Understanding Participation	*Connectivity*: Ability to reach and communicate with others as desired. *Skepticism*: Attitude of doubt or a disposition to incredulity either in general or toward a particular object. *Tolerance*: Possessing a fair, objective, and permissive attitude toward opinions and practices that differ from one's own.	Empowered individual Relocalization Integration of virtual-real

These consumers have core needs for understanding and participation; they feel that large institutions provide neither. They prefer to develop relationships with organizations they do business with. They seek and enjoy contact with people. While they may do some research online, they place their ultimate trust in people. Their skepticism runs deep, and they are inherently suspicious of a marketing angle or spin. Thus, they put their trust in people they know and people to whom they are referred by others they know.

How it shows up

These consumers seek to gather information. While they can do some of this by themselves, they are also avid users of networks. While gathering information, they will turn to friends and colleagues for experience or insight and ask if others know someone who might be able to help. They much prefer the raw intelligence of someone's experience with a product over a company's description. Many will use the various social media options or a blog with expertise in a question. They will visit discussion forums but will be skeptical about sites or messages they suspect of company sponsorship or influence. Organizations that have attempted this have been caught and publicly castigated.

What it means

Organizations cannot rely on their own good faith and assume that reason will prevail. These consumers have a deep distrust of organizations that can only be overcome by a sustained effort to be authentic in their dealings with them and their local community. This authenticity can be difficult, as it requires a frank admission of shortcomings and avoiding the temptation of bringing in the public relations team to try and put a positive spin on the news. Such admissions need to be accompanied by a sincere effort to undo any damage and a commitment to amend and improve behavior. While these admissions could cause short-term pain, over the long term, they will build trust in the organization, which these consumers will appreciate and reward. It may be possible to work more closely with the community and the networks within it to help communicate the organization's perspective. Instead of lecturing about benefits in traditional forums, organizations could work with social media and bloggers to get their perspective into the debate at the grassroots level—providing they don't dictate the message.

WE [REALLY] ARE THE WORLD

The title of this need state plays on the 1985 song "We Are the World," which was recorded to support charitable causes in Africa. That effort spurred some short-term attention, and while things soon returned to business as usual, the song lived on; the thought apparently touched something in these consumers that is now coming back to life; thus the "really" in parentheses. This time, the feeling of global responsibility or planetary consciousness is emerging as a stronger and more genuine force.

What has changed alongside the strengthening of the supporting values is the "flattening" [xxvi] of the world that enables easily accessible and real-time information about any event or situation almost anywhere in the world. Few geographies are beyond the reach of global media and communications. The connection to distant problems is more easily maintained and the options for action have increased as well. It has become much easier to act on these values now than it was back in 1985. So, while the values supporting this need state may well have been present 25 years ago, the supporting infrastructure was not but is now.

The two need states at the core of "global citizens" are these:

- *Global citizens.* Thinking of the ramifications of one's goals and activities beyond national borders, with a genuine concern for planetary welfare and willingness to act on that.

- *Making a difference.* Looking for ways to make a tangible difference in the pursuit of idealistic grand schemes.

---

xxvi   See Friedman, T. (2005). *The World is Flat: A Brief History of the Twenty-first Century.* Farrar, Straus and Giroux.

Global citizens

Thinking of the ramifications one's goals and activities beyond national borders with a genuine concern for planetary welfare and willingness to act on that.

The global citizens' sense of connectedness extends globally. They feel a sense of responsibility for the planet and all its inhabitants. They have a core need of self-transcendence in which they feel it is important to see beyond their individual concerns and consider the impact on the larger context. They see nationalism and national boundaries as artificial constructs that deflect attention away from the common destiny.

Table 31. Global citizens		
Needs	**Values**	**Catalysts**
Self-transcendence	*Integration*: Combining elements into a coherent whole. *Interdependence*: Sensitivity to how things depend on each other. *Thoughtfulness*: Characterized by careful reasoned thinking. *Transcendence*: Ability to rise above a particular circumstance in allegiance to a higher principle or principles.	Emerging markets arise Sustainable consumption Living within limits

Their sense of fairness and equality of opportunity chafes at the injustice for those who happened to have been born into a less advantageous situation. They see the interconnections among events and systems and are sensitive to how their actions influence and can have consequences far removed from them. They typically have a strong sense of environmental stewardship as well; it is about doing the best for other people and for the planet.

It is likely that global citizen consumers could be community-first consumers as well, and vice-versa. They are not mutually exclusive, although one orientation is likely to prevail often over the other.

How it shows up

Outer dimension changes have further crystallized this need state. The possibility of mutual destruction that arose from the capabilities of nuclear weapons brought home this point, albeit in a negative way. Since then, environmental issues such as the ozone hole and now climate change have reached a planetary scale and raised global consciousness. Similarly, the increasing interconnectedness of the global economy has reached the point where most nations are affected by the actions of others, whether they like it or not. Thus these consumers tend to be very concerned and involved with environmental issues such as climate change. They may organize recycling campaigns, "green" their organizations, or encourage their organizations or affiliations to adopt a carbon-neutral pledge.

What it means

These consumers will view an organization's behavior in terms of how it contributes to the benefit or detriment of the people and the planet. They will not be satisfied with an organization if it confines itself just to its own benefit. They feel that organizations have an obligation to make the world a better place, in the context of what is possible for the organization. They bring high standards, but merit attention in that their support is likely to be rewarded and their wrath to be feared.

Making a difference

Looking for ways to make a tangible difference rather than the pursuit of idealistic grand schemes.

These consumers are motivated to find ways to make a tangible difference in terms of making people's lives better or making the world a better place, even if that difference is a very small one. They value their personal creativity and seek to apply it in the service of contributing to positive outcomes. They may feel that every person can make a unique contribution to making the world a better place. They prefer to participate in practical activities that directly impact the lives of people and communities. They feel that grand schemes to change the world are not worth their time if they don't lead to positive action. They abhor all talk and no action.

Table 32. Making a difference		
Needs	**Values**	**Catalysts**
Creation	*Appropriateness*: Suitably designed for the task at hand and user capabilities. *Influential*: Ability to make a difference in an outcome. *Self-Expression*: Expression or assertion of one's own personality. *Thoughtfulness*: Characterized by careful reasoned thinking.	Re-localization Empowered individuals Consumer augmentation

They seek to influence others, and many are willing to do what it takes on their part to achieve positions of influence. They feel that if they want to change the world, they have a responsibility to do their part to be of maximum effectiveness. Others will be content with having a lesser impact, being satisfied with knowing they have done what is within their capabilities.

How it shows up

The desire to make a difference can be pervasive. For instance, these consumers may use it as a criterion of whether to take a job or not with a particular organization. "Does this company make the world a better place or does it contribute to problems?" Similarly, they may evaluate whether to engage with an organization using this criterion. They understand that how they spend their time and money in some small way makes a difference, and they gain satisfaction from doing so. In its extreme form, this can take on a moralizing tone in which any action, even simply having fun, may be viewed with apparent disapproval.

What it means

These consumers are interested in the story of the organizations they choose to do business with. They will be interested to know an organization's vision, mission, purpose, goals, etc. They'll want to know if there is a purpose of the organization beyond maximizing shareholder returns, as that is not enough for them. They will turn away from organizations with what they see as a narrow economic view. To attract these consumers, whose influence and vocal views make them a strong force in shaping public opinion, an organization will need to develop a story, backed with appropriate action, about how they serve a larger purpose and how they leverage their collection of people, skills, and capabilities to make a positive difference in the world.

GLASS HOUSES

These consumers are the activists and many will have an aggressive orientation. They are intolerant of behavior they deem wrong and are not afraid to let the offender, or any interested party, know about it. They feel they are not to be trifled with and that their values and beliefs are important and need to be respected.

These consumers are watching, often all the time. They are often savvy users of technology and expert in the world of information, and they use that to support their cause. Accountability is the buzzword; it won't always be pleasant, and it won't always be fair. The best an organization can do is stay consistent and true—or, closing the circle back to our first need state cluster, be authentic. "Spin" and message control and such tools will only get organizations into trouble. Telling the truth will, eventually at least, earn respect and credibility that will be appreciated and rewarded over the long haul.

The three need states at the core of "glass houses" are these:

- *Trusted partners for the new insecurity.* Requiring trusted partners in turbulent times, with the economy, terror, resource shortages, environmental issues, privacy invasion, identity theft, etc.

- *The truth, whole truth, and nothing but the truth.* Preference for the unvarnished truth, which increases credibility.

- *Expanding accountabilities.* Holding partners to high standards, such as the triple bottom line, community contribution, shared values and ethics.

Trusted partners for the new insecurity

Requiring trusted partners in turbulent times, with the economy, terror, resource shortages, environmental issues, privacy invasion, identity theft, etc.

These consumers are acutely aware of the problems and challenges facing the world. They feel that the world has become an increasingly insecure place, and they feel that insecurity personally. Security is thus a core need for this group.

Table 33. Trusted partners for the new insecurity		
Needs	**Values**	**Catalysts**
Security	*Assistance*: Seeking technological help in keeping up with increasing mental and physical demands. *Authenticity*: State of being genuine; not false or an imitation. *Commitment*: State of being bound emotionally or intellectually to a course of action or to another person or persons.	Living within limits Truth and truthiness Empowered individuals Emerging markets arise

They are not sure whom to trust, and thus they place great value on building trust and having trusting relationships. They are looking for help in navigating through an increasingly complex world, both from people, technologies, and organizations. They are looking for means of reassurance and will be appreciative of whatever the source of that might be.

How it shows up

They will carefully scrutinize potential partners, relationships, and products. They will be drawn to authenticity and turned off by attempts at spin control or managing what information is released and how it is stated. They seek partners who will tell them the truth. Their information skills mean they are not at the mercy of their partners. They will check up on them and do their best to ferret out whether the organization can be trusted. At the same time, they recognize their own need for help. They will appreciate products and services that help them with their problems and ease their burdens.

What it means

For organizations, this suggests that they must be on their best behavior at all times because if they offend these consumers, at best they lose their business, and at worst they become a target. They must act as if the consumer is in the room as they discuss policy options and decisions. Another way to think of it is to take the YouTube test; that is, if any actions were to be captured on camera or a smartphone and posted tomorrow on YouTube where millions of users could see it, would the organization still go ahead with it? The good news is that once these consumers establish a relationship, they are intensely loyal and often active advocates on behalf of their partners. They seek to reward the good behavior as well as punish the bad.

The truth, whole truth, and nothing but the truth

Preference for the unvarnished truth, which increases credibility.

These consumers have a strong sense of self and identity and are confident in their ability to handle problems or issues. They demand to be treated with respect and hate to be talked down to, and they are highly sensitive to this. They pride themselves on their realistic view of life and their ability to handle the truth, no matter how bad the news might be. They have a skeptical view, particularly of institutional authority, and they are likely to follow up and check on any information relayed to them either via sources on the Internet or with friends and their networks.

Table 34. The truth, whole truth, and nothing but the truth		
Needs	Values	Catalysts
Realism	*Authenticity*: State of being genuine, not false or an imitation. *Commitment*: State of being bound emotionally or intellectually to a course of action or to another person or persons. *Questioning*: Characterized by or indicating intellectual curiosity. *Skepticism*: Attitude of doubt or a disposition to incredulity either in general or toward a particular object.	Truth and truthiness Empowered individuals

They can handle bad news and would prefer it be given to them straight. They appreciate forthrightness and take it as a sign that an individual or organization can be trusted—and they reciprocate that trust. They will ask many questions and may seem overly demanding at times. This has both an information aspect and a trust and relationship building aspect. They will not get information about a product from one business and then go and buy the same product more cheaply from someone else; they value trust, and back it up with their spending.

How it shows up

Some of these consumers have developed a mistrust of corporate sustainability claims and efforts. They may become overwhelmed with myriad sustainability issues and initiatives and seek to get to the bottom of them. Many are now aware of the "greenwashing" campaigns promulgated by companies that want to appear to support sustainability and environmentalism but don't want to take any significant action. A general distrust of sustainable marketing has developed that could undermine brand loyalty despite the advertising dollars being spent on attracting green consumers.

What it means

While they are not tolerant of poor or sloppy work, these consumers recognize that mistakes can happen and will not be inclined to punish if individuals or organizations responding in good faith. They will appreciate an organization being forthright about its sustainability efforts, providing it does not attempt to make itself appear greener than it actually is. In fact, it behooves organizations to understand just what is expected from them in terms of green—as well as from their corporate behavior in general. Not every organization is held to the same standard. It is best to be true to what the organization believes than to jump onto every environmental bandwagon that drives by.

These consumers even recognize that the truth itself can be somewhat slippery—with so much information and so many viewpoints, it is often hard to tell. Thus, authenticity and consistency are key attributes in building relationships with these consumers.

Expanding accountabilities

Holding partners to high standards such as the triple bottom line, community contribution, shared values, and ethics.

High standards prevail among these consumers. They are demanding of themselves as well as others. Their system of morality is very important to them, and they feel others should share their concern. They have a set of expectations they bring to any potential transaction or relationship.

Needs	Values	Catalysts
System of morality	*Commitment*: State of being bound emotionally or intellectually to a course of action or to another person or persons. *Community*: Group of people with a common characteristic or interest living or working together within a larger society. *Sustainability*: Reducing the human footprint on the environment while maintaining quality of life.	Sustainable consumption Living within limits Truth and truthiness Empowered individuals Emerging markets arise Relocalization Continuum of ownership

Table 35. Expanding accountabilities

They will typically have a strong sustainability ethos, going beyond just the environment to include social and economic justice as well. They may favor local causes and investment in their community. They will typically have a long list of expectations and be drawn to people and organizations that share their concerns. When they find them, they will often form a strong bond and commitment.

How it shows up

Support for the triple bottom line has taken off as the next step in the evolution of sustainability, which in turn evolved from environmentalism. It expands the range of concerns from beyond being an environmental good citizen to being concerned for the economic and social well-being of the communities affected by an organization. They have a long list of causes they support and they back up their values with their time and money. Recent estimates suggest that 63 million Americans are spending $230 billion annually for products and services that fit this lifestyle pattern. Forest Ethics, a California nonprofit, is one example. It is spearheading the idea of a Do Not Mail list (resembling existing programs that keep consumers from getting phone solicitations) to save the more than 100 million trees per year it takes to produce unwanted catalogues and other junk mail—about 40 pounds per year for each American.[158]

What it means

Essentially, these consumers are looking for a complete package from the organizations they choose to do business with. They will scrutinize an organization from top to bottom and will identify and highlight any inconsistencies. It will not be enough to have a strong commitment to the environment if the organization is weak in others areas, such as not investing in the local community.

GATEWAY

ENTER

NINE

http://bit.ly/pCz899

To a degree, they foreshadow what is to come. They play a pioneering role in setting standards that may seem high or unreasonable at first but will eventually settle into the mainstream. This makes them an important group who fill the roles of leaders in public opinion and setters of standards.

Key points

- Need + situation = need states. Need states are needs within a specific context, situation, or set of activities, e.g., needs around breakfast. They provide an excellent target around which market researchers, product developers, and business strategists can devise plans. More organizations are realizing that the key to innovating and keeping customers happy is to understand the evolution of their needs, on which these need states provide an excellent head start.

- The 23 emerging need states are identified with one to three core needs, supplemented by three to five related values (the inner dimension component), and intersecting with two to four catalysts (the outer dimension component). The combination of inner and outer components helps to ensure a robust set of need states, grounded in both individual consumer changes and changes in the larger consumer landscape.

- Each need state is introduced and described with its components. Examples of how it shows up in consumer life are provided, as well as an interpretation of what it means. This treatment shows the "reality" of how these changes are already manifesting, and addresses the "so what?" by offering tangible suggestions on what organizations can do to respond.

- The 23 specific emerging need states are grouped into seven meta-needs or needs that cut across a wide swath of consumer life. The seven meta-needs provide a shorthand for capturing the big ideas behind these changes in consumer needs. They can help time-pressed organizations cut right to the chase while leaving the option open for digging into more specific need states that relate to the themes of interest.

7

FUTURE PERSONAS:
BRINGING THE FUTURE TO LIFE

Each of the seven emerging meta-needs is brought to life in the form of future personas. Personas are representative characters that fit a profile of someone who has that need. They are emerging today and forecast to become increasingly evident over the next decade. The seven personas each embody one of the seven meta-needs. They are each covered in a consistent format that includes the following:

- *Summary description*. The first few paragraphs characterize the persona in general.

- *Demographics*. A profile of a "typical" persona who embodies the meta-need, including gender, age, household income, education, and life stage.

- Illustration. A visual to help facilitate the "real-ness" of the persona.

- *Table*. A summary table that includes the supporting need states of the meta-need, the values this persona would likely embrace, and the related catalysts supporting the persona's emergence.

- *Committed time activities*. How the persona would likely approach several aspects of committed time—work, household and family care, shopping, and personal/biological necessities.

- *Free time activities*. Description of how the persona would likely approach free time—learning, leisure (entertainment/recreation), affiliation, and communication.

- *Vignette*. A brief day-in-the-life snapshot that provides insight into how the persona might operate in daily life.

It should be kept in mind that these personas are generalizations. As such, they will miss the diversity that will actually show up in how the meta-needs manifest in the future. For example, the demographics suggesting that Annie is a 35-year-old female does not imply that only 35-year-old females will have this meta-need. It is an attempt to find the center of the need, and some choices are made in providing details to help create a mental picture of the persona.

AUTHENTIC ANNIE: KEEPING IT REAL

Demographics

<u>Sex</u>: Female

<u>Age</u>: 35

<u>HHI</u>: $125,000

<u>Education</u>: MA, Public Health

<u>Life stage</u>: Midcareer, early parenthood

Annie is all about authenticity. She expects organizations to give it to her straight and trust her to be able to handle the truth. She rejects being protected and told things "for her own good." She understands that life can be difficult. She doesn't take things at face value and searches for the real story beneath the surface. She expects to be treated as an adult, as an equal, and with the respect she feels she has earned. She is sensitive to being manipulated and will react strongly against it. She thinks about how consumption fits in with her overall identity and sense of purpose and brings high expectations to her dealings with organizations.

Table 36. Authentic Annie: Keeping it real		
Need states	**Values**	**Catalysts**
	Authenticity	
	Appropriateness	
		Continuum of ownership
	Cool	
Au naturel		Enoughness
	Design	
Less is more		Life-shifting
	Experiences	
The authenticity premium		Living within limits
	Functionality	
		Sustainable consumption
The simplicity premium	Self-expression	
		Truth and truthiness
	Simplicity	
	Sustainability	

Committed=time activities

Work

Annie is grateful for the relative financial security that enables her to only have to work part time. This gives her enough time to spend time with her daughter while also enabling her to do work for a women's health NGO. She is happy to be a parent but is a strong believer in her work and expects to transition back to it full time when her daughter is old enough. She feels her work expresses who she is and what she is all about. That is not to say that it is not frustrating at times. She has to deal with government officials in countries they are trying to help, and it can be so difficult to get them to listen, never mind actually to do something. She sometimes feels that this frustration in dealing with less-developed countries makes her less tolerant of foolishness back home. She can be snappy after a hard day if she feels like she is getting the runaround from a salesperson. She feels she is too busy and life is too short to waste time on such nonsense.

Household and family care

Annie is officially part time at work, thanks to a job share she arranged with a colleague who is working on his degree. She is committed to her work, although she finds herself falling asleep at night in her rocking chair with her laptop open as she "is just going to catch up on a few things." She often feels the house is on the edge of chaos. Her husband does help out when he can, but he's busy, too, and working a very involving full-time job. Annie has decided that family and work are the top priorities—at least that's what she tells herself when the house looks a mess. She is willing to spend their money to save time, but she feels they don't quite have the financial strength to outsource everything they'd like to. She has put together a budget to help prioritize—actually it's more like a list of priorities as there isn't time to track it in detail.

A significant change in household care is that she has gradually converted to using natural cleaning remedies. She's even growing an ingredient in her herb garden and can hardly wait to try it out. She feels that she is not only protecting her family but also the environment, and she experiences a unique sense of cleanliness from these natural products—not that hospital antiseptic kind of clean, but a clean that makes you want to take a deep breath and enjoy. She's not afraid of spiders and is not above taking an ecosystem approach to cleaning—spiders do the job, much as their cat has taken care of the occasional mouse.

Shopping

Annie does not consider herself "born to shop." She views it as a necessity, and in light of her tight schedule it often feels as though it is both a luxury and a chore. She informally sorts her shopping into two types: purchases she judges should be done in the most efficient manner possible, and purchases deemed worthy of her time investment. For the efficiency items, she is thankful for the advent of e-commerce and is a great user of online ordering and delivery—she can't imagine how she'd get her Christmas shopping done otherwise, for example. She has also gradually converted most of her grocery shopping to Peapod. It took a while to "train" them on what she wanted, but they've done a good job in listening to her and she's converted more and more of her grocery shopping to them. She still reserves a weekend morning to visit the local farmer's market for fresh produce, but some weeks she even turns this over to Peapod as well.

She prefers wherever possible to shop at local stores where she knows the people and is willing to pay a little more for this convenience, as she feels it is the right thing to support local businesses. At the same time, she is also willing to support bigger businesses that she feels share her values. She recognizes that just because someone is local does not make them automatically a better option.

Personal/biological necessities

She feels it is important to trust products that she puts in or on her body—and that of her child as well. This is an area that she feels should not be skimped on. Thus, she is careful about what personal care products she uses. A long time ago, she started using Tom's of Maine toothpaste, for example, as she felt as though the brand and Tom himself were to be trusted. She has a tendency to use natural products where possible, again feeling that they are more trustworthy, although she is not averse to using a high-tech product that she trusts to do the job efficiently. For instance, she wonders about some of the chemicals in her hair products, but in this case, she trusts the salon and its admittedly pricey products because they work so well and save her time getting ready in the all-too-hectic morning rush out the door.

Free-time activities

Learning

One of the things Annie likes about the farmer's market is getting tips on how to improve her gradually increasing backyard garden. Whether it's from the farmers themselves or the patrons, she typically finds someone who has a tip she can use. Her husband wonders how it can take so long to buy some fruit; she spends as much time socializing as shopping, and it's often about the garden. This has become a release from her busy life, and she takes it very seriously for that reason. She also likes patronizing Smith & Hawken, even though they are a bit pricey, because the people there are so knowledgeable and they have been green from the get-go. She's even looking into a gardening course at the local community college. She's not sure if it's quite worth it, but one can dream.

Leisure (entertainment/recreation)

If you ask Annie about her leisure activities, you might get a puzzled look in response. It's not that Annie doesn't have or doesn't enjoy leisure, it's just that for her, work and home and leisure are so intertwined that it's hard to separate them out. She does enjoy occasionally tuning out and catching up on her latest copy of *Dwell* or *Real Simple*. She also enjoys nature shows, but she is not above the occasional indulgence in what she calls trashy TV, and she usually has at least one serial that she tracks voraciously, including chatting with others about past or upcoming episodes.

She's been planning a trip to Southeast Asia for months, working diligently to identify local contacts who can give her a "real" and personal experience. Sometimes she thinks she enjoys planning trips almost as much as taking them. She enjoyed her last trip, a "voluntourist" experience in which the team did a lot of digging as part of a public health project to improve the sewage system in a Latin American country. She helped coordinate that on behalf of her job. She's done several of these job-related voluntourist projects now, and this time would like to have an experience not related to work. She laughs when she reflects on being torn about getting an MBA—that wouldn't have done her much good digging ditches.

Affiliation

Annie does not consider herself much of a joiner. She will often participate in discussion forums or LISTSERVs when a topic catches her attention. She says her job is her interest. She does maintain a membership in the Sierra Club in the belief that she ought to do something for the environment, though she wishes she could do more. She is very active in the local PTA, as she believes parents should be actively involved in the education of their children.

Communications

She keeps up with friends on Facebook and was delighted to rediscover some old friends she'd lost contact with from both high school and college. Part of her commitment to being the best parent she can be is that she contributes to the "mommy blogs" that some of her neighborhood friends started. She was surprised at how it took off and has expanded well beyond the neighborhood. The fact that it has grown helps ease her guilt about not contributing enough, though sometimes she has to discipline herself to log off as she finds the real-life stories so compelling.

Day-in-the-life vignette

Annie's friends used to think she was so trendy. They laugh about it now, but parenthood changed her. Now it's more about what's *not* in the things she buys her family than the label or logo that the product carries. She likes simple products with simple messages and not a lot of fanfare. She doesn't spend much time getting dressed up for work. She's streamlined her wardrobe and whenever possible buys natural fabrics. Her view is to have fewer things, but of higher quality and durability.

She tries to bicycle to work once or twice a week, but that can be challenging. Her organization does allow her flextime, so if she has to jump in the VW bug, she plans her commute to avoid traffic. Today is a bike day, and the good thing about that is it gives her the option to skip yoga if the day gets too hectic. Most of her day at the office, today will be spent on the social media campaign they're devising to build support for increased foreign aid relating to public health.

After work, she's going to do some "research" for a backyard playset for her daughter. She's done some Internet searching and has ruled out anything plastic. Fortunately, her "mommy blogs" have given her some great tips. It's been years since she read a product review in the mainstream media. She's leaning toward a custom-built system but wants to check out a local outdoors store that might have some of the material she needs, and then she could do the rest. She figures it will depend on how helpful the people there are. If they'll be there for her when the inevitable questions come up, she may well take the plunge. She recognizes that the stuff she buys costs a little more, but that's okay. She likes to think her choices make a difference, and she likes the recognition that her choices are different—she looks forward to being the one giving advice about this on the mommy blog some day.

Annie's motto:
"Be true to yourself"

SUPER SAM: PUSHING THE ENVELOPE

Demographics

Sex: Male

Age: 24

HHI: $50,000

Education: BA, Biology

Life stage: Single, early career

Sam enjoys a challenge. He likes to win but is more interested in his own performance than in beating his fellows. He mixes with others to help him challenge himself—not that he needs too much pushing. His friends think he is crazy sometimes, and even worry about him, as when Sam heard about the futurist Ray Kurzweil taking over 200 supplements a day as a means to achieve longevity. Sam took that as something of a license to boost up his own already-substantial intake of vitamins and supplements. There is a bit of restlessness in his pursuits—he tends to jump from one obsession to another, always pushing the limits of his own performance; whether it's an extreme diet, or his ultramarathoning phase, or when he experimented with how little sleep he could get by with. He has already made it clear that he'll be the first one among his friends to get a brain or memory implant, as he was the first to have a smartphone with GPS and the first to have pretty much any gadget or innovation that could help him perform better. He is looking forward to a state-of-the art prosthetic knee, not just to deal with his aching football injury, but to give him greater speed and for training. And he is exploring a PhD in genetic engineering and jokes that he'll be his own lab rat.

Table 37. Super Sam: Pushing the envelope		
Need states	**Values**	**Catalysts**
Getting real with the virtual Performance enhancement	Authenticity Appropriateness Cool Design Experiences Functionality Self-expression Simplicity Sustainability	Empowered individuals Enhancement Life-shifting Ubiquitous connection Virtual-real-digital tribes

Committed-time activities

Work

Sam worked his way through his undergraduate studies as a personal trainer. His enthusiasm for self-improvement extends to helping other people do their best as well. He has to restrain himself sometimes as he sometimes forgets that not everyone shares his zeal. He has, nonetheless, amassed quite a clientele as his trainees know that Sam is on top of all the state-of-the art ideas and approaches. As he is fond of saying, he doesn't advocate anything that he hasn't tried and found worthwhile. He plans to continue this work as a graduate student and is confident that he can rebuild his clientele in a new city.

His current aspiration—admittedly, they change frequently—is to be a pioneer in gene therapies. He is fascinated by the possibilities of not only fixing disorders but improving people's performance capacity. He dreams of working with professional athletes in pushing beyond current limits. He recognizes that there are ethical questions involved, but frankly wonders what all the fuss is about.

Household and family care

Sam enjoys living with friends in a group house. They provide lots of opportunities for competition, whether it's video games or a morning bike ride. His friends sometimes complain that he pushes the pace too much, but they admire his tenacity. He is happy to have a room of his own where he keeps detailed files and records of the many different aspects of his performance that he tracks. He even has his own mini fridge where he stores his more expensive food items. He is happy to invest in his own performance, but doesn't want to have a roommate or friend casually grab one of his expensive protein bars in the group fridge. While he is meticulous about matters relating to performance, he does have a tendency to neglect the basics, such as cleaning. "I'll hire that out... someday."

Shopping

Sam fits the profile of a bimodal shopper. He is very conscientious about products relating to performance. He does due diligence in these areas and is not afraid to spend money on them, viewing them as an investment. He is very particular about the companies and brands he buys from, but once they earn his trust, he is very loyal and often becomes an enthusiastic advocate. On the flip side, he is a dangerous enemy to those products that he feels are inferior. He has earned the respect of people, such that his endorsement matters to them. He prefers to shop online so he can quickly do any additional research that he feels might aid his choice.

Personal/biological necessities

Sam feels that one should outsource those things that one doesn't like to do. And for him, cleaning fits that bill, whether it's his living space or his own body. He goes to a men's grooming salon on a weekly basis to treat himself right at least once a week. They tell him what to do and he does it. He doesn't want to waste his brainpower on thinking about the ordinary matters of daily life. Romantic partners complain that he won't spend money on clothes for a nice evening out, but there are practically no budget limits on athletic gear, whether it's shoes, a heart monitor, or a dive skin. Diet is, of course, highly important, and he wonders sometimes if he would have needed student loans if he cut down on his supplements, bars, and high-quality foods.

Free-time activities

Learning

Sam is probably going to be one of those perpetual students. He loves learning. His biggest challenge, school-wise, is to finish his degrees. His undergraduate studies took a year longer than they should have because he neglected taking several required courses as they didn't interest him. He gets impatient with professors he feels lack passion. He can't relate to people who see their jobs as jobs—for him, money is secondary to the pursuit of doing something you love.

Leisure (entertainment/recreation)

The distinction between work and school and leisure seems like artificial one to Sam. He divides the world into things he likes and the things he absolutely has to do because he cannot avoid them without severe consequences. He doesn't see the point of something like doing a jigsaw puzzle—he wonders why someone would want to turn their brain off. As far as standard recreation categories go, it's no surprise that he enjoys physical and mental challenges, from rock climbing to triathalons to ultramarathons, as well as a good book on the new possibilities emerging from science and technology.

Affiliation

Sam is prone to join discussion groups and online communities when he becomes interested in a particular topic. His typical pattern is a burst of participation and then it's on to the next interest. One of his recent fascinations has been around the "open prosthetics" community that takes an open-source software approach to prosthetics. He is usually the first of his group to try out new online innovations, from social networking to online gaming to virtual worlds. He just joined a Transhumanists group on Facebook. He thinks their ideas on the merger of people and technology are a bit mundane—he wants to go further and faster. No surprise there!

Communications

Sam is a gadget collector. He likes to be the first to figure out how to use new technologies. He tends to get bored quickly and look for the next new thing, which makes him a great customer for IT companies. Cool hunter groups, which search for the latest trends and fads, have approached him about participating and even offered to pay him to be an advocate. He has refused, however, as he feels that would taint him in the eyes of his colleagues, and he values his unofficial role as an opinion leader.

Day-in-the-life vignette

Maybe it was growing up playing lots of video games that made him feel this way... you know, where you have to build up your character's strength... but whatever it was, Sam always felt an intense drive to build himself up. During high school, it was all about pushing himself physically, and he tried every supplement he could get his hands on—legal and otherwise— in his effort to bulk up and build endurance for

Sam's motto:
"You only live once"

football. In college, he also started experimenting with cognitive enhancements— ways to make him more alert and to boost his memory for classes and big tests. Now that he's working full time again, he swears he'd get his Bluetooth earpiece implanted in his head if he could...

FREE SPIRIT FAITH: EVERY MOMENT MATTERS

Demographics

Sex: Female

Age: 43

HHI: $40,000

Education: BA, Art History; J.D.

Life stage: Divorced, switching careers

Faith had a life-changing experience—a moment or event that caused her to say, "Wait a minute, what am I doing with my life?" What may be different from others who have had similar experiences is that she did not let this opportunity pass her by. She walks the talk. She has made significant changes in an impassioned pursuit of a different way of life—one in which she is in control of her life and not being controlled by it. She felt herself heading down a "conventional" path in pursuit of success and confronted the question of what success really meant to her. She is no longer a slave to the pursuit of the dollar and values how she spends her time first and foremost. She has come to believe the aphorism, "do what you love, and the money will follow."

Table 38. Free Spirit Faith: Every moment matters		
Need states	**Values**	**Catalysts**
Investing time like money Living in real-time Whenever, wherever, whatever	Co-creation Connectivity Discovery Open-Mindedness Empowerment Nonconformity Personalization Spontaneity Transcendence	Co-creation Continuum of ownership Empowered individual Enoughness Life-shifting Ubiquitous connection

Committed-time activities

Work

The day before her final interview, Faith was scared. How could she walk away from the fast track she was clearly on with the Fortune 500 company? And to take a risk—and a large pay cut—with a start-up boutique graphic design firm? But once she got to the interview, she felt that familiar sense of ease she seemed to always get when she interacted with the people at the new place. She felt at home. She had always wanted to apply her love of art, and now she had the chance to do it.

She had talked with practically everyone she knew about this, and was surprised at how many supported her. Sure, a few old-timers lectured her about the opportunity she was tossing away, but most totally understood where she was coming from. If she wasn't happy climbing the ladder of success, what was the point of climbing it? They could see her eyes light up when she talked about the ideas she had for the new firm. The passion came through clearly. Most suggested that she would be good at whatever she put her mind to and told her to go for it.

Household and family care

Her divorce was a shock, as they usually are, but that wasn't the catalyst for the changes she's been making in her life. Sure, she had to downsize a bit afterward. She found herself working even harder to prove herself, and succeeding. But at what cost? So she found an apartment in the city within walking distance of the museums she so enjoyed. She sold the Lexus and joined the Zipcar car-sharing service. She found she could find most of what she needed within walking distance; public transportation and Zipcar filled in the gaps, such as visits to her mom in the suburbs. She discontinued her maid service and found, to her surprise, that the DIY aspects of housework and daily chores could be almost fulfilling and gave her a chance to turn her brain off. Some might suggest she still needed a maid, but her surroundings were clean enough to suit her purposes.

Shopping

One chore that she does not find very fulfilling is grocery shopping. One of her first moves was find an online shopping service. Peapod operates in the city and she loves it. Life's too short to spend pushing around a cart and standing in a grocery line. She is quite adept at online shipping in general and uses it for lots of things, especially gifts for out-of-town friends or relatives. She used to miss or send "belated" cards all the time, but no more—or at least a lot less. That said, for her there is still nothing like a day of shopping for the things she loves. Her love of design is expressed both in the items she carefully chooses for her apartment and in her clothes. She feels that both these areas are expressions of who you are. Rummaging through an antique shop, attending an art gallery opening, or even going to thrift shops to find that special item are among her greatest pleasures in life.

Personal/biological necessities

Faith does not consider herself a health nut, but she does maintain that yoga class is necessary for her sanity. Just because she has downsized her life does not mean she has downsized her type A personality. (She jokes that she's shooting for

B+). She has found that yoga is ideal for getting her centered again. Keeping that daily commitment has been an instrumental part of her "new" life. She used to do it for a while but then would fall off the wagon when work got busy. Now, she's pretty zealous about it. She needs a pretty strong reason to pull her away from yoga class.

She has been gradually moving toward using more natural products—not all the way, but incorporating them here and there. It makes her feel good that she's helping the environment in some small way. Even though she is picky about her personal appearance, she has been known to substitute natural products for many of her personal care needs. She's found that while there is a period of adjustment in getting used to them, they actually work just as well, if not better.

Free-time activities

Learning

Faith is a little concerned that her design skills may have gotten rusty as it's been too long since she used them. So, she is taking classes at DePaul to beef up her skills. It feels great to be learning in school again and so much more enjoyable and practical than many of the boring corporate training seminars she used to have to sit through. She recognizes the challenge of adapting her background in the arts to graphic design. Thankfully, the start-up saw her potential, but it sometimes freaks her out to imagine that being her job.

Leisure (entertainment/recreation)

Part of the promise that Faith made to herself in moving to the city and selling the Lexus was that she would use some of the money she saved to take trips. She loves to travel and has a "bucket list" of museums she hopes to visit someday. She uses services such as Lastminutedeals.com to find bargains. One of the advantages of being single again is that it's much easier to follow spur-of-the-moment impulses. She did a lot of business travel, but on some trips, she barely left the hotel or meeting room. She enjoys the spontaneity of just visiting a place and then deciding what to do.

Affiliation

Faith is not much of a joiner. She thinks of herself as a kind of free spirit. Maybe that was why she never felt quite right in the corporate world, even though she was so successful. She picks her spots carefully. One organization she really likes is the new Creative Chicago guild. It helped her to find her dream job and now she wants to help others do the same.

Communications

Faith previously shared the views of many of her corporate colleagues that social networking was a big waste of precious time. But one of her friends persisted and got her to try it. She felt kind of embarrassed at first when she shared what seemed to be the minutia of her new life. She had to admit, however, that she enjoyed the encouragement she received. It had something of an addictive quality about it, and she got over the initial awkwardness and is now a fairly avid Tweeter. She's expanded beyond "what I ate for breakfast" to discuss some design ideas, and this has put her in touch with several interesting people and groups. She was always a power networker in the corporate world, and those skills have helped in her new venture. She's already got a long list of potential clients from it.

Day in the life vignette

This wasn't exactly where Faith thought she'd be at age 43, starting over… single and with a new career; but it just felt right. Somewhere along the way, Eric and she grew apart… she admitted that her 80-hour weeks at the firm probably didn't help, but that was all in the past now. This time she was going to put herself first… not her work… and certainly not any man. Sure, it'd be a financial adjustment, but she

Faith's motto:
"It's never too late"

never had time to spend all that money, and she grew up simple… so in some ways it felt like "coming home" to be on a budget again. Now she was working to live… and the graphic design work was trickling in. She had even turned down her first gig from iFreelance.com last week because it was on too tight a turnaround… that felt really good to do! And then she found her dream job.

BECKY 2.0 AND BEYOND: THE [RELENTLESS] PURSUIT OF HAPPINESS

Becky has soooo much energy, and passion. So little time, so much to do! She loves what's she's doing and that's her fuel. She may tire you out as a friend, but she sure is great to have on your side. If she likes your products, service, organization, you can bet she'll let others know!

She believes that one has to take personal responsibility for one's life and happiness—happiness is not a birthright. She takes her own advice to heart. She has a zest for life that she

Demographics
Sex: Female
Age: 19
HHI: N/A
Education: Pursuing BA, Psychology
Life stage: Student

brings to everything she does. She has little use for complaining or complainers. You can see her fidget when someone starts to whine, or what she perceives as whining. She just does not understand why people spend so much time talking about what's wrong in their lives and so little time doing anything about it. At the same time, she enjoys helping people reach their potential, which is why she is pursuing a degree in psychology.

She likes to surround herself with positive people. She feeds off their energy—not that she needs much help. She has lots of friends and only wishes she could spend more time with them. Being on the go all the time can strain her ability to keep up with them. She feels that it is her purpose to make the world a better place and is very conscious of the products she buys and the organizations she associates with. She feels she votes with her feet and her wallet, and she is indeed a well-informed voter.

Table 39. Beckie 2.0: The relentless pursuit of happiness

Need states	Values	Catalysts
	Authenticity Contentment	
Help me help myself	Discovery	Co-creation
Identity products, services, and experiences	Enjoyment	Consumer augmentation
	Interdependence	Empowered individual
I'm not a consumer	Passion	Enoughness
Pursuit of happiness, a.k.a. well-being Reinventing the self	Questioning	Sustainable consumption
	Self-expression Spirituality	Truth and truthiness
Systematic and consistent	Sustainability	Virtual-real—digital tribes
	Wellness	

Committed-time activities

Work

It occasionally vexes Beckie that she seems to work so hard but has so little money. Not that she needs or even wants a lot, but one has to live! She often quips that "she's too busy to work." She takes a full load of five classes, has a couple of volunteer gigs—one is feeding the homeless and the other is playing guitar and singing—along with about a dozen student activities. When she says she's busy, she has a point. She does envision the day when she'll have to buckle down and get a "real" job. She is excited about a career as a therapist. The biggest challenge is what kind. Each time she learns about a new approach, that becomes her instant favorite… until the next one.

Household and family care

Beckie lives in the dorms—more like crashes there once in a while between activities. She often blames her roommate for her not wanting to be there—all she does is party and sleep. Beckie doesn't get how someone can pass up all the great opportunities life has to offer by being drunk half the time. She feels the room is full of negative energy and brings her down. She admits that she is not so good about keeping up with her share of the upkeep. She sees it as a waste of precious time. Her plan is to "outsource." When she has money from her practice, she'll use it to "buy time," which is far more precious to her.

Shopping

While some may call her a minimalist, Beckie has something of a bimodal approach to shopping. When she does care about a product or service, money is not an object. So while she buys most of her clothes at thrift shops, she is not shy about running up a bill for organic foods at Whole Foods or splurging at the local farmer's market. She likes the idea of supporting companies that share her values and are also trying to make the world a better place. And she will absolutely not buy anything from a company she judges is guilty of bad behavior. She likes to refer to herself as an "anti-sumer" as she thinks people put way too much emphasis on material goods. Of course, one needs to buy things to survive, but the least one can do is be conscientious about that.

Personal/biological necessities

Beckie aims to have all-natural products. She is opposed to products that involve animal testing and does not buy genetically modified foods. She limits her consumption of processed foods, but her busy lifestyle means that she has to occasionally compromise to avoid collapsing of starvation. She feels a little guilty about that occasional lapse and pledges to slow down, but it doesn't usually last for long. She is okay with spending a little more for natural and organic, since she doesn't spend a lot as a rule: quality, not quantity. She insists on natural fibers in any new clothes or accessories, although she will compromise occasionally if she is buying something secondhand since recycling is a good thing.

Free-time activities

Learning

She is training as a DJ for the campus radio station and has a voracious interest in a wide range of music. She has a great love of other cultures and feels that a culture's music is a great way to get to know it. She has aspirations of taking classes overseas and wants to do a field practicum there: no better way to learn than to immerse oneself. The tendency to favor action over theory is occasionally a shortcoming in her education. She has little time for "talking heads" and overly academic books or journals. She'd rather learn by doing; she's definitely not the type who reads the instructions or takes the tutorial. If she can't figure it out quickly, she's on to the next thing. There is always more to learn.

Leisure (entertainment/recreation)

Her love of music has inspired her to visit local cafes and small venues and beg for a chance to play. She is not above the occasional lunchtime "gig" busking near the train station—it is sometimes her best source of income. It's been the one constant among a wide range of experiments—from photography to meditation to rock climbing. The problem is that she starts a lot of hobbies but tends to lose interest quickly as competing activities invade. She actually thinks it more fun to participate in a "smart mob" protest against some corporate malfeasance than a traditional recreational pursuit. The spontaneity and camaraderie of the mob has so much energy, and it's usually for a good cause.

Affiliation

There seem to be few things Beckie hasn't volunteered for. It's where she has made most of her friends, except perhaps for school. But even within school, she is always volunteering. Her favorite was last summer doing day care for kids of local migrant farmworkers. It just felt so fulfilling to know firsthand that she was making a positive difference in the lives of others. She could see it in the smiles of the children and the appreciation from the workers. It is characteristic of her "joining" strategy that what she does needs to make a tangible difference. She is not into the big causes where it is next to impossible to change anything. She might believe in the cause, but she won't give her time to it if it looks like it's a lost cause.

Communication

Beckie was among the pioneers in social networking. She was such an avid connector. Her friends used to say she should get paid for it, but that is not the point with Beckie. She posts a little less than she used to—she's just too busy—and as with many things, her interest tends to peter out after a while. While she is tech-savvy, she sees technology as a tool—a means and not an end. She's not worried about having the latest gadget; she is happy to let others work out the kinks first. When she does find one she likes, she is surprisingly loyal to it. She doesn't like having to continuously upgrade. Her love of learning does not extend to how to operate things. She likes to joke that "she's a person, not an engineer."

Day-in-the-life vignette

The meeting with the dean went better than she expected. She had presented her vision for why the college should grow its own fruits and veggies and give up that portion of its corporate food service. Her premise is that connecting students to their food stream in this very tangible way will lower the school's carbon footprint and provide a psychological and health benefit that will pay off down the road. Thankfully she'd found the CampusGrows network on Facebook. She'd learned so much from other kids who were working on similar plans at their schools… getting crop/menu ideas, work plans, financial advice to make it self-sustaining, etc. She feels "there is always a better way." Next stop… a meeting with the college president! Rock on!

Beckie's motto:
"Life is short"

GOOD NEIGHBOR BOB: COMMUNITY FIRST

Bob has heard himself referred to as a boomerang, rejuvenile, kidult, etc. These are not necessarily compliments, but Bob doesn't care. He has a pretty solid sense of self and security, even though his family often wonders about him. They want him to settle down, finish school, and find a career path. They worry about his laissez-faire attitude toward life. He just doesn't seem to take anything seriously, except for his mountain biking and that computer stuff. For instance, while he might have holes in his jeans, he has a state-of-the-art bike that he is quite proud of. If you ask him what he does, he says he's a mountain biker—he doesn't want to be defined by his work, but by what he loves to do.

Demographics

<u>Sex</u>: Male

<u>Age</u>: 28

<u>HHI</u>: $34,000

<u>Education</u>: Some college, Self taught web guru

<u>Life stage</u>: Lives in group house with fiancé

The likelihood is that Bob is going to follow his own path. He sees life as a kind of soap opera, and he lets it unfold one day at a time. He doesn't get too worried about the future. He's really savvy about how to get by without too much money or working too hard. He relies a lot on his friends and acquaintances in the community. He gives as well as gets. He prefers to simply trade favors, and figures it all evens out in the end. He loves the local food co-op and also is reputed to be the biggest user of Ithaca Hours, the local currency.

Table 40. Good Neighbor Bob: Community first

Need states	Values	Catalysts
Community support Local preferences Trust the network	Appropriateness Collaboration Community Connectivity Influential Interdependent Questioning Skepticism Sustainability Tolerance	Emerging markets arise Empowered individuals Living within limits Relocalization Sustainable consumption Virtual-real—digital tribes

Committed-time activities

Work

Bob has adapted his self-taught skills in computer programming to become a studio engineer at the local recording studio. Business is kind of slow, so he is not making much money. But he likes doing it, and he's making enough to get by. He just fell into the job—a friend of a friend hooked him up. He gets annoyed at his parents harping on him to finish school, enough so that he recently moved out. He was also tired of people making fun of him for still living with his parents. He and his girlfriend moved into a group house with a few of his mountain biking buddies. He surprised them all when he proposed to his girlfriend immediately after they moved in… and she accepted. She shares his view that material security is not a big deal and doesn't worry that they don't have a place of their own—all in due time.

Household and family care

Bob and his fiancée don't have any immediate plans to have children, so they feel there is no hurry to get a place of their own. They like the sense of community they feel by living with others. They probably would have lived in a commune in the hippie days. They are pretty diligent about doing their fair share of the household maintenance. Their strong sense of community is such that they feel responsible to do their part. Bob won't admit it out loud, but he's glad that his fiancée is on a more solid career path—she's a recent law school grad planning to work in family law. In addition to providing some financial security, she also helped him out when he organized a protest movement about a proposed new site for a large retail chain that he and others felt would harm the local merchants.

Shopping

Bob tries to buy everything local. He is a big fan of the food co-op and thrift shops. After that, it's on to freecycle.org. He made a commitment to first try and buy everything used before buying anything new. He's heard all the jokes about recycled underwear and likes to shoot back "Who needs that anyway?" That keeps them off balance! He strongly believes that people are wasteful simply because they are too lazy. He's donated programming time to freecycle.org and to a few other ventures devoted to sharing in support of that belief.

Personal/biological necessities

Some say Bob has never met a trade he didn't like. For example, he has gone so far as to trade time in his recording studio after hours to a local herbalist in exchange for homemade toothpaste, deodorant, and medical advice after a particularly nasty mountain bike spill. He is wary of hospitals and clinics, preferring alternative medicine. He does wonder how much of it is the placebo effect, but he doesn't care. His sense is that there is wisdom in nature, and he believes strongly in the natural recuperative powers of the body. He's made some solid connections through the food co-op; many of the patrons are into natural remedies. He's networked his way into becoming pretty knowledgeable on the topic.

Free-time activities

Learning

Bob takes classes at the local community college, usually in whatever interests him at the moment. He feels a little guilty about not finishing his degree, but when he sits down to select classes, there is always something pretty interesting going on at the community college—much more interesting than "required core courses." Since he has a job, he figures it's his right to decide how he spends his time. And now that he's moved out of his parent's house, he doesn't have to listen to the "my rules in my house" speech.

Leisure (entertainment and recreation)

Mountain biking is his great love, and the thought of getting to the best trails in the country is the one time he wishes he made more money. But he figures he'll find a way to get to them eventually. He's mastered the local trails, at the cost of some bumps and bruises. His love of bikes has made him the go-to guy for bike repair and does his best to lend his friends a hand now and then without cutting into the business of his friends at the local bike shop. They don't mind too much as they know that he sends them plenty of business with his recommendations.

He plays in a band—admitted, they are not very good—but he enjoys it, so "whatever." They have recorded at his studio but haven't gotten too many customers beyond friends and family. He enjoys the camaraderie of the band. He simply enjoys the company of people.

Affiliation

Bob became the local coordinator for freecycle.org in his community because he really liked the service and felt that it was worth giving his time to. He enjoys promoting the groups he likes, not in a loud or "commercial" fashion, but in more of a quiet, word-of-mouth fashion. It is a bit ironic that for a noncommercial guy, he is actually a valuable customer as an opinion leader. He is on the board of the neighborhood association, feeling that he represents the interests of the non-establishment. He organizes an informal weekly mountain bike ride on Sunday afternoons, which has become hugely popular, though not many end up staying with him for the whole ride. And he pioneered the Locals ONLY iPhone app. These are just a few of his many affiliations. His parents are fond of saying that he's the world's busiest part-time man.

Communications

Bob blogs for the online version of the local alternative newspaper. His posts are usually really good, but he is not all that consistent in terms of submitting posts. He does it when the spirit moves him—it just doesn't move him that often. He is by no means anti-technology, despite the perception that a nature-loving naturalist like himself is hostile or at least skeptical of technology. He loves his iPhone and can't help but design a few apps of his own. He is not into gadgets for gadgets' sake—they need to have a practical purpose to be worth his time.

<u>Day-in-the-life vignette</u>

Bob remembered how proud he was of himself when he bought his first pair of pants from American Apparel. It was a start, but even that doesn't seem quite local enough for his taste anymore. That's why for the past two years, Bob's been on a mission to connect artists and craftspeople with people in the neighborhood through his new LocalsONLY iPhone app. Part eBay, part Epinions, its content is all local. And why not? Brooklyn has everything to offer, whether you're looking for artisan bread, an oil painting, or a handmade refurb'd bicycle. And the social aspects of the app take the guesswork out of who you're buying from… Bob's next challenge is to take his Locals ONLY movement to other cities.

Bob's motto:
"Chill out, dude"

STEWARTSHIP: WE [REALLY] ARE THE WORLD

Stewart can't deny that he "fits the profile" of a tree hugger. But he has to suppress a wry grin when he tells folks of his background in corporate America. He believes that the best way to change a system is to work within it. And he also believes that there is a lot more "goodness" to be tapped in the corporate sector than most of his fellow greens believe.

He vividly remembers the days of "We Are the World," and it remains his favorite song. He felt an energy in those times that he continues to believe in. His friends sometimes think he's a hopeless optimist. He can't imagine living any other way.

Demographics

Sex: Male

Age: 58

HHI: Living off nest egg

Education: BA, Yale, MA, Columbia

Life stage: Launching his "encore" career

What separates him from many of his colleagues, beyond his background, is that he firmly believes that environmentalists, or sustainabilists as he likes to say, must work with large corporations if they are going to "move the needle." While he sometimes felt smothered inside his organization, he has recognized the tremendous potential of all the resources that large multinationals bring to the table. If those resources can be directed to good purposes, he believes they can have a huge positive impact. He was happy to reach early retirement, and go to work for an environmental NGO. His first order of business: a phone call to his former company enlisting its support.

Table 41. StewartShip: We "really" are the world		
Need states	**Values**	**Catalysts**
Global citizens Making a difference	Appropriateness Influential Integration Interdependence Self-expression Thoughtfulness Transcendence	Consumer augmentation Emerging markets arise Empowered individuals Living within limits Relocalization Sustainable consumption

Committed-time activities

Work

Stewart is able to live comfortably off his retirement nest egg. He worked hard and saved well in anticipation of an early "retirement," and his plans fell into place nicely. He readily admits that retirement is an obsolete concept for him—he plans to keep on working as long as he's able. He already had his next move to the NGO mapped out and barely missed a beat, although he did sneak in a month-long ecotourist vacation with his wife in between. One of his principal projects is starting a microfinance foundation, and his connections in the corporate realm have proved valuable in making this happen.

Household and family care

While he is financially comfortable, the family is living on a real budget now, especially given the kids' plans for graduate school. Stewart wavered a bit on his plan when he realized how much it would cost. But his wife has taken on part-time work and that enabled him to stay the course. Part of that is necessary to feed their indulgence of frequent visits to the campus. They love the college atmosphere and they also find it necessary to "check up" on the kids. They have been accused of being helicopter parents, but they don't mind. They feel their kids have turned out really well—in spite of them!

Shopping

Stewart is generally a careful and informed shopper. It's not that he's cheap—he is not a price shopper—but he tends to be a little obsessive about knowing the background information of the products he buys and the organizations he does business with. He does his homework. He wants to be sure that his money supports his values. He is particularly interested in the origins of a product and is very pleased to support small businesses in emerging markets, such as fair trade coffee and TenThousandVillages.com.

Personal/biological necessities

Stewart was among the first to be aware of the carbon footprint issue and today seeks to be footprint-neutral in his choices. He acknowledges that he used to drive the corporate travel people crazy with his insistence that they provide a carbon offset option—in a tribute to his powers of persuasion, his organization was one of the first to do so.

There are so many simple choices that people can make. For instance, he uses a push mower instead of a power mower, a rake instead of a leaf blower, low-flush toilets, and a water-saving shower. The compost pile out back avoids the need for harmful chemical fertilizers—and the list goes on.

Free-time activities

Learning

Stewart's main education passion is to learn about other cultures. He loves to travel, primarily as an ecotourist, or in connection with some sort of business. His concern about carbon footprints means he doesn't take travel lightly—he doesn't travel just for pleasure. He offsets his carbon, and he likes to think he leaves wherever he visits a better place. He usually takes language classes in advance of the places he visits as he feels that he connects better with the locals and colleagues when he understands the basics of the language.

Leisure (entertainment/recreation)

Stewart tries to stay connected to the Yankees, but it seems to get tougher every year. He loves going to the park and experiencing the live event, but he's found himself more frequently relying on his handheld for updates on the score. He does a little walking and cycling—being in nature is always a favorite thing to do. He really enjoys sailing, but it's been several years since he's gotten to do it. In general, he prefers to get away from the hustle and bustle of daily life when he can: the simple things—playing Scrabble® with the kids, enjoying a good book.

Affiliation

Stewart joined the Unitarian church several years ago. He likes the "big umbrella" and its relaxed approach. It attracts a wide range of people from different backgrounds with really interesting views. It's so different from the dogmatic approach of the church he grew up in—even though he didn't attend very regularly, it did not inspire him. He's surprised to find himself back in church, but like many of his friends, he gets a sense of comfort from it.

Communications

Stewart uses technology to communicate but is fond of saying that he prefers old-fashioned face-to-face communication. He finds that virtual communication ends up stimulating his desire to meet more people. He laughs at the idea that they substitute for in-person communication—rather, they multiply it—but it has helped him to do his work more effectively although he still prefers human contact. For instance, he adapted a corporate training workshop he used to do on retirement savings for the general public. He developed an online version but never felt it had the same impact. He really enjoys doing it once again, working directly with people at the community center.

Day-in-the-life vignette

Stewart couldn't wait to get off the plane and hit the ground running. He'd heard from his team that the villages where they were going to launch the microfinance pilot program were really excited by the possibilities. This sure was going to be different than doing a deal on Wall Street, but he was glad he'd left that all behind. When he thought about it, his transformation probably started sometime after his church's mission trip to Haiti. He didn't go soft or anything... if anything, it reinforced his belief that free markets and commerce were the only answer. What it did do was make him realize that he could make a real difference. So... he took the nest egg he'd made in 20 years in the corporate world, set up a little foundation, and was going to do his part to bring people into the fold of the global economy by spreading the incredible power of the microloan.

Stewart's motto:
"We are all responsible"

HIGH TECH TINA: GLASS HOUSES

Tina thinks of herself as high tech– high touch. Her appearance might suggest a granola-eating, touchy-feely type, but watch out. She is very sophisticated in using technology in pursuit of her goals. While she came somewhat late to the technology world, she recognized its power as a difference-maker—it's about how to harness it in the right direction for the right purposes.

Demographics

<u>Sex</u>: Female

<u>Age</u>: 61

<u>HHI</u>: $65,000

<u>Education</u>: BA

<u>Life stage</u>: Empty-nester, husband retiring

Her grandchildren piqued her interest in the power of technology. She had always cherished the role of being something of a consumer activist. She organized boycotts, worked to protect local community interests, and was politically active. But she always felt outnumbered and overwhelmed. She remembers the day when her granddaughter was showing off a school project and the light bulb went off. Now here was an equalizer, at last!

Table 42. High Tech Tina: Glass houses		
Need states	**Values**	**Catalysts**
Expanding accountabilities The truth, whole truth, and nothing but the truth Trusted partners for the new insecurity	Authenticity Assistance Commitment Community Integration Questioning Skepticism Sustainability	Continuum of ownership Emerging markets arise Empowered individuals Living within limits Relocalization Sustainable consumption Truth and truthiness

Committed time activities

Work

Tina has had a long and satisfying career as a community college professor in political science. She had always instilled a sense of activism in her students—and she practiced what she preached. Some thought her a bit extreme, but even if they disagreed with her, they admired her passion. She has never been content to hide in the ivory tower. Her activism sometime troubled the administration, but they couldn't argue that she was perhaps the most popular instructor they had. She spent many of her nonwork hours working with the Watchtower Group, a consumer watchdog agency that monitored corporate malfeasance.

Household and family care

Tina has made the adjustment and enjoys the empty nest. Her great joy is spending time with her grandchildren. She never misses an opportunity to be with them, and her busy children are grateful for her help. They joke that she might as well move back in with them and have offered to build her a "granny flat." It sounds funny to her when she hears "granny"—after all, 60 is the new 50, or is it 40? She doesn't feel that old. Her place looks like kids are living there, and it makes her feel good to see toys strewn about the place. She has often thought of retiring to a warmer climate, but she can't imagine being away from the family.

Shopping

Tina is not much of a shopper. She usually doesn't have time for it, and she admits that neither she nor her husband is a great cook, so they eat out a lot. They are not foodies, for sure, so their primary criterion is atmosphere. But when she knows the grandkids are coming, she'll order up food online and have it delivered. In fact, she's found herself using online ordering for more and more things. She's become pretty adept at it and really cherishes the convenience.

Personal/biological necessities

She brings her watchdog mentality to the companies she does business with. She has adapted her monitoring techniques at work to her personal life. She cross-compares and checks up on all companies she does business with, as she does not want to be caught in the embarrassing situation of supporting an organization that she might later be working against.

She is a minimalist in terms of personal care. She prefers natural products and solutions where available but will not go to extremes. For her, convenience is the trump card. She believes in environmental protection, for example, but she'll compromise on that if saving time is involved.

Free-time activities

Learning

Her grandson has been teaching her mashups with Google Maps. She is astounded by the power of satellites and GPS. Being a teacher, she feels that she spends enough time in the classroom. She learns by doing and finds her grandkids a rich source of what's new and exciting. She likes to practice what she preaches in the classroom through her consumer and political activism. She's been toying with a book idea along the lines of "Activism in the Digital Age." She's queried a few publishers, but her grandkids are urging her to self-publish on the Internet and make it freely available for download.

Leisure (entertainment/recreation)

Tina does spend a lot of her free time doing her activist work. When she can, she enjoys being outdoors, ranging from easy hikes to occasional kayaking. She's noticed that spending so much time on the computer has led her to be entirely too sedentary, and she's put on a few extra pounds. She is not an exercise fanatic, so she needs to find activities that she enjoys that keep her on the move and active. There aren't enough protest marches these days to keep her in shape.

She's also "working" on a family genealogy and has managed to trace back four generations of family so far. Her Internet skills have served her well. When she's done, she's planning a physical trip to catalog the various locations. Again, the grandkids have suggested she create a blogsite that will chronicle not only the family past but the family present and future as well.

Affiliation

She occasionally attends the Friends Church (Quaker), although she is not too strict about that. She enjoys the calming effect it has on her to be among the congregation, and she really loves the events that they occasionally put together. She is a member of several activist groups. She is plugged into the community to the extent that she is quickly made aware of the latest group to form around an issue. She recognizes the need to capitalize on energy when it emerges around an issue, and will jump around as appropriate, while maintaining a few long-term relationships in the causes she deeply believes in.

Communications

Tina is careful about what she shares publicly. She may be Web-savvy, but she does not share the younger generation's less strict views about privacy. She is not above believing in the occasional conspiracy—maybe that's why The X-Files is her favorite TV show of all time. For example, she keeps her Facebook profile closed except to friends that she knows and can grant access to. She never provides her social security number online, which has caused her a problem or two. But she is not easily cowed, and in a battle of wills, people would be best advised not to bet against her.

Day-in-the-life vignette

It was fitting, she thought, that they launched their NGO on the 40th anniversary of Woodstock. It was where she and James met. They were so young then, but man, if they'd had the technology they have now back then.

The NGO—called the Watchtower Group—is going to build a web tool to help individuals track the social performance of their investments in real time. Users enter their stock and mutual fund holdings and pick from a list of 50-plus issues that they care about—such as the company's stance on fair trade, treatment of employees, environmental record, local vs. global sourcing, etc. They get a baseline report as well as real-time alerts. They'd also get the option to ping the investor relations departments to voice their support… or displeasure.

Tina's motto:
"Trust, but verify"

Key points

- The seven emerging meta-needs are brought to life in the form of seven future personas, which are representative characters that fit the profile of someone who has that meta-need.

- Each persona is described according to a summary description, demographics, an illustration, supporting need states, values, related catalysts, how they would likely pursue various activities, and finally, a brief day-in-the-life vignette, and a representative motto.

- The personas provide a tangible example of what future consumers who have the emerging need states will look like. While there will be a wide range of consumers who may have one or more of the aspects described, the examples are intended to help market researchers, product developers, and business strategists have a more tangible target to work toward.

8

CUSTOMIZING THE PERSONAS: PERSONA CONSTRUCTION KIT

This chapter is for those who would like to customize the seven personas from the previous chapter to better fit the specific context, customers or markets of their organization. The seven personas are intended to be generic and were developed with the understanding that they would be more useful with fine-tuning to suit a particular organization, markets, customers, products, etc. This chapter describes a "how-to process" for this customization.

The kit concept reflects a dish that the organization can prepare and cook itself, using the ingredients and recipe provided here. The seven personas were created using a minimum template—the basic recipe—that is often the basis for consulting project work. It contains the minimum basic amount of information to convey the essence of a persona in a useful way. Most of the time in our practice, the ingredients are varied according to needs of the particular client.

The process is iterative. One set of changes to ingredients has implications for the other ingredients. It's a personal preference whether you make changes along the way, or prefer to finish a round of changes and then double back to incorporate the effects throughout.

An important point is to start with a clear focus. This may sound obvious, but subtle differences here can be important. Some detail may have to be sacrificed in exchange for keeping the essence of the persona clear and memorable.

THE PROCESS

A workshop format is described to generate the customized personas. It is not the only way. A key aspiration is to get stakeholders involved and thereby increase the chances of buy-in down the road. People are less likely to disregard or criticize work if they had a hand in creating it.

To set expectations, people should not anticipate that the personas will be done by the end of the workshop, but will be further refined offline, and then the final product can be fed back to the group afterward. This is to make sure the group agrees with the changes and again supports buy-in.

There can be variations to the process described here that accommodate different levels of interest and time available.

Timing also assumes small groups (3–7 participants each) working on one persona. Following this ideal approach suggests a group of 20 people if the goal is to customize all seven. To reduce time, it may not be necessary to customize all seven. Groups can also customize more than one. This would probably add another hour or 90 minutes to the three-hour customization process—it won't take a full three hours to do another as the groups will likely be more efficient the second time around.

Three tasks are suggested to prepare:

1. Decide on the time and activities.

2. Prepare the materials.

3. Customize the script.

1. **Decide on the time and activities**

Quick and dirty	Explain personas only and then tweak.	3 hours
	Explain need states, then personas, and then tweak.	4 hours
	Explain inner and outer dimensions, need states, personas, and then tweak.	5 hours
The Full Monty	Explain model, inner and outer dimensions, need states, personas, and then tweak.	6 hours (or extend to whole day)

A sample "Full Monty" agenda with all the items is below, with the minimum time estimate. In other words, each module is estimated in terms of the least amount of time to sufficiently cover the material.

9:00   Inner Dimensions of Consumer Life

• Explanatory model of the inner dimensions of consumer life.

9:30   Needs-Values-Worldviews: Changes

• Explain changes in needs-values-worldviews.

10:00   Outer Dimensions: Mapping the Landscape

• Survey of key changes in outer dimensions of consumer life, e.g., lifestyle/culture, technological, economic, political, work and business, etc.

10:30   Emerging Need States and Resulting Personas

• Patterns of common needs that define core product/service/experience requirements.

12:00   Lunch

1:00   Persona Construction Kit

- Tips on how to customize generic personas via a how-to kit that can be used with your organization after the meeting.

4:00   Meeting Adjourns

2. Prepare the materials

The following materials should be prepared in advance:

- *Posters*: Posters for all the materials can be prepared, but at a minimum, the seven personas need to be created in poster form. It is recommended that they be printed in a size that covers a standard round table. (Please contact author ahines@uh.edu for access to electronic files.) We suggest printing one set of color posters for display in the workshop room so participants can familiarize themselves with them before the workshop or during breaks. The working versions can be black and white and have spaces for customization.

- *Stickers*: We recommend that any extra content to be added (described below) be applied to the poster in sticker format. Printing simple Avery® labels works fine; even quicker would be to print, cut, and tape, but the stickers provide a measure of convenience and consistency, and less time and mess.

- *Handouts*: These are clearly labeled guides to literally visit each piece of the persona poster real estate with instructions and options for what to do in each spot.

- Pencils for marking the posters directly.

3. Customize the script

The estimated timing for the customization piece of the workshop is roughly three hours (from 1:00–4:00 in the "Full Monty" version):

1. Introduce the personas (20 minutes).

2. Need states, values, and catalysts (20 minutes).

3. Demographic adjustments to preordained targets (30 minutes).

4. Generate list of appropriate activities and describe (60 minutes).

5. Identify additional items that are important and then describe (30 minutes).

6. See if all the changes fit and tweak initial description as needed (20 minutes).

1. Introduce the personas (20 minutes)

This approach suggests that small groups each do one persona. Even though they will read and discuss at the table, it is helpful to do the overview of all seven, as it cuts down on the possibility of groups mixing personas. One "danger" is that one persona ends up being modified in such a way that it effectively becomes another—e.g., Good Neighbor Bob is modified in such as way that he ends up looking like Stewart Ship. The process does guard against this to some extent—the overview of all seven is one way to help do that. It's not about overly constraining the customization but to keep clear the distinction between customization and reinvention. There is nothing wrong with reinvention, but it is not the purpose here, which aims to leverage existing work and invest valuable organizational time focused on tweaking and making them applicable—not having to start from scratch.

To review, the core elements of basic persona template (see Figure 11) are these:

- Need states, values, and catalysts

- Demographics

- Illustration (may need to be redone or tweaked in line with changes to demographics)

- Activities

- Motto (often optional)

2. Need states, values and catalysts (20 minutes)

The core need states (listed in Chapter 6) with supporting values (listed in Chapter 4) and catalysts (listed in Chapter 5)—captured in the tables accompanying each persona—should remain largely intact, with perhaps a slight tweak here or there. Beyond that, if it's a major overhaul, then one is in the territory of creating a new persona. This is also a second way to guard against persona creep, by keeping the core of the persona mostly intact. If teams can change half or more of this material, then they are reinventing rather than customizing; again, there's nothing wrong with that, but it's not the purpose here.

3. Demographic adjustments to preordained targets (30 minutes)

In contrast to the above, this component is highly customizable. There is a small degree of an intuitive feel for how the need states, values, and catalysts translate demographically, but it is not scientific or rigorous. Thus, the advice is to modify the demographics to suit particular needs and not to worry too much about how different it might be from the generic persona demographics.

Sometimes the demographics fit established or obvious targets. There may be a desire to create a set of generational personas, such as Gen Xers or Millennials, in relation to an offering. There could also be the goal of describing the existing customer base—along the lines of a segmentation study, or to use them to bring to a life a new, different, or emerging target. If an organization, for example, has not historically done well with, for example, 20-somethings or with a certain ethnic group or income level, these could be the focus of a persona or two.

There are several subcategories that can be tweaked within the demographic profile. The key test here is one of consistency. If, for example, a key values for the persona is less consumption and less emphasis on accumulating wealth, it would be inconsistent for the persona to earn half-a-million dollars a year. Several categories can be modified here to help sharpen the focus on the persona.

4.   Generate list of activities and describe (60 minutes)
The categories of activities provide a key opportunity for customization. The categories for the generic personas are basic to daily life. But most organizations will be looking to understand specific consumers likely to use their products and services in specific situations or while performing specific activities.

We recommend generating the list before the workshop as it could be very time consuming during the workshop. It is likely that the workshop organization and a small core team consisting of participants could generate at least the beginnings of a list offline, and then the group could fine-tune it in the workshop.

The list of key activities should be in relation to the focus of the inquiry. What are the half-dozen or dozen key activities around which one is seeking insight into the consumer? Using the food industry as an example, the focus could have a broad range of something like healthy snacking or a narrow range of something like portable breakfast occasions. For automotive, examples might relate to situations or activities important to a driver, from comfortable seating, to staying safe in traffic, to trying to find a new location. At this point, one can still be fairly generic about these, although it may make sense to later hone in on a particular activity or situation.

Once the list is agreed upon, then the team needs to provide examples of how the persona would likely carry out each of those activities. Using the healthy snacking example, how would the persona likely indulge in it? What representative snacks might they choose? As the list gets filled out, the team will begin to get a feel for what the persona is like. It may take an iteration or two to get it right.

5. Identify additional items that are important and then describe (30 minutes)

The next step is to add some new ingredients to further deepen the understanding of the persona. Teams may decide to go one at a time, deciding whether to keep an item, or to look at all the items and decide which are most relevant, and then select from the pool. It is not necessary to add all of the new ingredients—the key is to include those that provide insight around the issues or basis of the persona customization. It's helpful to think of this in terms of a menu and to select those items that are appropriate to the aspects of the target consumer. Each of the menu items is briefly described below.

Worldviews. The first item to consider is whether there is a particular worldview that seems to fit the profile of the target consumer. As described in Chapter 2, a consumer's worldview is closely related to his or her core needs and values—the three typically sync up.

The worldview examples used here come from Spiral Dynamics. In terms of emerging need states, the choices are fairly simple, as the consumers with these need states are likely to have one of the two newer worldviews—Communitarian or Integral.

- The Communitarian worldview (green on the spiral) fits with postmodern values. Consumers with this worldview join together for mutual growth and awareness. Greens seek peace within the inner self and sustainable health and well-being for the Earth and all its inhabitants. They value participation, and prefer dialogue, relationships, and reaching decisions through consensus, even at the expense of getting things done.

- The Integral worldview (yellow on the spiral) fits with integral values. Consumers with this worldview seek to live fully and responsibly, with flexibility, spontaneity, and functionality as the highest priorities. Yellows believe differences and pluralities can be integrated into interdependent, natural flows, with knowledge and competency superseding rank, power, status, or group. The yellow worldview sees life as being about doing what one can to make things better. They are focused on individual responsibility and pragmatic outcomes. They prefer to go with the flow and are skilled at adapting the worldview that makes sense in the given circumstances.

Styles. There may be occasions where organizations either wish to understand or appeal to a particular style. It could be, for instance, that a planned offering may best appeal to either introverts or extroverts. The recommendation here is to consider thinking styles and/or personality types. It is useful to keep in mind that styles or types do not coincide with the four levels of values (traditional, modern, postmodern, and integral) suggested in this work. As Wilber points out, "horizontal typologies... are not vertical levels... but rather different types of orientations possible at each of the various levels."[159] This degree of granularity may not be needed, and if so, it can be skipped over.

This work uses the KAI and HBDI as surrogates for thinking styles, and the popular Meyers-Briggs types for personality styles. There are many different systems and instruments for both that are excellent as well. Our recommendation is that if your organization has a preferred instrument in either of these areas, to by all means go with it.

- The KAI (Kirton Adaption-Innovation instrument, see http://www.kaicentre. com/). As described on the site, the Adaption-Innovation Theory and its associated psychometric instrument (KAI) provide insight into how people solve problems and interact when making decisions. They place people on a continuum of cognitive styles ranging from adaptor to innovator. The key to the distinction is that the more adaptive prefer their problems to be associated with more structure, and more of this structure to be consensually agreed than do the more innovative. The more innovative are comfortable solving problems with less structure and are less concerned that the structure be consensually agreed than are the more adaptive.

- The HBDI (Herrmann Brain Dominance Instrument, see http://www.hbdi. com/home/index.cfm). As described on the site, the HBDI® (Herrmann Brain Dominance Instrument®) profile is an assessment tool containing 120 questions that provide users with an in-depth understanding of their thinking preferences.

For a quick-and-dirty system, Gerald Haman of Solution People has devised a card-game variation of the fully HBDI system called the Know Your Brain game. For our purposes, the four principal thinking styles are these:

- *Investigator*: characterized by analytical and logical thinking. They are very good at solving a problem, particularly when you know what the problem is. They are also interested in digging deep into the problem and looking for root causes. The weakness of this quadrant is the tendency toward "paralysis by analysis."

- *Creator*: characterized by, of course, creativity, and an emphasis on the big picture and how things fit together. They are able to generate lots of ideas, many of which may seem unclear to folks in other quadrants. The weakness of this quadrant is not being very good at deadlines and following up on all the ideas they generate.

- *Evaluator*: characterized by folks who like to dot the Is and cross the Ts and get things done. They are very organized and like to run the show. The weakness of this quadrant is that they sometimes miss the big picture.

- *Activator*: characterized by the "people" people. They are in tune with what's going on between people in the room and are good at networking and getting along. Because of this, they are good at getting people working together and making things.

The MBTI (Myers-Briggs Type Indicator see http://www.myersbriggs.org). As described on the site, the purpose of this personality inventory is to make the theory of psychological types described by Carl Jung understandable and useful in people's lives. The 16 personality types can be found at http://www.myersbriggs. org/my-mbti-personality-type/mbti-basics/. They are as follows:

- *ISTJ (Inspector)*. Quiet, serious, earn success by thoroughness and dependability. Practical, matter-of-fact, realistic, and responsible. Decide logically what should be done and work toward it steadily, regardless of distractions. Take pleasure in making everything orderly and organized—their work, their home, their life. Value traditions and loyalty.

- *ISFJ (Protector)*. Quiet, friendly, responsible, and conscientious. Committed and steady in meeting their obligations. Thorough, painstaking, and accurate. Loyal, considerate, notice and remember specifics about people who are important to them, concerned with how others feel. Strive to create an orderly and harmonious environment at work and at home.

- *INFJ (Counselor)*. Seek meaning and connection in ideas, relationships, and material possessions. Want to understand what motivates people and are insightful about others. Conscientious and committed to firm values. Develop a clear vision about how best to serve the common good. Organized and decisive in implementing their vision.

- *INTJ (Mastermind)*. Have original minds and great drive for implementing their ideas and achieving their goals. Quickly see patterns in external events and develop long-range explanatory perspectives. When committed, organize a job and carry it through. Skeptical and independent, have high standards of competence and performance—for themselves and others.

- *ISTP (Crafter)*. Tolerant and flexible, quiet observers until a problem appears then act quickly to find workable solutions. Analyze what makes things work and readily get through large amounts of data to isolate the core of practical problems. Interested in cause and effect, organize facts using logical principles, value efficiency.

- *ISFP (Composer).* Quiet, friendly, sensitive, and kind. Enjoy the present moment, what's going on around them. Like to have their own space and to work within their own time frame. Loyal and committed to their values and to people who are important to them. Dislike disagreements and conflicts; do not force their opinions or values on others.

- *INFP (Healer).* Idealistic, loyal to their values and to people who are important to them. Want an external life that is congruent with their values. Curious, quick to see possibilities, can be catalysts for implementing ideas. Seek to understand people and to help them fulfill their potential. Adaptable, flexible, and accepting, unless a value is threatened.

- *INTP (Architect).* Seek to develop logical explanations for everything that interests them. Theoretical and abstract, interested more in ideas than in social interaction. Quiet, contained, flexible, and adaptable. Have unusual ability to focus in depth to solve problems in their area of interest. Skeptical, sometimes critical, always analytical.

- *ESTP (Promoter).* Flexible and tolerant, they take a pragmatic approach focused on immediate results. Theories and conceptual explanations bore them—they want to act energetically to solve the problem. Focus on the here and now, spontaneous, enjoy each moment that they can be active with others. Enjoy material comforts and style. Learn best through doing.

- *ESFP (Performer).* Outgoing, friendly, and accepting. Exuberant lovers of life, people, and material comforts. Enjoy working with others to make things happen. Bring common sense and a realistic approach to their work and make work fun. Flexible and spontaneous, adapt readily to new people and environments. Learn best by trying a new skill with other people.

- *ENFP (Champion).* Warmly enthusiastic and imaginative. See life as filled with possibilities. Make connections between events and information very quickly, and confidently proceed based on the patterns they see. Want a lot of affirmation from others and readily give appreciation and support. Spontaneous and flexible, often rely on their ability to improvise and their verbal fluency.

- *ENTP (Inventor).* Quick, ingenious, stimulating, alert, and outspoken. Resourceful in solving new and challenging problems. Adept at generating conceptual possibilities and then analyzing them strategically. Good at reading other people. Bored by routine, will seldom do the same thing the same way, apt to turn to one new interest after another.

- *ESTJ (Supervisor)*. Practical, realistic, matter-of-fact. Decisive, quickly move to implement decisions. Organize projects and people to get things done. Focus on getting results in the most efficient way possible. Take care of routine details. Have a clear set of logical standards; systematically follow them and want others to do so as well. Forceful in implementing their plans.

- *ESFJ (Provider)*. Warmhearted, conscientious, and cooperative. Want harmony in their environment and work with determination to establish it. Like to work with others to complete tasks accurately and on time. Loyal, follow through even in small matters. Notice what others need in their day-to-day lives and try to provide it. Want to be appreciated for who they are and what they contribute.

- *ENFJ (Teacher)*. Warm, empathetic, responsive, and responsible. Highly attuned to the emotions, needs, and motivations of others. Find potential in everyone and want to help others fulfill their potential. May act as catalysts for individual and group growth. Loyal, responsive to praise and criticism. Sociable, facilitate others in a group, and provide inspiring leadership.

- *ENTJ (Field Marshal)*. Frank, decisive, assume leadership readily. Quickly see illogical and inefficient procedures and policies; develop and implement comprehensive systems to solve organizational problems. Enjoy long-term planning and goal setting. Usually well informed, well read; enjoy expanding their knowledge and passing it on to others. Forceful in presenting their ideas.

Other influences. The last set of items to consider derive from the Inner Dimensions described in Chapters 2 and 3.

Emotions. Is there a specific emotion or emotional situation you want to appeal to, such as excitement?

- Disgust

- Fear

- Happiness

- Sadness

- Surprise

- Contempt

- Embarrassment

- Guilt

- Shame

- Envy

Roles. It may be, for instance, that you are appealing to consumers as parents.

- Sexual

- Generational

- Occupational

- Marital

- Parental

Skills. Do the consumers need to have a certain skill level or does the product/service need to be modified to fit the skill level of existing consumers? This work uses a grouping of four sets of skills devised by Brian Hall in his book *Values Shift*.[160]

- *Instrumental*: Read, write, and count; speak clearly and correctly; think logically; coordinate your physical self; master new skills in your profession; retain primary information sources; be competent in your work; logically integrate and process new technical data; manage a given amount of money per year; diet, exercise, and keep physically fit.

- *Interpersonal*: Show and share emotions appropriately, identify feelings accurately, identify another person's feelings accurately, state anger objectively; objectify your own and others' feelings and hold others accountable, articulate personal goals, remain calm in times of stress and anxiety, affirm the worth of others, project your imagination into another's world, be present with someone who is dying and reflect their feelings in a way that increases their comfort level, be creatively assertive, cope with conflict.

- *Imaginal*: Make your values conscious; combine and adapt new information; initiate totally new ideas from seemingly unrelated data; perceive hidden meaning in standard data; dream and imagine new futures that are possible; generate new ideas and images; utilize several modes of communication, such as poetry, music and dance.

- *System*: Use money as means; move comfortably with process; differentiate in small group settings between interpersonal and system needs; clarify group complexity; synthesize complex data, statements, and emotional input; set priorities creatively in the face of internal and external pressures; speak with clarity and be understood by people of different educational levels, cultures, and walks of life; engage in long-term system planning and goal setting; make sense of disparate data and see new possibilities; set limited design criteria.

Cultural (civilization): Is there a particular culture that you wish to appeal to— e.g., the Chinese (a.k.a. Confucian) market? This work uses the eight civilizations or culture identified by Huntington in his classic Clash of Civilizations:

- *Western (European, North American)*. Centered in Europe and North America.

- *Confucian (China and most of Southeast Asia)*. The common culture of China and Chinese communities in Southeast Asia. Includes Vietnam and Korea.

- *Japanese (Shinto, Buddhist, Confucian)*. Japanese culture as distinctively different from the rest of Asia.

- *Islamic (Arab, Turkic, Malay)*. Originating in the Arabian Peninsula spread across North Africa, Iberian Peninsula and Central Asia. Arab, Turkic, Persian and Malay are among the many distinct subdivisions within Islam.

- *Hindu*. Identified as the core Indian civilization.

- *Slavic-Orthodox*. Centered in Russia. Separate from Western Christendom.

- *Latin American*. Central and South American countries with a past of a corp-oratist, authoritarian culture. Most of its countries have a Catholic majority.

- *African*. While the continent lacks a sense of a pan-African identity, Hunting-ton claims that Africans are also increasingly developing a sense of African Identity.

Generations: It may be that a specific generation is being targeted. This work uses the U.S. generational profiles developed by Strauss and Howe as an example. The pattern of four generational archetypes coincides with the unfolding of a longer 80-year cycle composed of four eras, or "Turnings," that last about 20 years and always arrive in the same order with the same pattern of archetypes.[162]

- *Boomers (Prophet archetype)*. The First Turning is the High, a period of confident expansion as a new order takes root after the old has been swept away. The most recent High, which celebrated the end of World War II, was from 1946 to 1964, when today's "Prophet" baby boomers were born. These people grew up as increasingly indulged post-Crisis children, came of age as the narcissistic young crusaders of an Awakening, cultivated principles as moralistic midlifers and have emerged as wise elders guiding the next Crisis.

- *Xers (Nomad archetype).* The Second Turning is the Awakening, a time of spiritual exploration and rebellion against the now-established order. The most recent Awakening, characterized by the hippie culture rebellion in the 1960s was when the "Nomad" Generation X was born. Nomads are the underprotected children of an Awakening. They came of age as alienated young adults, mellowed into pragmatic midlife leaders during a Crisis, and aged into tough post-Crisis elders.

- *Gen Y or Millennials (Hero archetype).* The Third Turning is the Unraveling, an increasingly troubled era in which individualism triumphs over crumbling institutions. According to Strauss and Howe, America is currently in an Unraveling that began around 1984 and should have culminated around 2004. The "Hero" Millennial Generation is born. Heroes grow up as increasingly protected post-Awakening children, come of age as the heroic young team workers of a Crisis, demonstrate hubris as energetic midlifers, and emerge as powerful elders attacked by the next Awakening.

- *Gen Next??? (Artist archetype).* The Fourth Turning is the Crisis, when society passes through a great and perilous gate in history. The future "Artist" generation will then be born. Artists grow up as overprotected children during a Crisis, come of age as the sensitive young adults of a post-Crisis world, break free as indecisive midlife leaders during an Awakening, and age into empathic post-Awakening elders.

6. See if all the changes fit and tweak initial description as needed (20 minutes)

Do all the changes fit? This time is used to take a step back and see if all the additions and tweaks make sense when viewed together. Any conflicting pieces can be resolved here. For example, the age of a persona could have been set at 60, but later the group might decide to focus on the Gen Y "heroes." It may lead to some further adjustments and reconciliations. It may even lead to a tweak of the original description. If there have been significant changes to the persona, it might be helpful to sketch a new illustration.

In sum, the goal of this customization process is to create personas that approximate specific targets of the organization. The seven model personas are built from the research done in support of this work and thus have value as previews of future consumers. The approach is intended as an efficient way to build them with a readily available menu of "parts" to add or switch, thus it should be much faster than building personas from scratch. There are several timing options available to fit the needs of the organization.

Perhaps the principal challenge of this approach is to keep focused on customization and not reinvention. The choices of personas to customize, therefore, need to be "close enough" to the intended target where it is a matter of tweaking. The groups also need to be instructed to focus on what is really important to customize, that is, they need to know which menu items are important to add and which can be ignored. In other words, to focus on those items that really matter, and they should not get caught up in adding things just because they are there as this might distract from the important elements and blur the focus of the persona.

Key points

- This chapter provides a step-by-step guide for customizing the seven generic personas from the previous chapter to better fit with specific organizational consumers and needs. The generic personas are a good place to start, and using them as is is better than not using personas at all. Any organization is going to have different products, services, offerings, and customers, so it makes sense to customize the personas to fit those specific needs.

- In addition to the customization, "extra" types of information are provided as optional pieces to further deepen and enrich the personas. This is another opportunity to provide specificity for a particular organization. Most organizations will be skeptical of any generic segmentations, so the customization helps address that concern.

- Various options for the process are provided to accommodate different organizational needs, from quick and dirty to more comprehensive approaches. This is a convenience measure that recognizes that this area of concern/ activity will have a different level of priority in different organizations. For some it may be half-day activities, for others it could be the beginning of a major strategic revamping of their customer strategy.

9

CONCLUSION

This work is intended to fill a void in consumer understanding. First, because the consumer landscape is so complex and understanding it so daunting, it can be tempting to just give up, or to use the "spaghetti test" strategy of tossing a lot of offerings out there and see what sticks. The research here suggests that simply won't work in the emerging consumer landscape. The consumers driving change want authentic connections with the organizations they choose to do business with or associate with. They want to be heard and understood, not treated as lab rats.

Second, the consumer landscape is changing but in ways that are understandable if one is armed with the model, theory, and data provided in this work. The *New Dimensions of Consumer Life Model* provides a comprehensive framework around which to explore these changes, characterized as "the rethink." While the focus is on consumers, the findings here are applicable to "citizens" in general. This emerging consumer landscape is not incomprehensible; rather the outlines of it are quite clear.

The values changes at the heart of the consumer shift have been gaining momentum over the last generation. This work suggests that a critical mass is likely within the next decade. The postmodern and integral values that are the leading edge of change today will increasingly be seen as the mainstream in the affluent W1 nations. I hope that my clients who've heard and understood this message over the years have been making the necessary changes and are syncing up their organizations to be in tune with the emerging consumer landscape. I think they are, and seeing that this can work gave me the confidence to share these ideas with a much wider audience—the readers of this book.

This book was written to inspire action. The previous chapter captured the step-by-step mechanics of what to do. But my feeling is that unless the magnitude of these coming changes is grasped, the call to action will find itself on the bottom of ever-growing to-do lists and never make it to the top. Thus, the bulk of this work makes the case for change. The intent has been to paint as clear a picture as possible of how the future will be different. This detail is important as the future is viewed by most as some sort of nebulous, uncertain, and frankly scary terrain. Painting a picture of the future with detail helps demystify it, make it seem more real, less daunting, and perhaps even friendly. Readers can hopefully see themselves in this future. Perhaps they know someone like Good Neighbor Bob, or maybe they personally identify with Free Spirit Faith? At the very least, the goal has been to create personas that people can imagine emerging in the future. And perhaps most importantly, having this picture or image of the future would get the creative wheels turning and inspire ideas as to how one's business, school, government agency, or nonprofit could align themselves with a persona or personas.

Perhaps the most challenging aspect of the changes described here is that the emerging consumer landscape is not likely to be very kind to those caught in the "old paradigm." The activist orientation of the postmodern and integral consumers will have little time for those organizations trapped in the past. There will simply be too many other options to pursue. To speculate a moment on where these changes are taking us, the divide between customer and business, client and agency, student and teacher, and consumer and citizen will get increasingly blurry; "us and them" is evolving toward "we."

RECAP

At the core of the rethink are shifts toward postmodern values and in the distance behind those, integral values—reinforced by the Great Recession. In this work, these changes in values are combined with related external trends and captured in the form of emerging need states and future personas. Five key themes form the core of these changes: note the acronym "A CASE": *Authenticity, Connection, Anti-consumerism, Self-expression,* and *Enoughness.* Interesting, the Great Recession, rather than putting the brakes on change, appears to be accelerating it.

An important assumption of this work is that values come together in relatively coherent patterns and that understanding values shifts is central to understanding the changes in consumer life. The bulk of the research sources are in Chapters 2, 3, and 4, which lay the conceptual groundwork informing the rest of the analysis. In Chapter 5 on the outer dimensions, the data support comes primarily from research at the level of individual trends and values, which were subsequently synthesized into larger forces of change called catalysts. Chapters 6 and 7 rely on analysis based on the conceptual ideas referenced in the preceding chapters.

Chapter 1, *Introduction*, introduced the work and provided an overview of what the work intended to accomplish.

The next set of chapters in Part One: "Why the Consumer Landscape Is Changing" provided the case for change. It developed a conceptual model and framework for understanding why the consumers are changing.

Chapter 2 introduced the *New Dimensions of Consumer Life Model*, which provides a comprehensive framework to understand consumer life and how it is changing. Its intent is to provide a common understanding to help align organizational understanding of consumer life. The model divides consumer life into an inner and an outer dimension. This chapter focused on the inner dimension, putting identity at the center and suggesting that values, at the core of identity, are the key units for understanding how consumers change. The rest of the inner dimensions model was described and related to values.

Chapter 3 explored the exterior aspects of the inner dimension. Since they are at the boundary between the individual and the outside world, their influence is partly measured and partly subject to interpretation. Individuals are under almost continual pressure to conform to social views of the "right" values and behavior. While these influences are indeed powerful, it is still ultimately individuals who choose which values to hold and how to behave. Finally, a distinction is made between values in general and core values, with core values being those that an individual has acted upon (not just aspirational).

Chapter 4 further developed the research behind the creation of the *New Dimensions Values Inventory*. It overviews 20 previous systems for classifying values. The *New Dimensions Values Inventory* of 110 values, classified into four types: traditional, modern, postmodern, and integral, was described. The link between values and needs and worldviews was made, creating a powerful argument for a developmental model of relatively predictable change over time. A detailed explanation of the characteristics of values and patterns and how they evolve concluded the chapter.

Chapter 5 introduced the outer dimension of consumer life in the form of thirteen catalysts, groups of trends and related consumer values driving change in a particular direction. They were grouped in three sets with common themes: (1) *Engaged consumers*: Consumers shifting from a passive to an active orientation (2) *Blurring boundaries*: Consumers facing new challenges and opportunities in navigating the emerging virtual world and (3) *Bounded consumption*: Consumers confronting new limits to their lifestyle choices. Each catalyst was introduced and described, the key drivers behind it identified, and examples of what it looks like in the present were provided.

The second part, "What the Changing Consumer Landscape Will Look Like," built upon the theory described in the first part to paint a picture of how the future consumer landscape will be different. It mapped the future in two different ways, identifying emerging consumer need states, and then developing representative personas to help bring those need states to life. Finally, it provided a mechanism for individuals and organizations to customize the personas for their specific purposes.

Chapter 6 defined need states as needs within a specific context, situation, or set of activities, e.g., needs around breakfast, noting that they provide an excellent target around which market researchers, product developers, and business strategists can devise plans. The 23 emerging need states were identified with one to three core needs, supplemented by three to five related values (the inner dimension component), and intersecting with two to four catalysts (the outer dimension component). Each need state was introduced and described with its components. Examples of how it shows up in consumer life were provided as well as an interpretation of what it means. The 23 specific emerging need states were grouped into seven meta-needs or needs that cut across a wide swath of consumer life.

Chapter 7 brought the seven emerging meta-needs to life in the form of seven future personas, which are representative characters that fit the profile of someone who has that meta-need. Each persona was described with a summary description, demographics, an illustration, supporting need states, values, related catalysts, how they would likely pursue various activities, and finally, a brief, day-in-the-life vignette, and a representative motto. The personas provide tangible examples of what future consumers who have the emerging need states will look like. While there will be a wide range of consumers who may have one or more need state, the examples are intended to help market researchers, product developers, and business strategists have a more tangible target to work towards.

Chapter 8 provided a step-by-step guide for customizing the seven generic personas from the previous chapter to better fit with specific organizational consumers and needs. In addition to the customization, "extra" types of information are provided as optional pieces to further deepen and enrich the personas. Various options for the process are provided to accommodate different organizational needs, from quick and dirty to more comprehensive approaches.

Appendices, glossary, annotated bibliography, references and index conclude the work.

APPENDICES

NEW DIMENSIONS VALUES INVENTORY: VALUES DEFINED

Traditional	Description
Acceptance	Act of assenting or believing.
Authority	Respecting the decisions and role requirements of an institutionalized third party.
Balance	State of equilibrium.
Class	Having or reflecting high standards of personal behavior.
Comfort	Soothing, relaxation, and simple well-being.
Conformity	Adhering to an established or conventional creed, rule, or practice.
Down-to-earth	Practical and realistic.
Duty	Respectful and obedient conduct in fulfilling obligations.
Family-orientation	Family is of primary importance.
Heroism	Conduct exhibited in fulfilling a high purpose or attaining a noble end, often at great personal risk.
Home-orientation	Home is of primary importance.
Ordinariness	Having no special quality or interest, commonplace, unexceptional.
Patriotism	Devoted love, support, and defense of one's country; national loyalty.
Propriety	Conformity to what is socially acceptable in conduct or speech.
Protection	Safety and security.
Religion	Belief in and worship of a god or gods.
Security	Freedom from intentional harm.
Thrift	Careful management, especially of money.
Tradition	Customary pattern of thought, action, or behavior.

Modern

Achievement	Accomplishment of something noteworthy.
Action	Making things happen.
Adventure	Exciting or remarkable experience.
Affordability	Availability within one's financial means.
Ambition	Ardent desire for rank, fame, or power.
Attractiveness	Arousing interest or pleasure.
Belonging	Being part of and enjoying status within a group.
Challenge	Task or other activity requiring special effort or dedication.
Change	To experience or bring about alteration or transformation.
Choice	Options or alternatives.
Competition	Contest for some prize, honor, or advantage.
Confidence	Belief in oneself and one's powers or abilities.
Control	To have authority over oneself or another person or to direct the course of a situation.
Convenience	Freedom from effort or difficulty.
Curiosity	Desire to know.
Determination	Quality of being resolute, with firmness of purpose.
Do-it-yourself	Of or designed for construction or use by amateurs without special training.
Efficiency	Ability to do more with less.
Energy	Capacity for vigorous activity.
Equality	Corresponding in quantity, degree, value, rank, or ability.
Flexibility	Capable of adapting to a situation as needed.
Growth	Increasing capacity of an economy to produce goods and services.
Health	Soundness of body or mind.

Independence	Freedom from the control, influence, support, aid, or the like, of others.
Individuality	Being true to one's unique self.
Luxury	Indulgence in something that provides pleasure, satisfaction, or ease.
Materialism	Preoccupation with or emphasis on material objects, comforts, and considerations, with a disinterest in or rejection of spiritual, intellectual, or cultural values.
Performance	Accomplishment of work, acts, feats, etc.
Practicality	Focus on getting results.
Prestige	Distinction or distinguished reputation.
Pride	Feeling of deep pleasure or satisfaction derived from achievements, qualities, or possessions.
Quality	Superiority, excellence.
Realism	Viewing or representing things as they really are.
Recognition	Special notice or attention.
Resourcefulness	Ability to devise ways and means.
Secularism	Belief that religion should not be involved with the ordinary social and political activities of a country.
Speed	Swiftness in performance or action.
Style	Distinctive manner or custom of behaving or conducting oneself.
Subversion	Undermining the power and authority of an established system or institution.
Technology-orientation	Technology is of primary importance.
Time	Viewing time as a precious commodity.

Postmodern

Access	Freedom or ability to obtain or make use of something.
Appropriateness	Suitably designed for the task at hand and user capabilities.

Authenticity — State of being genuine, not false or an imitation.

Collaboration — Working jointly with others.

Community — Group of people with a common characteristic or interest living or working together within a larger society.

Cool — Fashionably attractive or impressive.

Creativity — Ability to come up with new and interesting ideas.

Customization — To build, fit, or alter according to individual specifications.

Design — Objects and environments thoughtfully constructed according to an aesthetic ideal.

Discovery — Pursuit of and deep interest in the unknown.

Diversity — Inclusion of different types of people, styles, and ideas.

Empowerment — Acquiring the tools, resources, and authority to get a task done.

Enjoyment — Experiencing satisfaction or delight in an activity.

Experiences — Collecting memorable activities instead of or along with material goods.

Experimentation — Trying out a new procedure, idea, or activity.

Fitness — State of being physically fit.

Freedom — Power to determine action without restraint.

Nonconformity — Refusal to adhere to an established or conventional creed, rule, or practice.

Novelty — Something new or unusual.

Open-mindedness — Freedom from prejudice, bigotry, or partiality.

Passion — Deep motivating interest in a topic.

Self-expression — Expression or assertion of one's own personality.

Simplicity — Freedom from intricacy or complexity.

Skepticism — Attitude of doubt or a disposition to incredulity either in general or toward a particular object.

Smartness	Innovations that increasingly shift information and decision-making burdens from the user to a device or service.
Sophistication	Process or result of becoming more complex, developed, or subtle.
Spirituality	Interest in and pursuit of the meaning and purpose of life.
Spontaneity	Acting on natural feeling or impulse, without effort or premeditation.
Sustainability	Reducing the human footprint on the environment while maintaining quality of life.
Thrill-seeking	Searching for a feeling of great excitement and pleasure.
Unconventionality	Not conforming to accepted rules or standards.
Understanding	Showing a sympathetic or tolerant attitude toward something.
Uniqueness	Having no like or equal.
Wellness	Advanced state of physical, emotional, and spiritual well-being.

Integral

Assistance	Seeking technological help in keeping up with increasing mental and physical demands.
Co-creation	Collaboration in the creation or augmentation of design and content, and sharing these creations with peers.
Commitment	State of being bound emotionally or intellectually to a course of action or to another person or persons.
Connectivity	Ability to reach and communicate with others as desired.
Contentment	Comfortable sense of well-being over time.
Functional	Serving an intended or useful purpose.
Influential	Ability to make a difference in an outcome.
Integration	Combining elements into a coherent whole.
Interdependence	Sensitivity to how things depend on each other.

Personalization	Alteration for the preferences of the individual.
Questioning	Characterized by or indicating intellectual curiosity.
Systematic	Methodical, given to having or following a plan.
Thoughtfulness	Characterized by careful reasoned thinking.
Tolerance	Possessing a fair, objective, and permissive attitude toward opinions and practices that differ from one's own.
Transcendence	Ability to rise above a particular circumstance in allegiance to a higher principle or principles.
Vision	Ability to how events or circumstances fit into the bigger picture.

THREE "WORLDS" OF NATIONS

The world's countries can be usefully divided into three groups based on demographic status and economic, human, and technological development. While countries are sorted into these three worlds, there is diversity within the countries. For example, World 2 countries are especially likely to have pockets of World 1 wealth and competency as well as World 3 poverty.

World 1 a.k.a. Affluent Nations

These are the technologically advanced and prosperous nations. With a population of about a billion, these countries produce most of the world's advanced technology. World 1 includes North America, much of Europe, Japan, and countries such as Australia, Israel, and Taiwan. Population growth in World 1 is slow to nonexistent.

Australia, Austria, Belgium, Canada, Denmark, Finland, France, Germany, Hong Kong, Iceland, Ireland, Israel, Italy, Japan, Luxembourg, Netherlands, New Zealand, Norway, Singapore, South Korea, Spain, Sweden, Switzerland, Taiwan, United Kingdom, United States

World 2 a.k.a. Emerging Markets

This is the vast middle, where resources more or less meet the needs of populations. Home to about four billion people, World 2 includes much of Asia, the former Soviet bloc, most of Latin America, and parts of Africa. World 2 is economically interesting as it includes most emerging markets and high-growth economies. World 2 countries include China, Russia, Brazil, Indonesia, and scores of small countries. By 2025, World 2 nations will be home to about five billion people.

Albania, Algeria, Antigua and Barbuda, Argentina, Armenia, Azerbaijan, Bahamas, Bahrain, Barbados, Belarus, Belize, Bolivia, Bosnia-Herzegovina, Botswana, Brazil, Brunei, Bulgaria, Cape Verde, Chile, China, Colombia, Congo–Brazzaville, Costa Rica, Croatia, Cuba, Cyprus, Czech Republic, Dominica, Dominican Republic, Ecuador, Egypt, El Salvador, Estonia, Fiji, Gabon, Georgia, Greece, Grenada, Guatemala, Guyana, Honduras, Hungary, India, Indonesia, Iran, Iraq, Jamaica, Jordan, Kazakhstan, Kuwait, Kyrgyzstan, Latvia, Lebanon, Libya, Lithuania, Macedonia, Malaysia, Maldives, Malta, Mauritius, Mexico, Moldova, Mongolia, Morocco, Namibia, Nicaragua, Oman, Palestine, Panama, Papua New Guinea, Paraguay, Peru, Philippines, Poland, Portugal, Qatar, Romania, Russia, Saint Kitts and Nevis, Saint Lucia, Saint Vincent, Samoa (Western), Saudi Arabia, Seychelles, Slovakia, Slovenia,

Solomon Islands, South Africa, Sri Lanka, Suriname, Swaziland, Syria, Tajikistan, Thailand, Trinidad and Tobago, Tunisia, Turkey, Turkmenistan, Ukraine, United Arab Emirates, Uruguay, Uzbekistan, Vanuatu, Venezuela, Vietnam, Yugoslavia, Zimbabwe

World 3 a.k.a. Poor Nations

Made up of the poorest parts of the world, including many African countries and places like Haiti and Afghanistan. Fast-growing populations, totaling about a billion, are mired in poverty, and will reach about 1.6 billion people by 2025.

Afghanistan, Angola, Bangladesh, Benin, Bhutan, Burkina Faso, Burma, Burundi, Cambodia, Cameroon, Central African Republic, Chad, Comoros, Congo–Kinshasa, Djibouti, East Timor, Equatorial Guinea, Eritrea, Ethiopia, Gambia, Ghana, Guinea, Guinea-Bissau, Haiti, Ivory Coast, Kenya, Laos, Lesotho, Liberia, Madagascar, Malawi, Mali, Mauritania, Mozambique, Nepal, Niger, Nigeria, North Korea, Pakistan, Rwanda, Sao Tome and Principe, Senegal, Sierra Leone, Somalia, Sudan, Tanzania, Togo, Uganda, Yemen, Zambia

GLOSSARY

Archetypes	The gut-level, deep, sense-making stories, deriving from the unconscious and emotive dimensions, that underlie worldviews and collective understanding and sense-making, e.g., Gaia, the American Dream, "Trust in Allah but tie your camel."
Attitudes	A predisposition or orientation (beliefs) with regard to a specific person, thing, or situation, e.g., "I don't trust airlines."
Behavior	What one does; a particular way of acting or conducting oneself that may be viewed as the manifestation of values and attitudes.
Beliefs	Things one holds to be true; an individual's knowledge base, e.g., "I believe in God."
Body	The physical aspect of self.
Character	The set of traits and virtues embodied in actions relating to one's conduct in terms of right and wrong.
Cognitive or	Preferred thinking or problem-solving style, e.g., Herrmann Brain Dominance thinking style instrument/Solution People: Investigators, Creators, Evaluators, Activators.
Cultural codes	According to Rapaille, the unconscious meanings applied to any given thing—a car, a type of food, a relationship, even a country—via the culture in which we are raised, e.g., "The code for health and wellness in America is 'movement'."
Culture	According to Inglehart, a system of attitudes, values, and knowledge that is widely shared within a society and is transmitted from generation to generation, e.g., Huntington's "civilizations": Western, Confucian, Japanese, Islamic, Hindu, Slavic-Orthodox, Latin American, African.

Emotions	Unconscious, biologically driven responses to stimuli, below the threshold of awareness; basic emotions are consistent cross-culturally; e.g., universal emotions: anger, contempt, disgust, envy, embarrassment, fear, guilt, happiness, sadness, shame, surprise.
Ethics	A subset of morals/norms that are codified rules or standards governing the conduct of members of specific groups, e.g., industry and professional codes of ethics.
External	Influences on an individual's values coming from the outside.
Feelings	An interpretation of emotions influenced by the individual's culture.
Generations	Idea of common patterns among a group that follows a historical sequence, e.g., U.S. example: Matures, Boomers, Xers, Millennials.
Genetic pre-	Possessing a gene or genes that increase the odds of having a certain trait or condition disposition.
Happiness	Long-term sense of well-being.
Identity	An individual's comprehension of self as a discrete, separate entity; how individuals define, think about, and describe themselves.
Ideology	A theory, or set of beliefs or principles, especially one on which a political system, party or organization is based, e.g., Communism, Socialism, Democracy.
Imprints	According to Rapaille, the combination of an experience and its accompanying emotions create a memory that subsequently strongly conditions our thought processes and shapes our future actions, e.g., "I'll never forget…"
Intuition	A problem-solving or decision-making approach that unconsciously draws on one's experience to immediately come to understand or know something without reasoning about it.

Life conditions	The context that one finds oneself in; the "best" values are those appropriate to the prevailing life conditions.
Lifestyles	A way of life or style of living that reflects the attitudes and values of a person, group, or culture, e.g., VALS: Innovators, Thinkers, Achievers, Experiencers, Believers, Strivers, Makers, Survivors.
Memory	Ability to store, retain, and recall information.
Mental model	The mind's framework and process for explaining and making sense of how the world works.
Mind	The mental aspect of self.
Moods	A slight but continuous emotional state that influences and activates certain emotions.
Morals/norms	Social, cultural, or community views on right and wrong that provide a guide to appropriate values and conduct for individuals.
Needs	Motivations; necessities; ranging from essential to survival to desires to improve one's life (serve one's purpose), e.g., needs systems from Maslow, Max-Neef, Reiss.
Paradigm	Basic ways of perceiving, thinking and valuing with accompanying set of rules and regulations that constitute a view of reality with an accompanying problem-solving system, e.g., Newton's mechanistic universe, Heisenberg's uncertainty principle.
Personality	The set of distinctive cognitive, emotional, and behavioral traits that distinguish an individual, e.g., Meyers-Briggs Profiles: Introvert-Extrovert, Sensing-Intuitive, Thinking-Feeling, Judging-Perceiving.
Purpose	Overarching goal or motivation, e.g., happiness, pleasure, enlightenment, greatest good, liberty, duty, creative expression, service to a cause.
Traits	Habitual patterns of behavior; a component of character and personality, e.g. shyness, sense of humor.

Values	An individual view about what is most important in life that in turn guides behavior; core personal values are those you think you have, feel at a deep level, and have acted on, e.g., Traditional, Modern, Postmodern, and Integral.
Virtues	The positive traits in relation to what is considered good or proper by the community, e.g., honesty, love, patience.
Worldview	Philosophy or framework that synthesizes the overall perspective from which one sees and interprets the world, e.g., Spiral Dynamics Blue (Order); Orange (Competition); Green (Participation); Yellow (Integration).

ANNOTATED BIBLIOGRAPHY

Barker, J. (1992). Paradigms: *The Business of Discovering the Future*. New York: HarperBusiness.

- Seminal work around the paradigm concept, which he defines as a problem-solving system, which in turn influences one's concept of values.

Beck, D. and Cowan, C. (1996). *Spiral Dynamics: Mastering Values, Leadership, and Change*. Malden, MA: Blackwell.

- Fundamentally important work that provides systemic explanations of how nine vMemes (value memes) a.k.a. worldviews evolve over time in a spiral fashion that alternates from internal to external orientation, in which each worldview builds upon the previous one. While the system is hierarchical, its authors note that an "appropriate" worldview is one that matches the "life conditions" in which an individual finds oneself. They have an assessment instrument and have created a global segmentation of the worldviews.

Beller, K., Weiss, S., and Patler, L. (2005). *The Consistent Consumer: Predicting Future Behavior through Lasting Values*. Sedona, AZ: LTS Press.

- Consulting firm approach that explores values through the lens of generational segments—Value Populations, in their terminology—that differ from traditional segments in emphasizing the unique cultural events and icons that occur during a generation's formative years and lead to different values being emphasized by different generations.

Berger, P. and Luckmann, T. (1967). *The Social Construction of Reality: A Treatise in the Sociology of Knowledge*. New York: Anchor Books.

- Classic work on the inter-subjective nature of reality, that is, reality is what we believe it is. Provides foundational understanding of how we come to understand reality, which in turn relates to how people come to develop their identity and, indirectly, their values.

Brooks, D. (2000). *Bobos in Paradise: The New Upper Class and How They Got There*. New York: Simon & Schuster.

- A somewhat tongue-in-cheek look at how intellectual prowess, rather than wealth or material goods accumulation, is the new measuring stick of status. The title blends the bourgeois world of capitalism and the bohemian counterculture. Provides some insight into the emerging culture context in the United States.

Brown, D. (1991). *Human Universals*. New York: McGraw-Hill.

- Makes the case that cultural anthropology's bias toward the influence of the external environment and cultural relativism has led to a neglect of universals. Some universals seem to be inherent in human nature, while others are cultural conventions that have come to have universal distribution. Culture, worldviews, and myths are universal, but this doesn't explicitly suggest that values are.

Cameron, J. (1992). *The Artist's Way: A Spiritual Path to Higher Creativity*. New York: Tarcher/Putnam.

- Relevance here centers around the discovery of one's purpose, in this case, a plan for discovering and unleashing our personal creativity via exercises and spiritual practice.

Campbell, J. (1949). *The Hero with a Thousand Faces*. Princeton, NJ: Princeton University Press.

- Explores the role of myth as a guiding force in culture. Also talks about the "hero's journey" concept, which is similar to Coelho's quest for one's personal legend. Both suggest a higher purpose which values may serve, and also touch on how values change, as the journey is a transformative process likely to change a person and his or her values.

Capra, F. (1992). *The Hidden Connections: Integrating the Biological, Cognitive, and Social Dimensions of Life into a Science of Sustainability*. New York: Doubleday.

- While the focus of book is on the implications of complexity, it has ties into decision-making and values. For example, it covers how our mental models of the present and future shape what we decide to pay attention to, thus shaping and being shaped by values. Individual mental models and values are in turn influenced by the collective mental model, i.e., the social construction of reality.

Coelho, P. (1988).*The Alchemist*. New York: HarperOne.

- A classic work about identifying and seeking one's purpose in life.

Ekman, P. (2003). *Emotions Revealed: Recognizing Faces and Feelings to Improve Communication and Emotional Life.* New York: Times Books.

- The author has done pioneering work in identifying universal human emotions. He disproved the previous claim that emotions were culture-specific and found that there were seven emotions with universal facial expressions and four others that were universal but with differing facial expressions. This work supports the validity of trying to understand universal or global patterns in values by making the case for universal emotions.

Encyclopedia of World Problems and Human Potential: Human Potential: Transformation and Values, Vol. 2. Union of International Associations, 1991.

- The Encyclopedia is an ongoing effort, begun in 1972, to collect and present information on the problems humanity confronts. It has a section on human values, organized in different ways. One approach, which lists 225 value polarities (constructive and destructive values are paired), is probably the easiest to follow.

Florida, R. (2002). *The Rise of the Creative Class: And How It's Transforming Work, Leisure, Community, and Everyday Life.* New York: Basic Books.

- Coming as if from an economic class perspective, the author essentially describes the postmodern values segment, also identified by Paul Ray at the Cultural Creatives. While both works focus exclusively on the US, the fact that researchers coming from different perspectives are finding common ground in identifying and characterizing this emerging group with shared values reinforces the core findings of the World Values Survey on the postmodern group.

Gendlin, E. (1978). *Focusing.* New York: Bantam.

- Explores the mind-body connection, in particular describing a technique for bringing one's "felt sense" about a topic or challenge to the surface. The felt sense is embedded deeper than emotion, in the sense that we can't access it without "going deeper," which is what the focusing technique enables one to do.

Gilbert, D. (2005). *Stumbling on Happiness*. New York: Vintage.

- Focus around how people imagine their own happiness, with a somewhat snarky tone jesting about our foibles in trying to do so. People are generally more optimistic about their own happiness than perhaps they ought to be in comparison to "reality," but at the same time this is a survival mechanism. The work has solid insights into motivation and decision-making and draws upon psychology, cognitive neuroscience, philosophy, and behavioral economics.

Goffman, E. (1959). *The Presentation of Self in Everyday Life*. New York: Doubleday, 1959.

- An interesting work that points out how the self we present to the outside world is heavily dependent on specific circumstances. For our purposes, values are not simply translated into action perfectly and consistently, but are influenced or perhaps filtered through the requirements of a particular circumstance, among other factors.

Hall, B. (1994). *Values Shift: A Guide to Personal and Organizational Transformation*. Eugene, OR: Wipf & Stock.

- Describes a system of 125 values the author developed in a collaborative effort. It is a development model that includes four phases in which values can emerge over time. Hall has an assessment instrument and uses it to help organizations understand and clarify their values.

Harman, W. (1998). *Global Mind Change: The Promise of the 21st Century*. San Francisco: Berrett-Koehler.

- Makes the case for a fundamental paradigm shift in which society's basic assumptions are being questioned, essentially shifting from a scientific, rational and reductive approach to one that is holistic, intuitive, and more spiritual. One of the better of several works on this theme.

Hawkins, D. (2002, revised). *Power vs. Force: The Hidden Determinants of Human Behavior*. Carlsbad, CA: Hay House.

- Asserts that one can use a form of "behavioral kinesiology" or muscle testing to test the truth or falsity of any statement. This is then used to create a calibrated scale of energy levels of human consciousness, suggesting an evolution from lower to higher levels. Does not directly address the role of values, but provides some interesting ideas on consciousness and decision-making. There are some serious questions on the methodology that one may not, and perhaps should not, get past.

Hines, A. (2006). Review: Inglehart, R. and Welzel, C. (2005). *Modernization, Culture Change and Democracy: The Human Development Sequence*. New York: Cambridge University Press. foresight, 8(3),65–68.

- Author's review of one of Inglehart's key works on the future of values that captures early thinking on several ideas presented in this work.

Hofstede, G. and G.J. (2005, 2nd ed.). *Cultures and Organizations: Software of the Mind*. New York: McGraw Hill.

- Focus is on the cultural level with excellent insight into the influence of culture, and in particular cultural dimensions, focusing in particular on five dimensions that stood out as significant in research survey carried out by the author.

Houston, J. (1982). *The Possible Human: A Course in Enhancing Your Mental, Physical and Creative Abilities*. New York: Tarcher/Putnam.

- How-to guide with lots of exercises to explore the enhancement of human capacities, with an emphasis on the mind-body connection. In particular, seeks to tap the neglected hidden images, ideas and sensory-based memories in order to enhance human potential and creativity.

Huntington, S. (1996). *The Clash of Civilizations and the Remaking of World Order*. New York: Simon & Schuster.

- Elaborates his thesis that people's cultural and religious identities—of which he identified eight groups or "civilizations" —will be the primary source of conflict in the future.

Inayatullah, S. Causal Layered Analysis: Unveiling and Transforming the Future. In Glenn, J. and Gordon, T. (2003). *Futures Research Methodology – V 2.0.*, Washington, DC: AC/UNU Millennium Project.

- Seminal article laying out an approach to depth in future thinking that includes steps for probing beneath the surface of events to understand the deeper driving forces of change, including values, worldview, and archetypes/myths/metaphors.

Inglehart, R. (1997). *Modernization and Postmodernization: Cultural, Economic, and Political Change in 43 Societies*. Princeton, NJ: Princeton U Press.

- Perhaps the single indispensible sourcebook on the topic. Launched the author on this quest a dozen years ago by providing a structure or model for how values change and supporting this with rich longitudinal data. This work is the most focused on laying out the theory. Several subsequent works have elaborated upon and enhanced this seminal work.

Inglehart, R. and Welzel, C. (2005). *Modernization, Cultural Change, and Democracy: The Human Development Sequence*. Cambridge, UK: Cambridge University Press.

- Makes the case for the continuing influence of culture on the expression of values. The author's previous work with World Values Survey has suggested the broad patterns in values changes. This raised the question of whether the globe is heading for a homogenization of values. This work suggests, to the contrary, that culture will continue to have an important influence on the expression of values. Thus two cultures may share the value of simplicity, but how they express it may be quite different.

Joas, H. (2001). *The Genesis of Values*. Chicago: University of Chicago Press.

- Excellent scholarly work that covers a wide range of thinkers—from Nietzsche to Durkheim to Dewey, among others, on the topic of how we come to hold our values. Interestingly, or perhaps disappointingly, few of them come directly at the topic of values, but we get their views as part of their larger philosophies. Nonetheless there are useful insights into the topic and we get a sense of what they think about values, even if it is not a front-and-center concern.

Kegan, R. (1994). *In Over Our Heads: The Mental Demands of Modern Life*. Cambridge, MA: Harvard University Press, 1994.

- Describes the development of one's consciousness or mental capacity over time. This capacity is a key factor to consider in the development of values, as one will be incapable of maintaining a more complex value system if one has not developed the sufficient mental capacity.

Klein, G. (2003). *The Power of Intuition: How to use your Gut Feelings to Make Better Decisions at Work*. New York: Currency Doubleday.

- Makes a compelling case for how intuition is a vital and necessary component of decision-making. He defines intuition as how experience gets translated into action. He also breaks down the decision-making process and outlines the role of mental models in helping us decide and provides us a means of understanding where and how values play a role in decision-making.

Klein, S. (2006). *The Science of Happiness: How Our Brains Make Us Happy—and What We Can Do to Get Happier.* Cambridge, MA: De Capo Press.

- Explores the role of neuroscience and, to a lesser extent, psychology, in happiness. As values are influenced by the pursuit of happiness, understanding it can shed light on the role of values, both from a motivational perspective (choosing values in relation to the pursuit of happiness) and as an influence in decision-making.

Layard, R. (2005). *Happiness: Lessons from a New Science.* New York: Penguin.

- A solid summary of much of the literature on happiness, though it contains more anecdotal observations and beliefs of the author than science. Relating to values, it provides perhaps the key potential motivation, i.e., the pursuit of happiness. The argument is that we choose and hold values—among other things—to maximize our pursuit of happiness.

Lehrer, J. (2009). *How We Decide.* New York: Houghton-Mifflin.

- Excellent and highly readable overview that relates advances in neuro-science to decision-making. Does a nice job of using stories to illustrate the important points.

Lewis, H. (1990). *A Question of Values.* New York: HarperCollins.

- Identifies six mental modes that determine how we come to hold our values. Four of these are internally derived, and two are externally derived. The author includes a list of 74 value systems, ranging from capitalism to Roman Catholicism to deconstructionism, logic, and science, but does not connect these systems to the mental modes' framework that is the subject of the bulk of the book.

Loehr, J. and Schwartz, T. (2003). *The Power of Full Engagement: Managing Energy, Not Time, Is the Key to High Performance and Personal Renewal.* New York: Free Press.

- As the title suggests, the central premise is that managing one's personal energy is a key purpose. The book recommends how to more effectively manage one's energy. Values in this context provide direction and guidance on the appropriate expenditure of one's energy. Includes a values inventory, though in our view, this mixes in other inner dimensions with values.

Maslow, A. (1968, 2nd Ed.). *Toward a Psychology of Being*. New York: Van Nostrand Reinhold Co.

- Focuses on self-actualization as the goal of healthy individuals. Includes a piece on related self-actualizing or "being" values. Notes that deficiency motivation focuses on basic needs, and once these are met the focus shifts to a growth motivation centered on self-actualization needs. Also discusses self-transcendence needs, which fits conceptually with the Integral Values and Worldview in this work.

Mitchell, A. (1983). *The Nine American Lifestyles*, New York: MacMillan.

- Uses a survey sample to devise a typology of nine segments centered on values that are expressed in lifestyles. It is a human development system in which people favor either an inner-directed or an outer-directed path with an integrated lifestyle at the pinnacle of psychological maturity.

Murphy, M. and Leonard, G. (1995). *The Life We Are Given: A Long-Term Program for Realizing the Potential of Body, Mind, Heart, and Soul*. New York: Tarcher/Putnam.

- A conceptual and "how-to" manual for personal transformation. Its description of how to achieve lasting long-term change is relevant to the work here.

Nutt, P. (2002). *Why Decisions Fail: Avoiding the Blunders and Traps that Lead to Debacles*. San Francisco: Berrett-Koehler.

- Readable and entertaining analysis of failed decisions with a clear analysis of why the decisions went awry by one of the leading thinkers in decision science. Nutt identifies three blunders and seven traps behind these failed decisions or debacles. Of particular interest to this work, one of the traps involves values that lurk behind an ethical position but are often not understood nor brought to the surface.

Ogilvy, J. (1979). *Many Dimensional Man*. New York: HarperCollins.

- A deep philosophical tome that tours the ideas of many great thinkers around the idea of the self. The key idea is that the individual is not a single self, but multiple selves.

Pearson, C. (1998, 3rd Ed.) *The Hero Within: Six Archetypes We Live By*. San Francisco: Harper.

- Draws upon Jungian ideas to identify six archetypes that one tends to follow on one's journey of individuation. They are prototypical roles or characters that people commonly follow, with some more or less favored by different cultures. They can be consciously chosen as mechanisms for self-transformation, with the types first identified by diagnostic questions or the author's assessment instrument.

Pink, D. (2005). *A Whole New Mind: Why Right-Brainers Will Rule the Future*. New York: Riverhead Books.

- Great read that is tangentially related to values in that one of six emerging senses or aptitudes includes the "search for meaning," which provides some insight into a possible directionality of values.

Rapaille, C. (2006). *The Culture Code: An Ingenious Way to Understand Why People around the World Live and Buy as They Do*. New York: Broadway Books.

- Focuses on how to uncover people's archetypes or the unconscious meanings they ascribe to various things—in particular focusing on areas of consumer interest. The archetypes are imprinted from a combination of experience and emotion and transmitted via the culture, usually at an early age. The author developed a three-hour workshop technique that identifies the "code" that taps into these imprints so that marketers can design products and services that succeed by tapping into these archetypes.

Ray, M. (2004). *The Highest Goal: The Secret That Sustains You in Every Moment*. San Francisco: Berrett-Koehler.

- Focused around finding one's purpose in life, which the author calls the "highest goal." It has a nice mix of theory, exercises, and case examples.

Ray, P. (2000). *The Cultural Creatives: How 50 Million People Are Changing the World*. New York: Harmony Books.

- In-depth exploration of this segment of US society, which mirrors the postmodern values segment referred to in this text. Readers looking for the short version may want to consult his excellent overview article: Ray, P. H. (February 1997). "The Emerging Culture," American Demographics.

Redfield, J. (1993). *The Celestine Prophecy*. New York: Grand Central Publishing.

- A somewhat clunky adventure story provides the mechanism to reveal nine insights important to an individual or an entire culture's spiritual awakening. Provides some insight into New Age thinking around spirituality and explores the idea that we are on the verge of a massive cultural awakening or transformation as people become aware of these insights.

Rokeach, M. (1973). *The Nature of Human Values*. New York: Free Press.

- Seminal work in the study of values that lays the foundation for much of this work. A comprehensive study that produced a conceptual framework and a significant system of values that remains one of the most influential works on the topic.

Rokeach, M. (1979). *Understanding Human Values: Individual and Societal*. New York: Free Press.

- Collection of articles with a couple that relate to this topic. Rokeach's own piece on how values change is very useful, and a piece by Williams citing Rokeach also covers the topic of how values change as well as some definitional concepts.

Scharmer, C.O. (2007). *Theory U: Leading from the Future as it Emerges*. Cambridge, MA: Society for Organizational Learning.

- A rich and more technical approach to many of the ideas in Presence (described below)—the textbook approach. Covers a lot of ground around purpose and mental models more than values.

Seligman, M. (1998). *Learned Optimism: How to Change Your Mind and Your Life*. New York: Free Press.

- Makes the case for how an optimistic thinking style makes one more successful and a negative style has harmful consequences, such as being more likely to become depressed. Suggests pessimists can learn to be optimists by learning a new set of cognitive skills, centered around combating negative thoughts as they arise.

Senge, P., Scharmer, C.O., Jaworski, J., and Flowers, B.S. (2004). *Presence: Human Purpose and the Field of the Future*. Cambridge, MA: Society for Organizational Learning.

- Emphasizes the need for individuals to question assumptions and see reality for what it is in order to fulfill their purpose. Notes how this kind of work is difficult and unsettling, which supports the notion of values change being difficult.

Simon, S., Howe, L., and Kirschenbaum, H. (1972). *Values Clarification: A Practical, Action-Directed Workbook*. New York: Warner Books.

- The introduction has some useful theory and ideas, and after that covers 73 different strategies, essentially tests or techniques, for individuals to assess their values. It offers an interpretative framework up front, but no help on interpreting how the results one gets from the various tests fit.

Strauss, W. and Howe, N. (1991). *Generations: The History of America's Future, 1584 to 2069*. New York: HarperCollins.

- The essential work on the concept of generations sharing a common ethos. The authors assert that four different types of generations are repeated sequentially in a fixed pattern of roughly one over 20 years for an 80-year cycle and that this pattern has predictive value. They published a follow-up, The Fourth Turning that goes into some of these predictions. I reviewed this work when it came out and found it thoughtful and intriguing, but had some concerns about its predictive power.

Thaler, R. and Sunstein, C. (2008). *Nudge: Improving Decisions about Health, Wealth, and Happiness*. New York: Penguin Books.

- Explores the role of context in influencing decision-making. In particular, shows how setting up a decision, what they call "choice architecture," can influence the results in a favorable way. Determining the default option for a choice, for instance, takes advantage of the role of inertia and thus is an important influence.

Trompenaars, F. (1998). *Riding the Waves of Culture: Understanding Diversity in Global Business*. New York: McGraw Hill.

- Focuses on the influence of culture around five dimensions similar to those identified by Hofstede. It has useful insights into the role of culture in general, but not much specifically on values.

Wilber, K. (1977). *The Spectrum of Consciousness*. Wheaton, IL: Theosophical Publishing House.

- Early work that lays out ideas for how consciousness evolves along a spectrum. Introduces many of the ideas that will be refined in later works. For our purposes, makes the point that one's values are related to one's position on the spectrum of consciousness.

Wilber, K. (2000, 2nd ed.). *Sex, Ecology and Spirituality: The Spirit of Evolution.* Boston: Shambhala, 2000.

- The author's magnum opus (so far) that details his integral philosophy and four-quadrant model for explaining the connectedness of all things in the context of evolutionary human development.

Wilber, K. (1996). *A Brief History of Everything.* Boston: Shambhala.

- An earlier "popularizing" effort that was perhaps less accessible than A Theory of Everything. Provides helpful insights into why people grow—or don't grow—from a human development perspective.

Wilber, K. (2000). *A Theory of Everything.* Boston: Shambhala.

- A popular version summarizing some of his core ideas developed in more detail in several other works. His integral perspective informs this work as an overall orientation to thinking about the topic. Of particular note is that he spends time exploring Spiral Dynamics which is used in this work as an exemplary system of worldviews.

Wilber, K. (2000). *Integral Psychology: Consciousness, Spirit, Psychology, Therapy.* Boston: Shambhala.

- The author applies his philosophy to developmental psychology and, of particular importance to this work, provides some theoretical background and insights to the emergence of postmodernism.

Zaltman, G. (2003). *How Customers Think: Essential Insights into the Mind of the Market.* Boston: Harvard Business School.

- Tremendously insightful into what really drives consumer behavior. Draws upon findings from brain science and the author's successful market research practice to make a convincing case that traditional market research misses a lot, and that one needs to go deeper to really understand how consumers think and decide.

REFERENCES

1. Mitchell, A. (1983). *The Nine American Lifestyles*. New York: MacMillan.

2. Rogers, E. (1962). *Diffusion of Innovations*. Glencoe, New York: Free Press, 150.

3. Hall, B. (1994). *Values Shift: A Guide to Personal and Organizational Transformation*. Eugene, OR: Wipf & Stock, 21.

4. Coates, J. (2004, Sept.-Oct.). *Coming to Grips with the Future from Research*. Technology Management, 47(5), 8.

5. Maslow, A. (1968). *Toward a Psychology of Being, 2nd Ed*. New York: Van Nostrand Reinhold Co., 177.

6. Rokeach, M. (1973). *The Nature of Human Values*. New York: Free Press, 216.

7. Joas, H. (2001). *The Genesis of Values*. Chicago: University of Chicago Press, 149.

8. Berger, P. & Luckmann, T. (1967). *The Social Construction of Reality: A Treatise in the Sociology of Knowledge*. New York: Anchor Books, 49.

9. Layard, R. (2005). *Happiness: Lessons from a New Science*. New York: Penguin, 24, 224.

10. Klein, S. (2006). *The Science of Happiness: How Our Brains Make Us Happy—and What We Can Do to Get Happier*. Cambridge, MA: De Capo Press, 200.

11. Florida, R. (2002). *The Rise of the Creative Class: And How It's Transforming Work, Leisure, Community, and Everyday Life*. New York: Basic Books, 4.

12. Cameron, J. (1992). *The Artist's Way: A Spiritual Path to Higher Creativity*. New York: Tarcher/Putnam, 3.

13. Berger, P. & Luckmann, T. (1967). *The Social Construction of Reality: A Treatise in the Sociology of Knowledge*. New York: Anchor Books, 44.

14. Kauffman, D. (1980). *Systems One: An Introduction to Systems Thinking*. Future Systems.

15. Beck, D. & Cowan, C. (1996). *Spiral Dynamics: Mastering Values, Leadership, and Change*. Malden, MA: Blackwell, 4.

16. Hall, B. (1994). *Values Shift: A Guide to Personal and Organizational Transformation*. Eugene, OR: Wipf & Stock, 43.

17. Houston, J. (1982). *The Possible Human: A Course in Enhancing Your Mental, Physical and Creative Abilities*. New York: Tarcher/Putnam, 2.

18. Houston, J. (1982). *The Possible Human: A Course in Enhancing Your Mental, Physical and Creative Abilities*. New York: Tarcher/Putnam, 5, 33.

19. Klein, S. (2006). *The Science of Happiness: How Our Brains Make Us Happy—and What We Can Do to Get Happier*. Cambridge, MA: De Capo Press.

20. Lehrer, J. (2009). *How We Decide*. New York: Houghton-Mifflin.

21. Zaltman, G. (2003). *How Customers Think: Essential Insights into the Mind of the Market*. Boston: Harvard Business School, 180.

22. Rapaille, C. (2006). *The Culture Code: An Ingenious Way to Understand Why People Around the World Live and Buy as They Do*. New York: Broadway Books, 5.

23. Rapaille, C. (2006). *The Culture Code: An Ingenious Way to Understand Why People Around the World Live and Buy as They Do*. New York: Broadway Books, 8.

24. Zaltman, G. (2003). *How Customers Think: Essential Insights into the Mind of the Market*. Boston: Harvard Business School, 9, 51.

25. Capra, F. (1992). *The Hidden Connections: Integrating the Biological, Cognitive, and Social Dimensions of Life into a Science of Sustainability*. New York: Doubleday, 61.

26. Klein, G. (2003). *The Power of Intuition: How to Use Your Gut Feelings to Make Better Decisions at Work*. New York: Currency Doubleday, 24.

27. Lehrer, J. (2009). *How We Decide*. New York: Houghton-Mifflin, 237.

28. Klein, G. (2003). *The Power of Intuition: How to Use Your Gut Feelings to Make Better Decisions at Work*. New York: Currency Doubleday, 17.

29. Gilbert, D. (2005). *Stumbling on Happiness*. New York: Vintage, 64.

30. Klein, G. (2003). *The Power of Intuition: How to Use Your Gut Feelings to Make Better Decisions at Work*. New York: Currency Doubleday, 28.

31. Scharmer, C.O. (2007). *Theory U: Leading from the Future as it Emerges*. Cambridge, MA: Society for Organizational Learning, xiv.

32. Hofstede, G. & Hofstede, G.J. (2005). *Cultures and Organizations: Software of the Mind. 2nd ed*. New York: McGraw Hill, 2-3.

33. Ekman, P. (2003). *Emotions Revealed: Recognizing Faces and Feelings to Improve Communication and Emotional Life*. Times Books, 46–47.

34. Lehrer, J. (2009). *How We Decide*. New York: Houghton-Mifflin, 89.

35. Klein, S. (2006). *The Science of Happiness: How Our Brains Make Us Happy—and What We Can Do to Get Happier*. Cambridge, MA: De Capo Press, 46.

36. Klein, S. (2006). *The Science of Happiness: How Our Brains Make Us Happy—and What We Can Do to Get Happier*. Cambridge, MA: De Capo Press, 45.

37. Layard, R. (2005). *Happiness: Lessons from a New Science*. New York: Penguin, 57.

38. Beck, D. & Cowan, C. (1996). *Spiral Dynamics: Mastering Values, Leadership, and Change*. Malden, MA: Blackwell, 52.

39. Inglehart, R. (1997). *Modernization and Postmodernization: Cultural, Economic, and Political Change in 43 Societies*. Princeton, NJ: Princeton University Press, 4.

40. Berger, P. & Luckmann, T. (1967). *The Social Construction of Reality: A Treatise in the Sociology of Knowledge*. New York: Anchor Books, 173-174.

41. Williams. R. (1979). *Change and Stability in Values and Value Systems: A Sociological Perspective. In Rokeach, M. Understanding Human Values: Individual and Societal*. New York: Free Press, 15.

42. Barker, J. (1992). *Paradigms: The Business of Discovering the Future*. New York: HarperBusiness, 32.

43. Barker, J. (1992). *Paradigms: The Business of Discovering the Future*. New York: HarperBusiness, 15–16.

44. Jung, C. (1936). The Archetypes and the Collective Unconscious. *Collected Works, Vol 9*, 87–110.

45. Inayatullah, S. (2009). Causal Layered Analysis: An Integrative and Transformative Theory and Method. In Glenn, J. & Gordon, T. (Eds.). *Futures Research Methodology–Version 3.0 CD-ROM*. Washington, DC: The Millennium Project, Chapter 35, 8–9.

46. Strauss, W. & Howe, N. (1991). *Generations: The History of America's Future, 1584 to 2069*. New York: HarperCollins.

47. Hofstede, G. & Hofstede, G.J. (2005). *Cultures and Organizations: Software of the Mind. 2nd ed*. New York: McGraw Hill, 3, 4.

48. Brown, D. (1991). *Human Universals*. McGraw-Hill, 40.

49. Trompenaars, F. (1998). *Riding the Waves of Culture: Understanding Diversity in Global Business*. New York: McGraw Hill, 7.

50. Hofstede, G. & Hofstede, G.J. (2005). *Cultures and Organizations: Software of the Mind. 2nd ed*. New York: McGraw Hill, 3.

51. Williams, R. (1979). *Change and Stability in Values and Value Systems: A Sociological Perspective. In Rokeach, M. Understanding Human Values: Individual and Societal.* New York: Free Press, 21.

52. Inglehart, R. & Welzel, C. (2005). *Modernization, Cultural Change, and Democracy: The Human Development Sequence.* Cambridge, UK: Cambridge University Press, 19.

53. Kluckhohn, C. (1979). *Values and Value Orientation in the Theory of Action. In Rokeach, M. Understanding Human Values: Individual and Societal.* New York: Free Press, 51.

54. Loehr, J. & Schwartz, T. (2003). *The Power of Full Engagement: Managing Energy, Not Time, Is the Key to High Performance and Personal Renewal.* New York: Free Press, 143.

55. Williams, R. (1979). *Change and Stability in Values and Value Systems: A Sociological Perspective. In Rokeach, M. Understanding Human Values: Individual and Societal.* New York: Free Press, 28.

56. Layard, R. (2005). *Happiness: Lessons from a New Science.* New York: Penguin, 57.

57. Loehr, J. & Schwartz, T. (2003). *The Power of Full Engagement: Managing Energy, Not Time, Is the Key to High Performance and Personal Renewal.* New York: Free Press, 142.

58. Mitchell, A. (1983). *The Nine American Lifestyles.* New York: MacMillan, vii.

59. Rokeach, M. (1973). *The Nature of Human Values.* New York: Free Press, 23.

60. Simon, S., Howe, L., & Kirschenbaum, H. (1972). *Values Clarification: A Practical, Action-Directed Workbook.* New York: Warner Books, 3.

61. Lewis, H. (1990). *A Question of Values.* New York: HarperCollins, 8.

62. Inglehart, R. (1997). *Modernization and Postmodernization: Cultural, Economic, and Political Change in 43 Societies.* Princeton, NJ: Princeton University Press, 154.

63. Inglehart, R. (1997). *Modernization and Postmodernization: Cultural, Economic, and Political Change in 43 Societies.* Princeton, NJ: Princeton University Press, 133.

64. Inglehart, R. (1997). *Modernization and Postmodernization: Cultural, Economic, and Political Change in 43 Societies.* Princeton, NJ: Princeton University Press, 31.

65. Joas, H. (2001). *The Genesis of Values.* Chicago: University of Chicago Press, 1.

66. Simon, S., Howe, L., & Kirschenbaum, H. (1972). *Values Clarification: A Practical, Action-Directed Workbook.* New York: Warner Books, 5–10.

67. Rokeach, M. (1979). *Understanding Human Values: Individual and Societal*. New York: Free Press, 3.

68. Rokeach, M. (1973). *The Nature of Human Values*. New York: Free Press, 11.

69. Williams, R. (1979). *Change and Stability in Values and Value Systems: A Sociological Perspective*. In Rokeach, M. *Understanding Human Values: Individual and Societal*. New York: Free Press, 17.

70. Inglehart, R. (1997). *Modernization and Postmodernization: Cultural, Economic, and Political Change in 43 Societies*. Princeton, NJ: Princeton University Press, 48.

71. Rokeach, M. (1973). *The Nature of Human Values*. New York: Free Press, 11.

72. Hall, B. (1994). *Values Shift: A Guide to Personal and Organizational Transformation*. Eugene, OR: Wipf & Stock, 3.

73. Hall, B. (1994). *Values Shift: A Guide to Personal and Organizational Transformation*. Eugene, OR: Wipf & Stock, 74.

74. Inglehart, R. (1997). *Modernization and Postmodernization: Cultural, Economic, and Political Change in 43 Societies*. Princeton, NJ: Princeton University Press, 111.

75. Wilber, K. (1996). *A Brief History of Everything*. Boston: Shambhala, 221.

76. Hall, B. (1994). *Values Shift: A Guide to Personal and Organizational Transformation*. Eugene, OR: Wipf & Stock, 84.

77. Beck, D. & Cowan, C. (1996). *Spiral Dynamics: Mastering Values, Leadership, and Change*. Malden, MA: Blackwell, 59–61.

78. Hofstede, G. & Hofstede, G.J. (2005,2nd ed). *Cultures and Organizations: Software of the Mind*. New York: McGraw Hill, 10.

79. Hofstede, G. & Hofstede, G.J. (2005, 2nd ed.). *Cultures and Organizations: Software of the Mind*. New York: McGraw Hill, 21.

80. Simon, S., Howe, L., & Kirschenbaum, H. (1972). *Values Clarification: A Practical, Action-Directed Workbook*. New York: Warner Books, 10.

81. Goffman, E. (1959). *The Presentation of Self in Everyday Life*. New York: Doubleday, 1959, 15, 21.

82. Loehr, J. & Schwartz, T. (2003). *The Power of Full Engagement: Managing Energy, Not Time, Is the Key to High Performance and Personal Renewal*. New York: Free Press, 143.

83. Rapaille, C. (2006). *The Culture Code: An Ingenious Way to Understand Why People Around the World Live and Buy as They Do*. New York: Broadway Books, 155.

84. Williams, R. (1979). *Change and Stability in Values and Value Systems: A Sociological Perspective. In Rokeach, M. Understanding Human Values: Individual and Societal*. New York: Free Press, 33.

85. Rokeach, M. (1979). *Understanding Human Values: Individual and Societal*. New York: Free Press, 7.

86. Maslow, A. (1968,2nd ed). *Toward a Psychology of Being*. New York: Van Nostrand Reinhold, 72.

87. Mitchell, A. (1983). *The Nine American Lifestyles*. New York: MacMillan, 41.

88. Wilber, K. (1996). *A Brief History of Everything*. Boston: Shambhala, 35–36.

89. Williams, R. (1979). *Change and Stability in Values and Value Systems: A Sociological Perspective. In Rokeach, M. Understanding Human Values: Individual and Societal*. New York: Free Press, 19.

90. Mitchell, A. (1983). *The Nine American Lifestyles*, New York: MacMillan, 46.

91. Rokeach, M. (1979). *Understanding Human Values: Individual and Societal*. New York: Free Press, 9.

92. Mitchell, A. (1983). *The Nine American Lifestyles*. New York: MacMillan, 3, 28.

93. Williams, R. (1979). *Change and Stability in Values and Value Systems: A Sociological Perspective. In Rokeach, M. Understanding Human Values: Individual and Societal*. New York: Free Press, 33.

94. Inglehart, R. (1997). *Modernization and Postmodernization: Cultural, Economic, and Political Change in 43 Societies*. Princeton, NJ: Princeton University Press, 84.

95. Inglehart, R. (1997). *Modernization and Postmodernization: Cultural, Economic, and Political Change in 43 Societies*. Princeton, NJ: Princeton University Press, 137.

96. Mitchell, A. (1983). *The Nine American Lifestyles*. New York: MacMillan, 52.

97. Beck, D. & Cowan, C. (1996). *Spiral Dynamics: Mastering Values, Leadership, and Change. Malden*, MA: Blackwell, 5.

98. Inglehart, R. & Welzel, C. (2005). *Modernization, Cultural Change, and Democracy: The Human Development Sequence*. Cambridge, UK: Cambridge University Press, 7.

99. Inglehart, R. (1997). *Modernization and Postmodernization: Cultural, Economic, and Political Change in 43 Societies.* Princeton, NJ: Princeton University Press, 142.

100. Beck, D. & Cowan, C. (1996). *Spiral Dynamics: Mastering Values, Leadership, and Change. Malden,* MA: Blackwell, 5.

101. Mitchell, A. (1983). *The Nine American Lifestyles,* New York: MacMillan, 27.

102. Wilber, K. (1996). *A Brief History of Everything.* Boston: Shambhala, 30.

103. Wilber, K. (2000). *Integral Psychology: Consciousness, Spirit, Psychology, Therapy.* Boston: Shambhala, 93.

104. Hines, A. (2006). *Review of Inglehart, R. & Welzel, C. Modernization, Culture Change and Democracy: The Human Development Sequence,* New York: Cambridge University Press, 2005. In Foresight, 8(3), 67.

105. Inglehart, R. & Welzel, C. (2005). *Modernization, Cultural Change, and Democracy: The Human Development Sequence.* Cambridge, UK: Cambridge University Press, 133.

106. Inglehart, R. & Welzel, C. (2005). *Modernization, Cultural Change, and Democracy: The Human Development Sequence.* Cambridge, UK: Cambridge University Press, 97–98.

107. Harman, W. (1998). *Global Mind Change: The Promise of the 21st Century.* San Francisco: Berrett-Koehler, 7.

108. Global Advertising: Consumers Trust Real Friends and Virtual Strangers the Most. (2009, July 7). *Nielsen.com.*

109. Wilson, D. & Purushothaman, R. (2003, October). *Dreaming with the BRICs: The Path to 2050.* Global Economics Paper No. 99, Goldman Sachs.

110. The Coming of "The TEN" Non-BRIC Economies. (2010, February 4). *Bangkok Post.*

111. Su, B. W. (2007, November). The US Economy to 2016: Slower Growth as Boomers Begin to Retire. *Monthly Labor Review.*

112. *Talkin' 'Bout My Generation: The Economic Impact of Aging US Baby Boomers.* (2008, June). McKinsey Global Institute. Available at www.mckinsey.com/ mgi/publications/Impact_Aging_Baby_Boomers/executive_summary.asp.

113. Mace, J. (2010, February 1). Emerging Markets: The New Drivers of Global Growth. *Money Management.*

114. Hariharan, K. (2005, July 22). Governments Lead the Charge for Nano's Development in Asia. *SmallTimes.com*.

115. Tata Nano Crash Test on Video. (2009, July 14). *AUTOCAR*.

116. The Year's Market Trends. (2010). *Greenercars.org*. Available at http://www.greenercars.org/highlights_mkttrends.htm

117. Driver, M. (2009, December 8). Open Source Predictions For 2010. *Gartner.com*. Available at http://blogs.gartner.com/mark_driver/2009/12/08/open-source-predictions-for-2010/

118. McDermott, N. (2008, May 17). Blade Runner Sprinter with No Legs Wins the Right to Compete in Olympics. *Daily Mail*.

119. Kurzweil, R. (2005). *The Singularity Is Near: When Humans Transcend Biology*. New York: Viking, 7.

120. Saxena, R. (2010, June 15). Now, Free Wifi Hotspots Available At All Starbuck Outlets. *Trend Updates*. Available at http://trendsupdates.com/now-free-wifi-hotspots-available-at-all-starbuck-outlets/

121. London-Wide Wi-Fi by 2012 Pledge. (2010, May 19.). *BBC News*.

122. Hokenson, C. (2010, April 14). HD/Video-On-Demand Investment Shows Growth. *HD Report*. Available at http://www.hd-report.com/2010/04/14/hdvideo-on-demand-investment-shows-growth/

123. Owyang, J. (2010, January 19). A Collection of Social Network Stats for 2010. Reporting on Nielsen data. *Web Strategy*. Available at http://www.web-strategist.com/blog/2010/01/19/a-collection-of-social-network-stats-for-2010/

124. Herring, C. (2009, April 19). Experts: Newspaper Closings Most Damaging In Smaller Towns. *Daily Staff Reporter*.

125. Fitzgerald, S. (2008, March 21). International Pillow Fight Day: Let the Feathers Fly! *National Post*.

126. Rosoff, M. (2010, September 7). Android App Is Like Foursquare Meets Pirate Bay. *Digital Noise: A Blog about Music and Technology*.

127. Surowiecki, J. (2005). *The Wisdom of Crowds*. Anchor.

128. Virtual Goods Mean Real Dollars. (2009, August 13). *eMarketer.com*.

129. Iozzio, C. (2010, January 27). Parrot AR Drone Turns Real Life into a Video Game. *PopSci.com*.

130. Parekh, R. (2009, January 26.) Zipcar Finds a Niche in Turbulent Economy. *AdAge.com.*

131. Social Technologies analysis.

132. Lowe, P. (2008, April 1). FAA: Long-Term Outlook Rosy for Business Aviation. *AIOnline.com.*

133. Pine, J. & Gilmore, J. (1999). *The Experience Economy: Work Is Theater & Every Business a Stage.* Harvard Business Press.

134. See Gross National Happiness on Wikipedia. Available at http://en.wikipedia.org/wiki/Gross_national_happiness

135. International Food Policy Research Institute (IFPRI) data cited in Rajendran, M. (2009, August 1). Food Habits: Meat of the Matter. *Businessworld.*

136. Mufson, S. (2010, March 16). As Economy Booms, China Faces Major Water Shortage. *Washington Post.*

137. Hsu, J. (2010, February 12). Shortage of Rare Earth Elements Could Thwart Innovation. *TechNewsDaily.com.*

138. Bradsher, K. (2009, August 31). China Tightens Grip on Rare Minerals. *New York Times.*

139. Donnan, D. (2009, June 8). Time to Reset Strategy for Post-Recession Consumer. *Chain Drug Review.*

140. Marketing to the Post-Recession Consumers. (2009, November). *NDecitica Marketing Strategy & Research.*

141. *Our Common Future, Report of the World Commission on Environment and Development.* (1987). World Commission on Environment and Development.

142. Elkington, J. (1998). *Cannibals with Forks: the Triple Bottom Line of 21st Century Business.* New Society Publishers.

143. *The Public and Climate Change (2009, July).* Spencer Weart & American Institute of Physics. Reporting on data gathered from Gallup.com, pollingreport.com. Pew Research Center for the People & the Press HSBC Climate Confidence Index 2007. Available at http://www.aip.org/history/climate/public2.htm.

144. TransFair USA's 2009 Coffee Impact Report. (2010, September 8). Transfair USA. Available at http://transfairusa.org/blog/?p=4906.

145. Personal Carbon. (2009, Fall). *Global Lifestyles, GL-2009-41.* Social Technologies.

146. Regmi, A. et al. (2001, January). *Cross-Country Analysis of Food Consumption Patterns/WRS-01-1*. Economic Research Service/USDA. Available at http://www.ers.usda.gov/publications/wrs011/wrs011d.pdf

147. Rubin, J. (2008, May 27). The New Inflation. *Strategic Economy*.

148. See http://www.ithacahours.com/success.html

149. Zwaniecki, A. (2008, November 28). Portland, Oregon, Adjusts as Experiment with Smart Growth Goes On. *America.gov*. Available at http://www.america.gov/st/business-english/2008/November/20081126142028sai kceinawz0.3590357.html

150. Max-Neef, M. (1989). Human Scale Development: An Option for the Future. *development dialogue*, 1, 20.

151. Max-Neef, M. (1989). Human Scale Development: An Option for the Future. *development dialogue*, 1, 27.

152. Max-Neef, M. (1989). Human Scale Development: An Option for the Future. *development dialogue*, 1, 20.

153. Reiss, S. (2004). Multifaceted Nature of Intrinsic Motivation: The Theory of Basic Desires. *Review of General Psychology, 8*(3), 179.

154. Reiss, S. (2004). Multifaceted Nature of Intrinsic Motivation: The Theory of Basic Desires. *Review of General Psychology, 8*(3), 185.

155. Max-Neef, M. (1989). Human Scale Development: An Option for the Future. *development dialogue*, 1, 29.

156. Robinson, J.P & Geoffrey, G. (1997). *Time for Life: The Surprising Ways Americans Use Their Time*. Pennsylvania State University Press.

157. Too Busy for Errands? Outsource! (2008, June 26). *Associated Press*.

158. Caplan, J., (2008, December 15). De-Cluttering Your Mailbox. *Time*.

159. Wilber, K. (2000). *Integral Psychology: Consciousness, Spirit, Psychology, Therapy*. Boston: Shambhala, 53.

160. Hall, B. (1994). *Values Shift: A Guide to Personal and Organizational Transformation*. Eugene, OR: Wipf & Stock.

161. Huntington, S. (1996). *The Clash of Civilizations and the Remaking of World Order*. New York: Simon & Schuster.

162. Strauss, W. & Howe, N. (1991). *Generations: The History of America's Future, 1584 to 2069*. New York: HarperCollins.

INDEX